<small>ADVANCE PRAISE FOR</small>

Asians Loving Asians: Sticky Rice Homoeroticism and Queer Politics

"In *Asians Loving Asians*, Shinsuke Eguchi offers a much needed intervention into the exploration of gay sexual cultures and the meaning attributed to whiteness and white desires within gay communities both nationally and globally and the impact such desires have on multiple different arenas. Through adapt use of various methods and theoretical perspectives, this work demonstrates the ways that 'sticky rice,' the coupling of two Asian men in sexual relationships, can both be powerful and problematic. This book is a major accomplishment that will shape how we perceive inter and intra racial desire and the wide reaching impact of such desires beyond personal intimacies."

—**Chong-suk Winter Han**, Professor of Sociology, Middlebury College and Author of *Geisha of a Different Kind: Race and Sexuality in Gaysian America* and *Racial Erotics: Gay Men of Color, Sexual Racism, and the Politics of Desire*

"Written in Eguchi's distinctive and compelling voice, *Asians Loving Asians* will make you rethink your assumptions about race, gender, sexuality, and nation. Bringing together the fields of communication, Asian American studies, and Queer studies, the book displays an astonishing intellectual breadth. At the same time, it provides a template for pushing the boundaries of qualitative methods and demonstrates the transformative possibilities of critical, cultural, and auto-ethnographic methods."

—**LeiLani Nishime**, Professor of Communication, University of Washington and Author of *Undercover Asian: Multiracial Asian Americans in Visual Culture* and Co-Editor of *Racial Ecologies*

"It's 2022, and we're all in favor of post-colonial, non-Western, intersectional investigations of gender, sexuality, and ethnicity. But, alas, easier said than done. Luckily, Shinsuke Eguchi is showing us how this can be done, in the best possible way, by doing it. *Asians Loving Asians* is a pathbreaking work that will enlighten us all, and that will inspire new directions in queer scholarship."

—**Larry Gross**, Professor of Communication, Annenberg School for Communication and Journalism, University of Southern California and Founder and Editor of the *International Journal of Communication* and the Annenberg Press Book Series

"*Asians Loving Asians: Sticky Rice Homoeroticism and Queer Politics* takes the vernacular discourse of 'sticky rice,' which refers to same sex desire between Asian men, from aphorism to theoretical frame and political activist affect. It is part confessional and part critically embodied theory building that deconstructs internalized racism perpetuated in the hegemony of colonialism of same sex desire.

In *Asians Loving Asians*, Shinsuke Eguchi deftly engages queer color critique with an unwavering voracity that does not drift in abstract theoreticality, but is made manifest in the embodied practices of queer Asian men and their performative resistance against exoticism and the return to self-love. In the process there are close readings of media representations of queer Asian desire; ethnographic interviews with queer Asian male subjects; and the criticality of self-affirmations to create a counter hegemonic queer Asian-futurism that calls us all to attend.

Eguchi establishes a fierce postcolonial queer of color critique that expands the focus of inquiry, discovery and positionality with the queer Asian subject. The work emerges from the body of the author, and thus both centers and it decenters staid presentations and proclamations of queer theory. *Asians Loving Asians: Sticky Rice Homoeroticism and Queer Politics* reads as critical autoethnographic discovery and offers a new template of sociality from a transnational Asian queer perspective. *Asians Loving Asians* is a must read for anyone seeking to explore the most bracing aspects of queer of color critique, by exploring a more expansive focus on racialized queer diversity. The book as a whole is liberating for the author and will be so for all who engage it. And like Marlon Riggs, who wrote about the audacity of Black men loving Black men, maybe Shinsuke Eguishi could also argue that 'Asian men loving Asian men is a revolutionary act.'"

—**Bryant Keith Alexander**, Dean, College of Communication and Fine Arts, and
Interim Dean, School of Television and Film, Loyola Marymount University,
Co-Author of *Collaborative Spirit-Writing Performance in Everyday Black Lives* and
Still Hanging: Using Performance Texts to Deconstruct Racism, and
Co-Editor of *The Routledge Handbook of Gender and Communication*

Asians Loving Asians

Critical
Intercultural
Communication
Studies

Thomas K. Nakayama and Bernadette Marie Calafell
General Editors

Vol. 29

The Critical Intercultural Communication Studies series
is part of the Peter Lang Media and Communication list.
Every volume is peer reviewed and meets
the highest quality standards for content and production.

PETER LANG
New York • Bern • Berlin
Brussels • Vienna • Oxford • Warsaw

Shinsuke Eguchi

Asians Loving Asians

Sticky Rice Homoeroticism and Queer Politics

PETER LANG
New York • Bern • Berlin
Brussels • Vienna • Oxford • Warsaw

Library of Congress Cataloging-in-Publication Data

Names: Eguchi, Shinsuke, author.
Title: Asians loving Asians: sticky rice homoeroticism
and queer politics / Shinsuke Eguchi.
Description: New York: Peter Lang, 2022.
Series: Critical intercultural communication studies; vol. 29 | ISSN 1528-6118
Includes bibliographical references and index.
Identifiers: LCCN 2021038301 (print) | LCCN 2021038302 (ebook)
ISBN 978-1-4331-8306-5 (hardback) | ISBN 978-1-4331-8305-8 (paperback)
ISBN 978-1-4331-8307-2 (ebook pdf) | ISBN 978-1-4331-8308-9 (epub)
Subjects: LCSH: Asian American gay men—Social life and customs. | Asian
Americans in mass media. | Gay men in mass media.
Classification: LCC HQ76.2.U5 E38 2022 (print) | LCC HQ76.2.U5 (ebook) |
DDC 306.76089/95073—dc23
LC record available at https://lccn.loc.gov/2021038301
LC ebook record available at https://lccn.loc.gov/2021038302
DOI 10.3726/b17438

Bibliographic information published by **Die Deutsche Nationalbibliothek**.
Die Deutsche Nationalbibliothek lists this publication in the "Deutsche
Nationalbibliografie"; detailed bibliographic data are available
on the Internet at http://dnb.d-nb.de/.

©2022 Peter Lang Publishing, Inc., New York
80 Broad Street, 5th floor, New York, NY 10004
www.peterlang.com

Table of Contents

Acknowledgments   vii

Introduction: Asians Loving Asians: Sticky Rice Homoeroticism
    and Queer Politics   1

Part I: Reading Media Representations
Chapter One: Queerness of Sticky Rice: In and Across *Yellow Fever* and
    Front Cover   27
Chapter Two: Queering Gender Borders of Sticky Rice: On *Koreatown*   49

Part II: Speaking with Racialized Asian Queer Male Subjects
Chapter Three: Living in Paradox: Seeing "Alternative Cartographies"
    through Sticky Rice   77
Chapter Four: Pedagogy of Unfreedom: Building Queer Relationalities
    through Sticky Rice   105

Part III: Returning to the Self
Chapter Five: Monstrous Onē Performance: Sticking
    with *Hikawa Kiyoshi* [氷川きよし]   135

Coda: Turning Points: Queer Desire in Progress   159

Appendix I   169
About the Author   171
Index   173

Acknowledgments

Since the summer in 2014, writing *Asians Loving Asians: Sticky Rice Homoeroticism and Queer Politics* has been a quite challenging journey for me as a scholar. Without receiving various supports from many people whom I have come across, I could not have completed this monograph book project. There have been multiple moments when I wanted to give up pursuing this project. I felt I was so disconnected from the trope of sticky rice at times. Hence, having been able to complete this book monograph projects is one of the major personal life accomplishments. And I want to take some time to acknowledge and honor people who have been supportive of me and this monograph book project throughout its various manifestations.

I want to begin by extending a very special note of my gratitude to people who have tremulously helped this particular book monograph project. First, I cannot thank you enough to Peter Lang's *Critical Intercultural Communication Studies* series co-editors Tom Nakayama and Bernadette Marie Calafell who are my scholarly mentors and worships.

Tom, since my undergraduate study in Intercultural Communication, you have been someone I want to be like when I grow up as a scholar. Hence, I am so honored that my book is included in your editing series. Thank you so much for your presence and distinguished scholarly works in the discipline.

Bernadette, while my post-doctoral training at University of Denver, you changed my life SO MUCH as you suggested me to read *Black Queer Studies* co-edited by E. Patrick Johnson and Mae G. Henderson (2005 – Duke University Press). I was so lucky to have you as my post-doc mentor, Bernadette! Thank you so much for everything you have done for me since then. And additional thanks to you for publishing this monograph book. I am VERY proud of this book published by two key Critical Cultural Communication scholars I look up to.

I also appreciate Claire Sisco King who has published my preliminary work from this book monograph project titled, "Sticky rice politics: Impossible possibilities of queerness in and across *Yellow Fever* and *Front Cover*," under her editorship for *Women's Studies in Communication* (2020). Along with two of your kind, amazing, and intelligent reviewers, you have intellectually pushed me to articulate my thoughts during the numbers of revisions. Also, special thanks to Taylor & Francis for granting permission to reprint my previously published essay described above as Chapter I of this book.

In addition, I extend a special note of gratitude to all of the seven co-researchers who have willingly participated in interviews with me for this monograph book project. Moreover, I thank the entire Peter Lang team for their support and for making sure the quality of this monograph book throughout the publication process.

I am also grateful of the fact that I have been given various speaking opportunities to present some aspects of *Asians Loving Asians: Sticky Rice Homoeroticism and Queer Politics* throughout the years. I thank for having received the productive feedback from the audience in the following venues: National Communication Association's International and Intercultural Communication Division; University of Washington's Communication Department; University of Denver's Communication Studies' Department; and Gonzaga University's Critical Race and Ethnic Studies' Department.

At this juncture, I appreciate scholars who served as my professors, advisors, and/or mentors during my undergraduate and graduate programs in Communication (2001–2011) through which my scholarship was originated from. I cannot thank you enough for Victoria Chen who served as my undergraduate faculty adviser at San Francisco State University. Without your help, I could have never really gone to the graduate program. And thank you to Deborah J. Borisoff who invested in mentoring me to go on to a Ph.D. program during my M.A. program in Culture and Communication at New York University. You were such a great adviser and mentor who was willing to connect me to scholars in the discipline such as late James W. Chesebro, David McMahan, and William J. Starosta. Because of you (Debbie and Jim), I am so grateful of having gone to work on a Ph.D. in Communication and Culture from Howard University in Washington DC. I am forever grateful of having worked with scholars such as Carolyn Stroman, Chuka

Onwumechili, and Wei Sun who were so supportive of my scholarship. And, my dissertation chair Melbourne S. Cummings and my dissertation adviser William J. Starosta, I cannot thank you two enough for putting up with wild Shinsuke. Without you two, I would never have been a scholar like myself today.

I also want to extend a sincere note of gratitude to the Department of Communication and Journalism at University of New Mexico where has thus far provided an opportunity for me to grow as a Critical Cultural Communication scholar for last decade. While my faculty experience has been and is quite stressful, I appreciate I am learning how to struggle and survive with the harsh-realities of the U.S. higher education industry which cannot be simply ignored. I first thank to Ilia Rodríguez, David Weiss, Tamar Ginossar, Susana Martinez Guillem, Marco Briziarelli, and Judith White whom I have been working together since my first day at University of New Mexico. I also appreciate the opportunity to work with colleagues who inspire me to keep going as a scholar. Thanks to Jaylen deMaria, Cleophas Muneri, Yangsun Hong, Michael LeChuga, Mohammed Yousef, Evan Ashworth, and Dave Keating. Moreover, I thank to colleagues from my affiliated departments and programs such as Nancy López, Assata Zerai, Glenabah Martinez, Bee Chamcharastr, Shiv Dasai, and Steven Verney.

Furthermore, I thank to our former department colleagues Mary Jane Collier, Myra S. Washington, Marissa Floyd, and Shadee Abdi who have moved on to other jobs.

In addition, I want to thank to all students whom I am working with and have worked with before. Teaching keeps me sane! I appreciate my former and current Ph.D. advisees who makes me feel why I need to stay in New Mexico. Thanks to Zhao Ding, Hannah Long, Anthony Zarinana, Sophie Jones, Kamela Rasmusen, Keisuke Kimura, Cassidy Ellis, Austin Miller, Ruoning "Arrow" Xia, Emerson "Kai" Armstrong, Anh Nguyen, Tomide Oloruntobi, and Olivia Roe. I also thank two of my former MA advisees Resile Cortes and Benjamin Bradley who both have gone to pursue Ph.D. degrees in Communication at Arizona State University at different times. Special thanks to Erin Watley, Godfried Asante, Myra "Nikkie" Roberts, Santhosh Chandrashekar, Seonah Kim, and Lindsay Scott whom I have worked with as their dissertation or thesis committee member.

Now I recognize scholar-friends or colleagues who have been supportive of me during my working of this particular monograph book project. Thanks to my quarantine squad and Howard University friends Nicole Files-Thompson and Sean Upshaw who regularly meet up for Facetime gatherings with drinks during nights. And thanks to my academic family members (of choice), Bernadette Marie Calafell, Dawn Marie D. McIntosh, Andy Kai-Chun Chuang, Sara Baugh, and Miranda D. Olzman who are regularly in contact with me. Without all of you,

I do not know how I could have gotten through the COVID-19 pandemic when I had to write most of this monograph book project while staying home. I also do not know how I can have fun in my tenured faculty life without you! You all know how to deal with wild Shinsuke! Thank you for your unconditional, loving, and supportive friendships. Love you all!!!!

There are also many scholar-friends or colleagues who have supported me during the course of this particular monograph book project whether they know this or not. Thanks to Leilani Nishime, Tina M. Harris, Bryant K. Alexander, Rachel A. Griffin, Rona T. Halualani, Fatima Zahrae Chrifi Alaoui, Diane Grimes, Gloria Pindi Nziba, Sarah Amira de la Garza, Ahmet Atay, Satoshi Toyosaki, Jeffrey Q McCune, Jr., Raquel Moreira, Chuck Morris, Amber Johnson (also known as Cypress Amber Reign), Lore/tta LeMaster, Elizabeth Whittington, Cerise Glenn, Marnel Niles Goins, Richie Neil Hao, Tony Adams, Aisha Durham, Robin M. Boylorn, Karma R. Chávez, Ralina L. Joseph, Kristina Scharp, David Oh, Lisa Flores, Ashely Mack, Kent A. Ono, David McMahan, Robert Gutierrez-Perez, Haneen Ghabra, Bryan McCann, Stacey Sowards, Javon L. Johnson, Gust A. Yep, Andrew Spieldenner, Stacey Holman Jones, Pavi Prasad, Sachi Sekimoto, Aimee Carrillo Rowe, Larry Gross, Christopher Brown, Chuyun Oh, Ako Inuzuka, Richard Craig, Mark C. Hopson, Kathryn Sorrells, Anthony Cuomo, Daniel Stern, Sandra Faulkner, Pamela J. Lannutti, Lucy Miller, Meshell Sturgis, Anjali Vats, Jason Wrench, Heather Hundley, Gina Castle-Bell, Late Dan Brouwer, Mohan Dutta, Jaime McDonald, James Welker, C. Winter Han, Jesús Gregorio Smith, Kimberlee Pérez, Lisa Hanasono, Shuzhen Huang, Terrie Wong, Megan Morrisey, Trina Wright-Dixson, Truman Keys, Jenna Hanchey, Jessica Johnson, Robert Meija, Dana Cloud, Nina Maria Lozano, Shaunak Sastry, Roberta Chevrette, and Meina Liu.

Before closing this acknowledgment section, I want to thank my personal friends such as Kiyoko & Bill Simmons, Marie Kuroda, Mika Oh, Fujiyo Ogata, Hiroe Takahashi, Nanako Onoue, Yukiko Kanatani, Etsuko Shinohara, Michiko Tamura, Paul Scotto di Pompeo, and Keiko Yoshi for having listened to my struggle of writing this monograph book project throughout the years. Now that this book is published, you won't need to hear me complaining. Furthermore, I dedicate my efforts on *Asians loving Asians: Sticky Rice Homoeroticism and Queer Politics* to all who struggle every day to fight for intersectional queer politics of race in and across local, national, and global contexts. Lastly, I so appreciate my mother, Yukari Eguchi and my father, Itsuro Eguchi for their lifelong support system. There is no word on this planet I can use to thank you two.

Thank you, everyone!!!!!! Love you!!!!

Introduction: Asians Loving Asians: Sticky Rice Homoeroticism and Queer Politics

In the mid July 2000, I attended *the 9th Tokyo International Lesbian and Gay Film Festival* (currently known as Rainbow Reel Tokyo) that took place in Omotosesandou (表参道). The film session I attended was a collection of short films. One of them was the UK/Hong Kong-produced 26-minute short film *Yellow Fever* directed by Hong Kong-born filmmaker Ray Yeung. This film represents how a British Chinese man living in London, Monty (played by Adrian Pang), struggles to accept his queer desire toward a Taiwanese neighbor Jai Ming (played by Gerald Chew). As the narrative progressed, *Yellow Fever* introduced me to a gay vernacular "sticky rice" for the first time. Sticky rice refers to an "Asian" man who is interested in building sexual and romantic relationships with other "Asian" men. At that time, I was confused with the intraracial queer storyline. I did not quite understand what really made this film so unique. So, I said to myself, *why does Monty struggle to fall in love with Jai Ming? Falling in love with someone who looks like me isn't a problem here [implying Japan]. What is wrong with this film?* Apparently, I was quite naïve. Little did I know that I would feel connected to the trope of sticky rice through which Yeung represents in *Yellow Fever* later in my life.

In the present moment, I do not even remember the last time when I click to view the profiles of "Asian" in gay online dating sites. Maybe, I have done so for a few times after I moved to the U.S in 2001. Viewing "Asian" online profiles have been *very, very rare*. The racialized Asian men initiating to chat with me have been also rare. For almost two decades, I have rarely invested in meeting, dating, and relating with other Asian men in person after I chatted with them briefly online. As I think of my past dating experiences, the men I met have been neither Asian nor foreign. *Does this mean I hate someone who look like and sound like me?* Wait. I grew up and raised in Japan during 80's and 90's. My first queer crash was a high school cisgender male classmate who was a masculine-presenting swimmer. Apparently, he looks like me. My body still remembers how I was confused with *Yellow Fever's* sticky rice narrative I had been exposed to in 2000. *Still, when did I lose my interest in someone who look like and sound like me? What really got into me?*

Perhaps, the longer I am in the U.S., the more I internalize ongoing histories of anti-Asian racism or anti-Asian hate that support White supremacy. The COVID-19 pandemic that reproduces anti-Asian racism working with xenophobia, sexism, cisheteronormativity, and more points to the pervasiveness of America's race problem. Hence, internalizing racism is a never-ending process of culture and communication that requires ongoing disruptions. At the same time, my U.S.-based Japanese scholar friends such as Sekimoto (2014) and Toyosaki (2011) have showcased, I may continue to participate in the way Japanese people are structurally aspired to become and be Americans in the historical continuum of the Pacific War through which Japan "lost." So, my transnational embodiment of Japanese upward mobility reshapes the way I have been seeking a "husband" material who does not look like and sound like me in the U.S. Indeed, a relationship is the social capital. Either way, I am still interested in meeting, dating and relating with non-Asian men no matter how much I study about the way the politics of race organize the social, political, and economic hierarchy of queer desires. *So, ironic.* As I almost always critique scholars who hide their bodies under the language, I must also turn my critical gaze to myself. I am required to trouble how I engage in my queer desires. Hence, I am going to ask myself, *why am I stuck in the temporal space through which racialized Asian male sexual minoritarians are known to seek out interracial romances?* I'd better find ways to answer my own question. Otherwise, as I said in McIntosh and Eguchi (2020), I am afraid of letting my research hide my body as a central platform of knowledge and analysis.

*****

The trope of sticky rice operates as a vernacular discourse that counters the *mundane* of gay sexual cultures. Sticky rice points out the material realities through which the White masculine ideal is a normative currency that shapes the historical marginalization of racialized Asian identities, performances, and politics in and across gay sexual cultures. Ono and Sloop (1995) suggest that "vernacular discourse is speech that resonates within local communities.… However, vernacular discourse is also culture: the music, art, criticism, dance, and architecture of local communities" (p. 20). The settler colonialist logics of whiteness that organize gay sexual cultures orient and reorient an ongoing stigmatization of racialized Asian male subjects as *unattractive and undesirable Others*. Here, the White phallus is the invisible and universal power that maintains the feminization and subordination of racialized Asian men in and across local, national, and global contexts (e.g., Nakayama, 1994; Shimizu, 2012; Wu, 2018). The historical matrix of anti-Asian racism that works with xenophobia has been castrating Asian and Asian American men and their masculinities (Eng, 2001). Consequently, the cisnormative masculinist architectures of gay sexual cultures that worship the White phallus contextualize the normative social and performative path for the racialized Asian male subjects to desire the White male. Han (2015) reiterates that "the obsession with White beauty leads some gay Asian American men to reject all aspects of themselves as Asian" (p. 124). Because the logic of whiteness is a discursive practice that maintains the hierarchal production and constitution of differences (e.g., Jackson, 1999; Nakayama & Krizek, 1995), it actively pressures Asian men to meet, date, and have sex with the White male as a symbol of upward social mobility. Only with this material condition, sticky rice functions as a gay vernacular that offers a brief moment of sexual and gender transgression against the settler colonialist power of White masculine beauty standard.

Having participated in White/Western/U.S. gay sexual cultures described above, I value the counter-normative vernacular significance of sticky rice. Gay sexual cultures that privilege the phallic hegemony of anal sex penetration confine Asian men to be sexual bottoms who get penetrated and dominated (e.g., Han 2015; Lim, 2014; Nguyen, 2014; Wu, 2018). Asian men are rarely imagined to be tops (meaning, the insertive partners) and/or versatiles (meaning, both insertive and receptive partners). Nguyen (2014) observes that "Asian characters are not conferred gay membership due to their effeminacy, desexualization, and exclusive bottom role (rather than the standard gay sexual versatility accorded to White men)" in gay pornography (p. 42). The gay sexual cultural operation of White supremacy perpetuates the historical stigmatization of Asian men who desire other Asian men. A sticky rice coupling of two Asian men who are racially gendered as two sexual bottoms is not counted as properly gay (Nguyen, 2014). At the same time, the racialized gender implication of sticky rice coupling can decenter the cisnormative masculinist architectures of gay sexual cultures that worship the White phallus. In the words of Nguyen (2014), sticky rice has the potential to be "a political stance against White racism and [is] a collective affirmation of gay Asian identity" (p. 156). Hence, I turn my critical attention to complexities and contradictions of sticky rice in this monograph book.

I find that, while some scholars (i.e., Han, 2015; Nguyen, 2014; Wu, 2018) have interrogated the trope of sticky rice before, the historically specific and culturally saturated formations of sticky rice emerged from White/Western/U.S. gay sexual cultures require further attention. While sticky rice can marginalize the whiteness of gay sexual cultures that subordinates racialized Asian male subjects, it can simultaneously sustain the cisnormative relational paradigm. More precisely, the trope of sticky rice still works within the logics of gay sexual cultures that reify the White cisheteropatriarchal paradigms of sex, desire, intimacy, and relationship. The gay vernacular paradox of sticky rice can maintain certain normative acts, performances, and processes of *business-as-usual* ingrained in the political and economic institution of whiteness as a settler colonialist power (Wu, 2018). Thus, multiple, unstable, and dynamic assemblies of sticky rice that constitute, complicate, and differentiate the stickiness (or sameness) of two Asian men in and across particular temporalities, spatialities, and relationalities require full, careful examination.

By analyzing the trope of sticky rice displayed in and across various personal, relational and communal, and media communication contexts, this book *Asians loving Asians: Sticky Rice Homoeroticism and Queer Politics* enters into the intellectual and political landscape described above. I am interested in examining media representations and everyday interpersonal intercultural negotiations of vernacular discourses around sticky rice. To actualize my interest, I interrogate following specific elements of sticky rice; the way sticky rice recycles, rethinks, and shifts the settler colonialist logics of whiteness that sustain ongoing histories of anti-Asian racism; the way sticky rice resists and reifies the *mundane* operation and execution of whiteness that organizes gay sexual cultures; the way sticky rice reproduces, reconstitutes, and/or challenges intra-regional political rivalries, economic hierarchies, and historical tensions in and across Asia and Asian diasporas; and the way sticky rice suggests alternative mappings of queer sex, desire, intimacy, and relationality. By taking further steps to unpack complexities and contradictions of sticky rice as a gay vernacular, I aim to offer an additional and alternative space to question and critique of "Asians loving Asians" further.

In what follows, I describe the genealogy of a queer of color critique as my methodology first. While laying out the genealogy, I also elaborate the way three specific sites of knowledge and analytics (i.e., *quare studies*, *disidentification* and *intersectionality*) are central to my methodological orientation. Then, my justification of how this book contributes to Critical Intercultural Communication studies follows. Lastly, I present organizations and specific contents of this book. In so doing, I set the scene/stage for unpacking the trope of sticky rice in and across various personal, relational and communal, and media communication contexts.

Queer of Color Critique

To begin *Asians Loving Asians: Sticky Rice Homoeroticism and Queer Politics*, I centralize a queer of color critique as my methodology. The genealogy of a queer of color critique (e.g., Cohen; 1997; Eng, Halberstam, & Muñoz, 2005; Ferguson, 2004; Johnson, 2016; Johnson & Henderson, 2005; Muñoz, 1999) began with efforts to (re)locate multi-dimensional issues of power, privilege, and oppression in the emergence of queer theory around late 1980's and early 1990's. The pioneers of queer theory such as Butler (1990, 1993), Sedgwick (1985, 1990), and Warner (1999) did not fully and carefully account complex and contradictory particularities of differences (i.e., race, gender, sexuality, nation, class, language, coloniality, indigeneity, and the body) shored under "queer." They omit to consider the material realities of sexual and gender minoritarians of color, for example. Alexander (2002) has observed that "Queer studies is unacceptably Euro-Americans in orientation" (p. 1288). Hence, by examining the connections between queer politics, theory, and praxis, Cohen (1997) expresses the following concern:

> I am concerned with those manifestations of queer politics in which the capital and advantage invested in a range of sexual categories are disregarded and, as a result, narrow and homogenized political identities are reproduced that inhibit the radical potential of queer politics. (p. 441)

The concept of queer that is politically supposed to be inclusive of all people reifies the historical marginalization of people who stand outside of the White, cisgender, able-bodied, and middle-upper class (Cohen, 1997). Queer politics that challenges the logics of heteronormativity erase people from raced, gendered, classed communities under the concept of "queer" (e.g., Anzaldúa, 1991; Ferguson, 2004; Johnson, 2001). The supremacy of whiteness working with cispatriarchy and capitalism organizes race-less, gender-less, and class-less paradigms of queer politics, theory, and praxis (e.g., Eng, 2001; McBride, 2005; Muñoz, 1999).

This situation implicates what Ferguson (2019) says is that multi-dimensions of queer politics concerning with political and economic struggles such as race, class, poverty, globalization, colonization, and capitalism have been almost "forgotten" over the years. The logic of capitalism requires new market for consumption incorporates a particular version of queerness organized by White, cisgender, able-bodied, and middle-upper class into the U.S. settler colonial nation-state (Eng, 2010). As a consequence, the gay liberation movement that is solely concerned with the issue of (homo)sexuality pushes the multidimensional queer politics to margin. So, the supremacy of White middle-upper class cisgender sexualities continues. Ferguson (2005) articulates the following:

[S]ociological arguments about the socially construed nature of (homo)sexuality index the contemporary entrance of white gays and lesbians into the rights and privileges of American citizenship. As they extend such practices and access racial and class privileges by conforming to gender and sexual norms, White gay formations in particular become homonormative locations that comply with heteronormative protocols (p. 53).

The gay liberation movement that promotes the structural assimilation of homosexuality into the cisheteronormative institution is indeed the politics of homonormativity. It is a replication of cisheteronormative ideals, values, and systems such as nuclear family, marriage, monogamy, reproduction, and private sex among queer people, cultures, and spaces and places (Duggan, 2002). As a consequence, the politics of homonormativity is to maintain the cisnormative power and privilege of heterosexuality working with the logic of whiteness as a property (Eng, 2010). The politics of homonormativity strategically ignores, erases, and marginalizes historically particular and culturally specific issues and concerns of people of color who deal with multilayered oppressions of differences to negotiate their queer sexualities everyday (e.g., Chávez, 2013b; Cohen, 1997; Ferguson, 2019). The non-White, non-Western paradigms and organizations of minoritarian sexualities and genders are almost erased (Puar, 2007).

Accordingly, a queer of color critique centralizes nuanced particularities of race, gender, and class to question and critique whiteness of queer politics that dismantles the macro-structural productions and constitutions of heteronormativity working with patriarchy, cisgenderism, capitalism, and more (Alexander, 2008). Cohen (1997) reminds, "A model of queer politics that simply pits the grand 'heterosexuals' against all those oppressed 'queers' is ineffectual" (p. 458). To embrace the genealogy of a queer of color critique, I must be attentive to multiple political, economic, and historical struggles that produce specialized and resistant knowledges embedded in the material realities of Asian men who build sexual and romantic relationships with other Asian men. Hence, I privilege three following specific analytics, *quare studies*, *disidentification* and *intersectionality* that organize my queer of color critique on *Asians Loving Asians: Sticky Rice Homoeroticism and Queer Politics*. Next, I direct the attention to *quare studies*.

Quare Studies

Performance studies scholar E. Patrick Johnson (2001) proposes quare studies to explicate racialized, gendered, and classed knowledge(s) embedded in the material realities of sexual and gender minoritarians of color. It pushes scholars and practitioners to interrogate the way sexual and gender minoritarians of color develop historically specific and culturally saturated knowledge(s) of queerness (e.g., Alexander 2008; Eguchi, 2021; Eguchi, Calafell, & Files-Thompson, 2014; Eguchi & Roberts, 2015; Johnson, 2014; McCune, 2014). Here, queerness is an alternative temporal optic of sexualized and gendered minoritarian knowledge(s) that denaturalizes the cisheteronormative logics of knowing, being, and acting (e.g, Chambers-Letson 2018; Gopinath, 2018; Keeling, 2019; Muñoz, 2009). To establish the genealogy of quare studies, Johnson (2001) situates his grandmother's accent of *queer* as *quare* to represent the racialized, gendered, and classed knowledge(s) that counter the *normal* and *ordinary*. "Quare" is a Black/African American vernacular soundscape of "queer" having commonly spoken in the U.S. region, South. Johnson reiterates, "'Quare' offers a way to critique stable notion of identity and, at the same time, to locate racialized and gendered knowledges" (2001, p. 3). Unpacking historically specific and culturally nuanced complexities of differences (i.e., race, ethnicity, gender, sexuality, class, and more) shored under a term queer is quare.

This Johnson's move toward a queer of color critique builds on Moraga and Anzaldúa's (1983) *theories in flesh* that accounts the way racism, sexism, and classism shape and reshape sexual and gender minoritarians of color to experience and make sense of their everyday lives. The methodological foundation of theories in flesh rooted in women of color feminism is to interrogate the way everyday lived experiences produce and reproduce specialized and resistant knowledge(s) among minoritized people like women of color (Calafell, 2015). Theories in flesh that privileges a relationship between theory, politics, and practice embrace and highlight how diverse standpoints produce and constitute alternative ways of knowing about the world (e.g., Chávez, 2009b; Madison, 1993). Accordingly, theories in flesh that examines historical and contemporary realities of sexual and gender minoritarians of color pay close attention to the way materials of vernacular discourse (i.e., art, criticism, literature, performance, theater, and dance) manifest the embodied politics of resistance (e.g., Calafell, 2015; Gutierrez-Perez, 2018; McIntosh & Hobson, 2013; Moreman & McIntosh, 2010). Everyday lived experiences through which sexual and gender minoritarians of color struggle with, resist, and dismantle historically imbalanced power relations of differences are the major fields through which possibilities of queerness are reimagined.

Building on theories in flesh described above, quare studies denaturalizes the whiteness of queer studies in order to create a culturally inclusive space (Johnson, 2001). By problematizing a fixed, essentialist construction of a gay-straight binary paradigm, queer studies theoretically assumes the logic of individualism, agency, and sexual freedom through which people can become and be who they want to be (e.g., Anzaldúa, 1991; Calafell & Nakayama, 2017; Johnson, 2001). The major asset of queer studies that destabilizes the normative ideas, values, and categories ignores the contradictory way in which macrostructures of power such as race, gender, and class continue to produce structural constraints (e.g., Alexander, 2008; Chávez, 2013a, b; Eguchi & Calafell, 2020; Yep, 2013). Particularly for sexual and gender minoritarians of color, they cannot simply dismantle the collective mechanisms of identity categories that produce ongoing histories of relational and communal ties (e.g., Johnson, 2001; McBride, 2005; McCune, 2014; Snorton, 2014). The politics of race also operate as historically necessary products for people of color to fight against ongoing histories of racism working with sexism, classism, capitalism, and more (e.g., Alexander, 2012; Cohen, 1997; Johnson, 2001). Consequently, quare studies that diversifies the whiteness of queer studies emphasizes specialized and resistant knowledge(s) that produce historically specific and culturally saturated performances of queerness as the everyday life practices (e.g., Eguchi, 2021; Eguchi, Calafell, & Files-Thompson, 2014; Eguchi, Files-Thompson, & Calafell, 2018; Eguchi & Roberts, 2015).

Disidentification

Quare studies that gestures toward such an inclusive space for a queer of color critique exemplified above draws Muñoz's (1999) theorizing of disidentification as the major methodological component (Johnson, 2001). Disidentification is an analytic that identifies subtle nuances of the way sexual and gender minoritarians of color perform their queer desires, identifications, and affiliations *within* and *against* the normative sets of ideas, belfies, and values (e.g., Alexander, 2008; Chambers-Letson 2018; Rivera-Servera, 2012). It is neither an assimilation nor resistance politics (e.g., Eguchi, 2021; Eguchi & Asante, 2016; Eguchi, Files-Thompson, & Calafell, 2018). Muñoz (1999) asserts, "Disidentification is the third mode of dealing with the dominant ideology, one that neither opts to assimilate within such a structure nor strictly opposes it; rather, disidentification is a strategy that works on and against dominant ideology" (p.11). Sexual and gender minoritarians of color creatively put together their multiple fragmentations of differences to make sense of who they are and what they do depending on where they are. Consequently, they develop their coping mechanisms of performance that are simply neither assimilative or oppositional. So, they can navigate the spatial and contextual arrangements of power. Sexual and gender minoritarians of color who occupy multiple fragmentations of differences are not structurally privileged *enough* to simply buy into or refuse the majoritarian codes of belonging (Muñoz, 1999).

To exemplify this theory of disidentification, I turn the attention to the way racialized Asian male subjects are known to cope with the historical feminization of Asian men in and across gay sexual cultures that sustain the supremacy of whiteness. According to Han (2015), the White cisgender masculinist architecture of gay sexual cultures positions racialized Asian male subjects to be feminine and submissive. There is a limited space for an alternative gay Asian optic. This condition implicates the mainstream White settler colonialist imagination of Asian and Asian American men constructed as having failed to meet the standard of (White) masculinity and manhood (e.g., Chen, 2019; Eguchi, 2021; Nakayama, 1994). Consequently, some racialized Asian male subjects work hard to meet the physical standard of (White) masculinity and manhood. However, masculine-presenting Asian male subjects struggle to receive the approvals from their non-Asian peers because they are still judged and evaluated as *Asian who just try* (Han, 2015). Thus, some racialized Asian male subjects capitalize their femininized presentations to navigate in and across gay sexual cultures (Eguchi, 2011, 2021). They are best known for becoming and being drag queens because of the historically constructed perception around racialized Asian men (Poon & Ho, 2008). As Han (2015) emphasizes, the logic of whiteness that organizes gay sexual cultures celebrates and praises Asians as long as they are stereotypically feminine and submissive. The whiteness of gay sexual cultures chastises, disciplines, and controls Asians to stay in their lane. Therefore, the racialized Asian male subjects who embrace their feminine presentations can be read as a performative mode of disidentification (Han, 2015).

Intersectionality

At the same time, it is important to highlight that Muñoz's (1999) theory of disidentification values, draws, and embraces legal and critical race theorist Crenshaw's (1989, 1991) proposal of intersectionality emerged from the Black feminism. Muñoz (1999) says, "Disidentification is meant to offer a lens to elucidate minoritarian politics that is not monocausal or monothematic, one that is calibrated to discern a multiplicity of interlocking identity components and the ways in which they affect the social" (p. 8). Coining the term intersectionality, Crenshaw (1989, 1991) calls to account for the way the simultaneous technologies of race, gender and class produce and reproduce institutional experiences constructed for Black women. The legal institution emphasizes on women as *White women* while it also highlights the racialized issues and concerns for Blacks that mainly signal *Black men* (Chávez, 2012). The legal institution systematically overlooks how the issues and concerns of Black women implicate the interlocking power relations of racism, sexism, and classism (Calafell, Eguchi, & Abdi, 2020). Consequently, the conception of intersectionality is meant to complicate how differences among differences produce and constitute women of color experiences. This Crenshaw's proposal methodologically shapes the way Muñoz (1999) expands intersectionality to be inclusive of sexual and gender minoritarian identifications working with race, gender, sexuality, class, and the body in his theorizing of disidentification.

Mirroring Muñoz's (1999) move toward the concept of intersectionality, Johnson's (2001) quare studies concerns with how differences produce and constitute intersectional experiences for sexual and gender minoritarians of color. Johnson utters, "Quare studies addresses the concerns and needs of gay, lesbian, bisexual, and transgendered people across issues of race, gender, class, and other subject positions" (p. 20). This suggestion that points to the conception of intersectionality prompts its genealogical expansions. For example, Lee (2003) engages in a transnational, women of color turn of Johnson's (2001) quare studies. By situating a Chinese/Mandarin sounding and pronunciation of queer as "kuare," Lee calls to account how nation, language, and geopolitics complicate intersectional queer experiences of race, gender, sexuality, class, and the body. An ongoing interplay of complex and contradictory tensions between local politics and globalization politics shapes the contemporary arrangements and organizations of queer sexualities in Taiwan. This sets a scene to expand quare studies beyond Black queer studies as an original site of theorizing through which quare studies has developed from. At the same time, Alexander (2008) builds on quare studies to propose a critical interpretive queer methodology that gestures toward a postcolonial queer of color critique. This methodology denaturalizes the intersections of queerness, gender, race, nation-state, settler colonialism, and the body. Later, Johnson (2014) picks up both quare and kuare studies as the methodological optics to write their Black queer experience of becoming a video vixen, that is, a model performer in hip-hop music videos. These methodological extensions of quare studies point to the state of quare studies that cannot be separated from the conception of intersectionality. Indeed, quare studies is much bigger than Black queer studies.

Simultaneously, quare studies that politically centralizes vernacular discourses as the referencing points to diversity queer studies initiate other methodological emergences. McRuer (2006) proposes to "crip" queer studies to examine the intersections among queerness and dis/ability. "Crip" that reclaims the derogatory word cripple accounts how the healthism of able-bodiedness underlies normative assumptions of gender, sexuality, sex, and the body. In addition, some scholars (e.g., Green, 2016; Snorton, 2017; Stryker, S., Currah, P., & Moore, 2008) argue for trans* as an analytic that denaturizes the temporal and spatial arrangements of gender intersecting with differences such as race, sexuality, class, nation, and settler colonialism. Here, the asterisk symbolizes inclusive approaches to transgender embodiments, performances, and politics (Halberstam, 2018). The social constructions of gender are ongoing assemblages of historical and existing power relations that organize social institutions, interactions, and processes. These emergences of crip and trans* that diversify the circumference of queer studies point to the methodological usefulness of quare studies that complicates the conception of intersectionality.

Being sensitive to the fruitful expansions of quare studies described above, I engage in questions and critiques of sticky rice as a gay vernacular in *Asians loving Asians: Sticky Rice Homoeroticism and Queer Politics*. My scholarly commitment builds on Johnson's recommendation that "quare studies must also focus on interracial dating and the identity politics such coupling invokes" (2001, p. 19). While some readers may claim sticky rice is not interracial, I argue that sticky rice can be indeed *interracial* depending on a specific spatial dynamic of coupling. For example, there are multiple layers of skin color, ethnic, and cultural differences among the subjects racialized as Asian in and across local, national, and global contexts (e.g., Eguchi & Ding, 2017; Prasad, 2018). The multiracial Asian subjects also transgress the racially essentialized category of Asian (Nishime, 2014). Considering these complexities of "Asian" as a racial category point to the reality through which certain couplings of sticky rice are interracial. At the same time, even when two racialized Asian men who look similar stick together, its sticky rice coupling can be intercultural and international. The literal and figurative concept of Asia is never a singular, stable, and fixed concept (e.g., Chiang & Wong, 2017; Gopinath, 2018; Yue, 2017). Thus, sticky rice coupling is multiple, unstable, and dynamic in and across historical and ideological contexts. Therefore, my examination of sticky rice builds on the genealogy of quare studies that interrogates the historically specific and culturally saturated knowledge(s) of queerness embedded in the material realities of sexual and gender minoritarians of color.

Contributions to Critical Intercultural Communication Studies

Given my methodology described above, I believe that *Asians loving Asians: Sticky Rice Homoeroticism and Queer Politics* may be an interest of academic audiences coming from various disciplines such as Cultural studies, Critical Race and Ethnic studies, Women, Gender, and Sexuality Studies, Sociology, Education, and more. Still, it is important for me to situate that this book that has the potential for interdisciplinary contribution is housed in Communication studies through which my undergraduate, graduate, and post-doctoral trainings have taken place. This book specifically contributes to expand the circumference of Critical Intercultural Communication studies proposed by scholars such as Calafell (2021), Halualani (2014), and Nakayama (2008). To demonstrate the disciplinary contribution of this book, I lay out the foundation of Critical Intercultural Communication studies next.

Critical Intercultural Communication studies is meant to question and critique the intersection of culture and communication as the multiple, unstable, and dynamic site of power through which differences are constantly altered, shaped, and reinforced (e.g, Calafell & Moreman, 2010; Chávez, 2009a; Collier, Hegde, Lee, Nakayama, & Yep, 2001; Halualani & Nakayama, 2010; Halualani, Mendoza, & Drzewiecka, 2009; McIntosh & Eguchi, 2020; Toyosaki & Eguchi, 2017). More precisely, *communication* is a process of articulation and re-articulation about *culture* (Halualani & Nakayama, 2010). *Culture* is a contested site of struggle in which discourses around ideologies of differences are in tension with each other in and across intersecting webs of social, political, economic, and historical contexts (Sorrells, 2010). At the same time, *Inter* of *Intercultural* is to enter into historically contingent and structurally produced relations of power that organize the politics of differences (Carrillo Rowe, 2010). Thus, *criticality* in Critical Intercultural Communication studies not only examines the way macro-structural conditions of power materialized through differences impact on processes of communication between/among members of cultural groups. But it also explicates how processes of communication between/among members of cultural groups reify and/or resist with macro-structural conditions of power. The analytical layers of Critical Intercultural Communication studies emphasize an ongoing interplay of multilevel tensions of power between macro (structures/systems/institutions), meso (communities/organizations/groups), and micro (individuals/relationships/families) (e.g., Halualani & Nakayama, 2010; Sekimoto, 2012; Sorrells, 2010).

Because of the conceptual formations described above, Critical Intercultural Communication studies is an intellectually and politically important space where historically specific and culturally nuanced examinations of queerness in and across intercultural communication contexts have been happening (Eguchi & Asante, 2016). In the past, Communication scholars including but not limited to Alexander (2010), Calafell (2007a, b, 2009), Corey and Nakayama (1997), Holman-Jones (2005), Martinez (2003), Moreman and McIntosh (2010), and

Nakayama, (1994) examined ambiguous, ambivalent, and subtle intersections between queerness and intercultural communication. These scholarships have collectively promoted Chávez's (2013a) proposal of *Queer Intercultural Communication* as a subfield of Critical Intercultural Communication studies. This intellectual move has followed Yep, Lovass, and Elia's (2003) outline of queering Communication studies. Situating queer, Chávez argues to problematize the White, Western intelligibility of LGBTQIA+ (Lesbian-Gay-Bisexual-Transgender-Questioning-Intersex-Asexuality-Plus) identities, performances, and politics. Said differently, Chávez calls to study non-White, non-Western sexual and gender minoritarians in and across local, national, and global contexts. Picking up Chávez's (2013a) call, Eguchi and Asante (2016) reiterate their global, transnational visions for Queer Intercultural Communication in order to denaturalize the cisheteronormative landscape of Critical Intercultural Communication. The labeling of Queer Intercultural Communication as a field of inquiry is gradually emerging (Eguchi & Calafell, 2020). Still, the genealogy that gestures toward a global and transnational direction of queer studies is growing in and across multiple venues of Communication studies (e.g., Cruz, 2020; Hill & Chávez, 2018; Huang & Brouwer, 2018).

Asians loving Asians: Sticky Rice Homoeroticism and Queer Politics enters into the aforementioned landscape of Communication studies in order to make its interdisciplinary contributions. To accomplish the goal, I deploy following critical cultural qualitative methods; *close reading of text* (Chapters 1 and 2); *in-depth interview* (Chapters 3 and 4); *performative writing* (Chapter 5); and *critical reflexivity* (Coda). The intersection of these multiple methods points to how this book emerges from my body as a central platform of knowledge and analysis. As I began this introductory chapter with my narrative, I unapologetically choose not to ignore, erase, and marginalize the personal that prompts the intellectual and political. Hiding myself under the name of research is ingenuine (see, for example, McIntosh & Eguchi, 2020). Consequently, I position this book as *a critical, cultural, and auto/ethnographic approach.*

By auto/ethnographic, I mean a form of critical cultural interpretive method through which a researcher starts from the personal to perform an investigation of culture in and across historical and ideological contexts (Alexander, 2012). As Boylorn (2008) reinforces, "Autoethnographic research combines the impulses of self-consciousness with cultural awareness reflecting the larger world against personal lived experiences oftentimes blurring the lines between them" (p. 413). This methodological implication that orients connections and disconnections between the personal and the cultural reinforces what Yep (2013) calls for in theorizing Queer Intercultural Communication. Yep maintains:

Intercultural communication research must create new spaces for "other [meaning non-White, non-Western, and queer] bodies" to articulate their embodied experiences and to speak as subjects rather than objects of knowledge. Such spaces suggest "other" ways of theorizing, researching, and living through the production of their own "living theory," co-creation of research techniques, and engagement in embodied resistance. (p. 124)

This call politically reiterates what Communication scholars such as Alexander (2010), Boylorn (2008), Calafell (2009), Chávez (2009a) and Moreman and McIntosh (2010) have previously argued to locate the body as a major site of knowledge and analysis in critical, cultural approaches to communication. Following this genealogy, I make known the personal as a referencing point of *Asians loving Asians: Sticky Rice Homoeroticism and Queer Politics* to question, critique, and shift the trope of sticky rice in and across various personal, relational and communal, and media communication contexts.

Orchestrating *Asians Loving Asians: Sticky Rice Homoeroticism and Queer Politics*

Mirroring the frameworks of Critical Intercultural Communication studies described above, the organization of the chapters that starts from macro- (media) to meso- (relational and communal) and to micro-level (personal) analysis is intentional. I begin this book's first two chapters included in "Part I Reading Media Representations" as I engage in a close reading of media representations of sticky rice that explicate, elucidate, and elaborate the macrostructural relations of power. In the following two chapters under "Part II Speaking with Racialized Asian Queer Male Subjects," I interrogate discourses around sticky rice emerged from my in-depth interviews with the co-researchers. Here, I examine the representation, negotiation, and performance of sticky rice in and across relational and communal ties. In the last theme "Part III Returning to the Self," I explicate my body as a site of auto/ethnographic knowledge to critically analyze impossible possibilities of genderqueerness performed by an Enka/Japan's classical style music singer Hikawa Kiyoshi [氷川きよし]. Following the chapter, a coda critically reflects my writing of this book that has mostly taken place under the COVID-19 pandemic, highlighting ongoing histories of American's race problems. With the collections of these chapters, I address complexities and contradictions of macro/meso/micro-level processes of communication around sticky rice as a gay vernacular.

More specifically, I engage a close reading of the concept of sticky rice exemplified in and across the films *Yellow Fever* (1998) and *Front Cover* (2015) in Chapter one titled "Queerness of Sticky Rice: In and Across *Yellow Fever* and *Front Cover*." Both *Yellow Fever* and *Front Cover*, directed by Hong-Kong born filmmaker Ray Yeung, revolve around the juxtaposition between "old" and "new" immigrant subjects. Accordingly, of particular interest here are the ways the old–new immigrant dynamics of sticky rice display impossible possibilities of queerness – that is, a temporal moment of counterhegemonic transgression. The three following themes organize this analysis: the mobility of the "old" immigrant subject; the denaturalizing of racialized gender; and queer kinship and relational structures. In this chapter, I reevaluate the overall implications of the constructions of sticky rice that *Yellow Fever* and *Front Cover* offer.

In Chapter two "Queering Gender Borders of Sticky Rice: On *Koreatown*," I mobilize queer as a practice or verb to disrupt the White cisheteropatriarchal logics of gay phallic masculinity that arrange temporal and spatial specificities of sticky rice in *Koreatown* (2017), an episode of *HERE TV's Falling for Angeles* (S1E2). Of particular interest here are the ways in which *Koreatown* represents a gay phallic masculinist economy of desire that re/organize a *trans-Asian* intercultural encounter between a Taiwanese-American Kevin and an adopted Korean-American Gino. Simultaneously, I unpack how *Koreatown* displays a brief moment of transgression against the social orders. The intersectionality of gay and Asian, constrained by White cisheteropatriarchal ideals, produces vernacular possibilities of sticky rice. The following four themes organize this analysis; *Cisnormative Phallic Competition, Relational Juxtaposition, Stickiness of Collective Pain*, and *the Unknowable Future*. Overall, this chapter challenges the *always already-ness* of gay phallic masculinity as the normative social capital.

In Chapter Three "Living in Paradox: Seeing 'Alternative Cartographies' through Sticky Rice," I orient queer diaspora as a border-crossing methodology to analyze vernacular discourses around sticky rice emerged from my in-depth interviews with the seven racialized Asian/American queer male co-researchers. More specifically, through a queer diasporic analytic, I map out alternative cartographies of the social orders which the co-researchers see through their negotiations with vernacular discourses around sticky rice. I pay careful attention to the way they struggle with and resist images associated with the gay sexual category of "Asian." Simultaneously, I critically look into the way they fail to transgress the "settled" boundaries of whiteness that organizes the hierarchy of gay sexual cultures. By examining the paradox, this chapter draws how vernacular discourses around sticky rice emerged from the interviews allude to impossible possibilities of queerness.

The Chapter Four "Pedagogy of Unfreedom: Building Queer Relationalities through Sticky Rice" continues to analyze discourses around sticky rice emerged from my in-depth interviews with the co-researchers. However, this chapter deploys *queer Asia as critique* to unpack how interview discourses around sticky rice generate possible pathways toward a moment of coalitional possibility. Specifically, I examine the way the co-researchers articulate the gay sexual cultural stigmatization of sticky rice as *inadequately gay* and *un-American*. At the same time, I analyze how the co-researchers are aware of coalitional possibilities of sticky rice that represent the *stickiness* of the racialized Asian queer male subjects in order to trouble the constraints and restraints of (queer) freedom. In so doing, I interrogate how queerness of sticky rice can generate pathways to develop *the collective* among the racialized Asian queer male subjects.

In Chapter Five "Monstrous Onē Performance: Sticking with *Hikawa Kiyoshi* [氷川きよし]," I draw on my auto/ethnographic knowledge to examine impossible possibilities of Hikawa's genderqueerness that indexes the *onē-kei* talent genre. It is an essentialized, umbrella term of minoritized sexual and gender performers, including but not limited to male-to-female (MTF) transgender, nonbinary, cross-dressing, and cismale same-sex loving subjects. To analyze Hikawa's genderqueerness, I deploy a method of performative writing that juxtaposes my narrative of being a transnational Japanese effeminate queer with Hikawa. Here, I methodologically operate the trope of sticky rice to examine my *Japanese-to-Japanese* attraction to Hikawa as an idolized worship of the celebrity representing some aspects of who I am and what I do. From this analytic, I question and critique discourses around impossible possibilities of Hikawa's genderqueerness. And I unpack the way Hikawa's genderqueerness offers a brief moment of transgression against the majoritarian codes of (cis)gender conduct.

Following the chapter that refashions Hikawa's genderqueerness as a form of revolt, a coda titled "Turning Points: Queer Desire in Progress" ends *Asians loving Asians: Sticky Rice Homoeroticism and Queer Politics*. Here, I return my attention to the *behind-the-door* story of writing about and analyzing the trope of sticky rice to create an intersubjective space between the reader (you) and the author (me). I share my embodied performance of racialized queerness that prompts me to write this monograph book project. Simultaneously, I reflect the way the COVID-19 pandemic shapes my desire to complete writing this book. The overall goal of this closing chapter is to leave some possibilities for both the readers and me to continue to question and critique the trope of sticky rice in the future.

As you read, I ask you to keep in mind that all of the chapters included in this book emerge from my body as a major platform of knowledge and analysis. Accordingly, each of the chapters that have their own intellectual and political limitations showcases the way I must continue to engage in critical reflexibility of my knowledge and analysis. Because I am who I am, I am missing *somethings* that implicate the way I am not seeing, feeling, and sensing at this moment. At the same time, I hope that you embrace impossibilities of my knowing, being, and acting with me. My impossibilities teach me what I, as a transnational queer of color critic, continue to study in the future. Hence, this book is never meant to showcase the perfection of my research trajectory and academic journey. Instead, this book is a new/alternative beginning of what I will be doing next. With this intellectual and political commitment in mind, I begin *Asians loving Asians: Sticky Rice Homoeroticism and Queer Politics* by opening the first chapter on *Yellow Fever* and *Front Cover*.

*****

I feel my body is so tensed right now….
   I feel my anxiety is getting high (and high) right now….
The topic I am going to write is…
   …what my body has almost already "forgotten"about…
SO
I need to push (and push) the boundaries of my comfort zone.
WELL
I better be ready to fuck up my comfort zone!
LET'S DO IT!

References

Alexander, B. K. (2002). Reflections, riffs and remembrances: The Black queer studies in the millennium conference. *Callaloo, 23*, 1285–1302. https://muse.jhu.edu/article/6316

Alexander, B. K. (2008). Queer(y)ing the postcolonial through the western. In N. K. Denzin, Y. S. Lincoln, & L. T. Smith (Eds.), *Handbook of critical and indigenous methodologies* (pp. 101–133). Sage Publications.

Alexander, B. K. (2012). *The performative sustainability of race: Reflections on Black culture and the politics of identity.* Peter Lang.

Anzaldúa, G. (1991). To(o) queer the writer: Loca, escrita y chicana. In B. Warland (Ed.), *Inversions: Writing by dykes, queers, and lesbians* (pp. 251–273). Press Gang.

Boylorn, R. M. (2008). As seen on TV: An autoethnographic reflection on race and reality television. *Critical Studies in Media Communication, 25*(4), 413–433. https://doi.org/10.1080/15295030802327758

Butler, J. (1990). *Gender trouble: Feminism and the subversion of identity.* Routledge.

Butler, J. (1993). *Bodies that matter: On the discursive limits of "sex."* Routledge.

Calafell, B. M. (2007a). *Latina/o Communication studies: Theorizing performance.* Peter Lang.

Calafell, B. M. (2007b). Mentoring and love: An open letter. *Cultural Studies <=> Critical Methodologies*, *7*(5), 425–441. https://doi.org/10.1177/1532708607305123

Calafell, B. M. (2009). "She ain't no diva!": Reflections on in/hospitable guests/hosts, reciprocity, and desire. *Liminalities; A Journal of Performance Studies*, *5*(5). http://liminalities.net/5-4/diva.pdf

Calafell, B. M. (2015). *Monstrosity, performance, and race in contemporary culture.* Peter Lang.

Calafell, B. M. (2021). On invitations and possibilities. *Journal of International and Intercultural Communication*, *14*(1), 1–2. https://doi.org/10.1080/17513057.2020.1748881

Calafell, B. M., Eguchi, S., & Abdi, A. (2020). Introduction: De-whitening intersectionality in intercultural communication. In S. Eguchi, B. M. Calafell, & S. Abdi (Eds.), *De-Whitening intersectionality: Race, intercultural communication, and politics* (pp. xvii–xxvii). Lexington Press.

Calafell, B. M., & Moreman, S. (2010). Iterative hesitancies and *Latinidad*: The reverberances of raciality. In R. Halualani & T. K. Nakayama (Eds.), *Handbook of critical intercultural communication* (pp. 400–416). Wiley-Blackwell.

Calafell, B. M., & Nakayama, T. K. (2017). Queer theory. In K. B. Jensen & R. T. Craig (Eds.), *International encyclopedia of communication theory and philosophy* (pp. 1–6). John Wiley & Sons.

Carrillo Rowe, A. (2010). Entering the inter: Power lines in intercultural communication. In T. K Nakayama & R. T. Halualani (Eds.), *The handbook of critical intercultural communication* (pp. 216–226). Wiley-Blackwell.

Chambers-Letson, J. (2018). *After the party: A manifesto for queer of color life.* New York University Press.

Chávez, K. R. (2009a). Embodied translation: Dominant discourse and sommunication with migrant bodies-as-text. *Howard Journal of Communications*, *20*(1), 18–36. https://doi.org/10.1080/10646170802664912

Chávez, K. R. (2009b). Remapping Latinidad: A performance cartography of Latina/o identity in rural Nebraska. *Text and Performance Quarterly*, *29*(2), 165–182. https://doi.org/10.1080/10462930902774866

Chávez, K. R. (2012). Doing intersectionality: Power, privilege, and identities in political activist communities. In N. Bardhan, N. & M. P. Orbe (Eds.), *Identity research and communication: Intercultural reflections and future directions* (pp. 21–32). Lexington Books.

Chávez, K. R. (2013a). Pushing boundaries: Queer intercultural communication. *Journal of International and Intercultural Communication*, *6*(2), 83–95. https://doi.org/10.1080/17513057.2013.777506

Chávez, K. R. (2013b). *Queer migration politics: Activist rhetoric and coalitional possibilities.* University of Illinois Press.

Chen, J. N. (2019). *Trans exploits: Trans of color cultures & technologies in movement.* Duke University Press.

Chiang, H., & Wong, A. K. (2017). Asia is burning: Queer Asia as critique. *Culture, Theory and Critique, 58*(2), 121–126. https://doi.org/10.1080/14735784.2017.1294839

Cohen, C. J. (1997). Punks, bulldaggers, and welfare queens: The real radical potential of queer politics? *GLQ: A Journal of Lesbian and Gay Studies, 3*(4), 437–465. https://doi.org/10.1215/10642684-3-4-437

Collier, M. J., Hegde, R. S., Lee, W. S., Nakayama, T. K., & Yep, G. A. (2001). Dialogue on the edges: Ferment in communication and culture. In M. J. Collier (Ed.), *International and Intercultural Communication Annual 24: Transforming communication about culture: Critical new directions* (pp. 219–280). Sage.

Corey, F. C., & Nakayama, T. K. (1997). Sextext. *Text and Performance Quarterly, 17*(1), 58–68. https://doi.org/10.1080/10462939709366169

Crenshaw, K. (1989). Demarginalizing the intersection of race and sex: A black feminist critique of antidiscrimination doctrine, feminist theory, and antiracist policies. *The University of Chicago Legal Forum*, 139–167. https://chicagounbound.uchicago.edu/uclf/vol1989/iss1/8/

Crenshaw, K. (1991). Mapping the margins. *Stanford Law Review, 43*, 1241–1299. https://doi.org/10.2307/1229039

Cruz, J. (2020). Introduction: African feminist and queer coalitions. *Women's Studies in Communication, 43*(2), 101–105. https://doi.org/10.1080/07491409.2020.1745582

Duggan, L. (2002). The new homonormativity: The sexual politics of neoliberalism. In R. Castronovo & D. Nelson (Eds.), *Materializing democracy: Toward a revitalized cultural politics* (pp. 175–194). Duke University Press.

Eguchi, S. (2011). Negotiating sissyphobia: A critical/interpretive analysis of one 'femme' gay Asian body in the heteronormative world. *Journal of Men's Studies, 19*(1), 37–56. https://doi.org/10.3149/jms.1901.37

Eguchi, S. (2021). Gaysian fabulosity: Quare(ing) the *normal* and *ordinary*. In M. Niles Goins, J.F. McAllister, & B. K. Alexander (Eds.), *The Routledge handbook of gender and communication* (pp. 45-58). Routledge.

Eguchi, S., & Asante, G. (2016). Disidentifications revisited: Queer(y)ing intercultural communication theory. *Communication Theory, 26*(2), 171–189. https://doi.org/10.1111/comt.12086

Eguchi, S., & Calafell, B. M. (2020). Introduction: Reorienting queer intercultural communication. In S. Eguchi & B. M. Calafell (Eds.), *Queer intercultural communication: The intersectional politics of belonging in and across differences* (pp.1–16). Rowman & Littlefield.

Eguchi, S., Calafell, B. M., & Files-Thompson, N. (2014). Intersectionality and quare theory: Fantasizing African American men's same-sex relationships in *Noah's Arc: Jumping the Broom. Communication, Culture, & Critique, 7*(3), 371–389. https://doi.org/doi:10.1111/cccr.12054

Eguchi, S., & Ding, Z. (2017). "Uncultural" Asian Americans in ABC's *Dr. Ken. Popular Communication, 15*(4), 296–310. https://doi.org/10.1080/15405702.2017.1326604

Eguchi, S., Files-Thompson, N., & Calafell, B. M. (2018). Queer (of color) aesthetics: Fleeting moments of transgression in VH1's *Love & Hip-Hop: Hollywood Season 2. Critical Studies in Media Communication, 35*(2), 180–193. https://doi.org/10.1080/15295036.2017.1385822

Eguchi, S., & Roberts, M. N. (2015). Gay rapping and possibilities: A quare reading of "*Throw That Boy P***y.*" *Text and Performance Quarterly, 35*(2/3), 142–157. https://doi.org/10.1080/10462937.2015.1025820

Eng, D. L. (2001). *Racial castration: Managing masculinity in Asian America.* Duke University Press.

Eng, D. L. (2010). *The feeling of kinship: Queer liberalism and the racialization of intimacy.* Duke University Press.

Eng, D. L., Halberstam, J., & Muñoz, J. E. (2005). Introduction: What's queer about Queer studies now? *Social Text, 23*(3/4), 1–17. https://doi.org/10.1215/01642472-23-3-4_84-85-1

Ferguson, R. A. (2004). *Aberrations in black: Toward a queer of color critique.* University of Minnesota Press.

Ferguson, R. A. (2005). Race-ing homonormativity: Citizenship, sociology, and gay identity. In E. P. Johnson & M. G. Henderson (Eds.), *Black queer studies: A critical anthology* (pp. 52–67). Duke University Press.

Ferguson, R. A. (2019). *One-dimensional queer.* Polity.

Gopinath, G. (2018). *Unruly visions: The aesthetic practices of queer diaspora.* Duke University Press.

Green, K. (2016). Troubling the Waters: Mobilizing A Trans* Analytic. In E. P. Johnson (Ed.), *No tea, No shade: New writings in Black queer studies* (pp. 65–82). Duke University Press.

Gutierrez-Perez, R. (2018). Theories in the flesh and flights of the imagination: Embracing the soul and spirit of critical performative writing in communication research. *Women's Studies in Communication, 41*(4), 404–415. https://doi.org/10.1080/07491409.2018.1551695

Halberstam, J. (2018). *Trans*: A Quick and quirky account of gender variability.* University of California Press.

Halualani, R. T. (2014). Editor's introduction: Critical interventions in urgent times. *Journal of International and Intercultural Communication, 7*(4), 259. https://doi.org/10.1080/17513057.2014.964143

Halualani, R. T., Mendoza, S. L., & Drzewiecka, J. A. (2009). "Critical" junctures in Intercultural Communication studies: A review. *Review of Communication, 9*(1), 17–35. https://doi.org/10.1080/15358590802169504

Halualani, R. T., & Nakayama, T. K. (2010). Critical intercultural communication studies: At a crossroads. In T. K. Nakayama & R. T. Halualani (Eds.), *The handbook of critical intercultural communication* (pp. 1–16). Wiley-Blackwell.

Han, C. W. (2015). *Geisha of a different kind: Race and sexuality in gaysian America.* New York University Press.

Hill, A., & Chávez, K. R. (2018). Introduction: Inciting communication across Queer Migration studies and Critical Trafficking studies. *Women's Studies in Communication, 41*(4), 300–304. https://doi.org/10.1080/07491409.2018.1544000

Holman Jones, S. (2005). (M)othering loss: Telling adoption stories, telling performativity. *Text and Performance Quarterly, 25*(2), 113–135. https://doi.org/10.1080/10462930500122716

Jackson II, R. L. (1999). White space, white privilege: Mapping discursive inquiry into the self. *Quarterly Journal of Speech, 85*(1), 38–54. https://doi.org/10.1080/00335639909384240

Johnson, A. (2014). Confessions of a Video Vixen: My autocritography of sexuality, desire, and memory. *Text and Performance Quarterly, 34*(2), 182–200. https://doi.org/10.1080/10462937.2013.879991

Johnson, E. P. (2001). "Quare" studies or (almost) everything I know about Queer studies I learned from my grandmother. *Text and Performance Quarterly, 21*(1), 1–25. https://doi.org/10.1080/10462930128119

Johnson, E. P. (2016). Introduction. In E. P. Johnson (Ed.), *No tea, no shade: New writings in Black queer studies* (pp. 1–26). Duke University Press.

Keeling, K. (2019). *Queer times, Black futures.* New York University Press.

Lee, W. (2003). Kuaering queer theory: My autocritography and a race-conscious, womanist, and transnational Turn. In G. A. Yep, K. E. Lovaas, & J. P. Elia (Eds.), *Queer theory and communication: From disciplining queers to queering the discipline(s)* (pp. 147–170). Harrington Park Press.

Lim, E.-B. (2014). *Brown boys and rice queens: Spellbinding performances in the Asias.* New York University Press.

Madison, S. D. (1993). "That was my occupation": Oral narrative, performance, and black feminist thought. *Text and Performance Quarterly, 13*(3), 213–232. https://doi.org/10.1080/10462939309366051

Martinez, J. M. (2003). Racisms, heterosexisms, and identities: A Semiotic phenomenology of self-understanding. In G. A. Yep, K. E. Lovaas, & J. P. Elia (Eds.), *Queer theory and communication: From disciplining queers to queering the discipline(s)* (pp. 109–127). Harrington Park Press.

McBride, D. A. (2005). *Why I hate abercrombie & fitch: Essays on race and sexuality.* New York University Press.

McCune, Jr. J. Q. (2014). *Sexual discretion: Black masculinity and the politics of passing.* University of Chicago Press.

McIntosh, D. M. D., & Eguchi, S. (2020). The troubled past, present disjunctures, and possible futures: Intercultural performance communication. *Journal of Intercultural Communication Research, 49*(5), 395–409. https://doi.org/10.1080/17475759.2020.1811996

McIntosh, D. M. D., & Hobson, K. (2013). Reflexive engagement: A white (queer) women's performance of failures and alliance possibilities. *Liminalities: A Journal of Performance Studies, 9*(4), 1–23. http://liminalities.net/9-4/reflexive.pdf

McRuer, R. (2006). *Crip theory: Cultural signs of queerness and disability.* New York University Press.

Moraga, C., & Anzaldúa, G. (Eds.). (1983). *This bridge called my back: Writing by radical women of color.* Kitchen Table.

Moreman, S. T., & McIntosh, D. M. (2010). Brown scriptings and rescriptings: A critical performance ethnography of Latina drag queens. *Communication and Cultural/Critical Studies*, *7*(2), 115–135. https://doi.org/10.1080/14791421003767912

Muñoz, J. E. (1999). *Disidentifications: Queers of color and the performance of politics*. University of Minnesota Press.

Nakayama, T. (2008). Editor's statement: On (not) feeling rebellious. *Journal of International and Intercultural Communication*, *1*(1), 1–2. https://doi.org/10.1080/17513050701837865

Nakayama, T. K. (1994). Show/down time: "Race," gender, sexuality, and popular culture. *Critical Studies in Media Communication*, *11*(2), 162–179. https://doi.org/10.1080/15295039409366893

Nakayama, T. K., & Krizek, R. L. (1995). Whiteness: A strategic rhetoric. *Quarterly Journal of Speech*, *81*(3), 291–309. https://doi.org/10.1080/00335639509384117

Nguyen, H. T. (2014). *A View from the Bottom: Asian American masculinity and sexual representation*. Duke University Press.

Nishime, L. (2014). *Undercover Asian: Multiracial Asian Americans in visual culture*. University of Illinois Press.

Ono, K. A., & Sloop, J. M. (1995) The critique of vernacular discourse. *Communication Monographs*, *62*(1), 19–46. https://doi.org/10.1080/03637759509376346

Poon, M. K.-L., & Ho, P. T-T. (2008). Negotiating social stigma among gay Asian men. *Sexualities*, *11*(1/2), 245–268. https://doi.org/10.1177/1363460707085472

Prasad, P. (2018). Sunburned: Color lines in Sand. *Departures in Critical Qualitative Research*, *7*(1), 101–122. https://doi.org/10.1525/dcqr.2018.7.1.101

Puar, J. K. (2007). *Terrorist assemblages: Homonationalism in queer times*. Duke University Press.

Rivera-Servera, R. (2012). *Performing queer Latinidad: Dance, sexuality, politics*. University of Michigan Press.

Sedgwick, E. K. (1985). *Between men: English literature and male homosocial desire*. Columbia University Press.

Sedgwick, E. K. (1990). *The epistemology of coming out*. University of California Press.

Sekimoto, S. (2012). A multimodal approach to identity: Theorizing the self through embodiment, spatiality, and temporality. *Journal of International and Intercultural Communication*, *5*(3), 226–243. https://doi.org/10.1080/17513057.2012.689314

Sekimoto, S. (2014). Transnational Asia: Dis/orienting identity in the globalized world. *Communication Quarterly*, *62*(4), 381–398. https://doi.org/10.1080/01463373.2014.922485

Shimizu, C. P. (2012). *Straight sexualities: Unbinding Asian American manhoods in the movies*. Stanford University Press.

Snorton, C. R. (2014). *Nobody is supposed to know: Black sexuality on the down low*. University of Minnesota Press.

Snorton, C. R. (2017). *Black on both sides: A racial history of trans identity*. University of Minnesota Press.

Sorrells, K. (2010). Re-imagining intercultural communication in the context of globalization. In T. K Nakayama & R. T. Halualani (Eds.), *The handbook of critical intercultural communication* (pp. 171–189). Wiley-Blackwell.

Stryker, S., Currah, P., & Moore, L. J. (2008). Introduction: Trans-, trans, or transgender? *Women's Studies Quarterly, 36*(¾), 11–22. https://doi.org/10.1353/wsq.0.0112

Toyosaki, S. (2011). Critical complete-member ethnography: Theorizing dialectics of consensus and conflict in intercultural communication. *Journal of International and Intercultural Communication, 4*(1), 62–80. https://doi.org/10.1080/17513057.2010.533786

Toyosaki, S., & Eguchi, S. (2017). Powerful uncertainty for the future of Japan's cultural diversity: Theorizing Japanese homogenizing discourses. In S. Toyosaki & S. Eguchi (Eds.), *Intercultural communication in Japan: Theorizing homogenized discourse* (pp. 1–23). Routledge.

Warner, M. (1999). *The trouble with normal: Sex, politics, and the ethics of queer life*. Harvard University Press.

Wu, C. (2018). *Sticky rice: A politics of intraracial desire*. Temple University Press.

Yep, G. A. (2013). Queering/quaring/kauering/crippin'/transing "other bodies" in intercultural communication. *Journal of International and Intercultural Communication, 6*(2), 118–126. https://doi.org/10.1080/17513057.2013.777087

Yep, G. A., Lovaas, K. E., & Elia, J. P. (2003). Introduction: Queering communication: Starting the conversation. In G. A. Yep, K. E. Lovaas, & J. P. Elia (Eds.), *Queer theory and communication: From disciplining queers to queering the discipline(s)* (pp. 1–10). Harrington Park Press.

Yue, A. (2017). Trans-Singapore: Some notes towards Queer Asia as method. *Inter-Asian Cultural Studies, 18*(1), 10–24. https://doi.org/10.1080/14649373.2017.1273911

PART I

READING MEDIA REPRESENTATIONS

CHAPTER ONE

Queerness of Sticky Rice: In and Across *Yellow Fever* and *Front Cover*[1]

Media images of Asians and Asian Americans, largely by those who are neither, are typically constructed in relation to others, especially Whites; however, these representations are not racial alone, but use other forms of difference to construct hierarchical relations. (Nakayama, 1994, p. 165)

In gay vernacular, "sticky rice" refers to an Asian man who is primarily interested in developing sexual and romantic relationships with other Asian men. Calafell and Delgado (2004) assert that vernaculars are culture-specific and text-specific ways in which historically marginalized groups perform uses of language to counter the *normal* and *ordinary*. The concept of sticky rice points to gay racial politics privileging White phallic masculinities at the expense of Asian men. Whiteness is an exceptional power that organizes the inner workings of gay sexual cultures (e.g., Han, 2015; McBride, 2005; Wu, 2018). Images of youthful, gym-going, White, cismale able-bodies are circulated as the ideal gay masculine norm, for example. Whiteness has also castrated Asian men as feminine *Others* (e.g., Eng, 2001; Nakayama, 1994; Nishime, 2017). In consequence, there is an ideological disincentive for an Asian man being intimate with another Asian man. Nguyen (2014) reasons, "Sex between two Asian men (read two effeminate gay men, two bottoms [meaning anal-receptive partners]) does not quite count as properly homosexual" (p. 155). As a result, many Asian men find themselves competing for attention from the small pool of "rice queens" – or, White men who are exclusively interested in dating Asian men – so they gain the social capital that attends to the whiteness that organizes gay sexual cultures (Han, 2015). This interracial aspiration maintains divisions between Asian men that the concept of sticky rice implies.

Directed by Hong-Kong born filmmaker Ray Yeung, *Yellow Fever* (1998) and *Front Cover* (2015) implicate gay sexual cultures in and across different times, spaces, and contexts. The UK/Hong Kong-produced 26-minute short film *Yellow Fever* focuses on Monty (played by Adrian Pang), a British Chinese man living in London and struggling to fall in love with a Taiwanese neighbor, Jai Ming (played by Gerald Chew), who recently moved to England from Taiwan. A queer cinema studio, Frame Line, released *Yellow Fever* on June 20, 1998 at San Francisco's International Lesbian & Gay Film Festival. Other lesbian-gay-bisexual-transgender (LGBT) film festivals in Tampa, Chicago, Boston, Tokyo, and Vancouver also featured it. The DVD *Asian Queer Shorts* (2009) includes *Yellow Fever* as one of the short films. Currently, it is accessible through venues such as YouTube and Amazon.

The US-produced one hour and 27-minute film *Front Cover* is a remake of *Yellow Fever*. This extended version, produced by NewVoice and distributed by Strand Releasing, focuses on Chinese American male fashion stylist Ryan Fu (played by Jake Choi), who develops feelings for Chinese male actor Qi Xiao Ning (played by James Chen), who is visiting New York City. It was first released for screening at the Seattle International Film Festival on May 28, 2015. Then other film festivals such as the Chicago International Film Festival, Toronto LGBT Film Festival, and FilmOut San Diego featured it. On August 5, 2016, *Front Cover* was officially released in New York. Netflix also distributed *Front Cover* for streaming between October 18, 2016 and April 18, 2018. Currently, it is accessible through streaming services similar to Amazon. As a transnational queer of color critic, I am drawn to these rare Western gay media texts that exclusively feature the vernacular of sticky rice.

Yellow Fever and *Front Cover* revolve around the juxtaposition between "old" and "new" immigrant subjects. In an interview with Dee (2016, September 28), Yeung talks about gay racial politics pressuring Asian men to turn their sexual and romantic attentions toward the whiteness that structures gay sexual cultures. Explaining the remake process from *Yellow Fever* to *Front Cover*, he says that "for me to fit in [to the mainstream gay sexual culture] was to not hang out with any Asian gay boys.... the only thing to do was to date a White guy; that would make you feel like less of an outsider." Accordingly, Yeung remarks, "I wanted to film in a Western setting because I wanted to play with that old immigrant and new immigrant dynamic" (Dee, 2016, September 28). The shared storyline of *Yellow*

Fever and *Front Cover* is about a racially shifting moment for the "old" immigrant subject as he moves to, through, and away from falling in and out of love with the "new" Asian immigrant subject. While defining the mobility of the "old" immigrant subject in contrast to the relative immobility of the "new" immigrant subject, both *Yellow Fever* and *Front Cover* offer narratives of two Asian men falling in love.

I critique Yeung's old-new immigrant dynamic because it implies a linear growth expectation of immigrants. Its expectation normalizes the naturalization of immigrants wherein White supremacy actively forces immigrants to neutralize their performative aspects of foreignness to adopt whiteness. In fact, the historical feminization of Asian men, intersecting with anti-Asian immigrant rhetoric, continues to marginalize both "old" and "new" Asian immigrant subjects in and across gay sexual cultures organized by whiteness (Eguchi, 2015; Han, 2015; Lim, 2014; Nguyen, 2014; Wu, 2018). This racialized gender space is in fact a borderland where immigrant subjects categorized as *Asian* meet and relate to one another. Chicana feminist queer theorist Anzaldúa (2012) reminds us, "A borderland is a vague and undetermined place created by the emotional residue of an unnatural boundary. It is in a constant state of transition" (p. 25). A borderland is a constantly shifting and ambiguous space of in-betweenness that can denaturalize a linear growth expectation of immigration. It is *both* a metaphoric and material site that troubles the conventional modes of living (Gutierrez-Perez, 2018). Yet Yeung's old-new immigrant dynamic not only erases the active forces of White supremacy that foreignize Asians, but it also revitalizes the colonial-transnational dichotomy of homoerotic encounters between the West and the East. Thus, by centralizing the old-new immigrant dynamic, Yeung depoliticizes the vernacular possibilities of sticky rice that might form a coalition between/among Asian men to challenge the whiteness organizing the inner workings of gay sexual cultures.

For that reason, in this chapter I trouble the textual displays of sticky rice in and across *Yellow Fever* and *Front Cover*. More specifically, I interrogate Yeung's old-new immigrant dynamic as a complex and contradictory product of power. It both reifies illusions of essentialist binary paradigms (e.g., West-East, domestic-foreign, and center-margin) and represents the ahistorical, unspecified notion of China as a homeland. However, despite these ideological constraints, *Yellow Fever* and *Front Cover* are rare Western gay media texts that represent the vernacular of sticky rice in and across times, spaces, and contexts. Accordingly, I value some aspects of Yeung's visions of two Asian men falling in love, which may articulate and rearticulate the disruptive or resistant possibilities of sticky rice as racialized gender politics. Thus, in my critique I am simultaneously interested in re-politicizing Yeung's displays of sticky rice, which push the boundaries of the whiteness that structures the inner workings of gay sexual cultures.

In the following, I first introduce impossible possibilities of queerness as a conceptual lens for reading the paradoxical layers of sticky rice in and across *Yellow Fever* and *Front Cover*. While discussing my conceptualization of queerness, I also elaborate on the significance of reading *Yellow Fever* and *Front Cover* in relation to one another. I compare the two films to see if and how their rhetorics about Asian men and gay sexual cultures have changed. Following analysis of the films, I close this chapter by reevaluating the overall implications of sticky rice that *Yellow Fever* and *Front Cover* offer.

Methodology: Queerness and Intersectionality

Drawing on Alexander (2008), I engage in a close reading of the trope of "sticky rice" in and across *Yellow Fever* and *Front Cover* as texts that require an intersectional queer of color analysis of racialized cisheterosexism. Of particular interest here are the ways in which the old-new immigrant dynamic of sticky rice displays *impossible possibilities* of queerness. Queerness is a utopian mode of sexual minoritarian politics that denaturalizes hierarchal relations of power (e.g., cisheterosexism, racism, classism, xenophobia, and/or colonialism) as the dominant sets of knowledge (Keeling, 2019). Muñoz (2009) clarifies this conceptualization by asserting that "queerness [is] a temporal arrangement in which the past is a field of possibility in which subjects can act in the present in the service of a new futurity" (p. 16). Considering the future as a temporal destination, attention to the impossible possibilities of queerness may allow queers to recognize that "something" is missing from the present, which remains depressive and toxic for them. The process of articulating and rearticulating what constitutes "something" is intellectually and politically imperative for queers to identify gaps in the present (Chambers-Letson, 2018). Thus, I conceptualize queerness as a temporal moment of counter-hegemonic transgression in and across the lines of power differentials (e.g., race, ethnicity, gender, sexuality, nation, class, language, and the body).

In line with feminist queer scholarship (e.g., King, 2016; LeMaster, 2015; Morrissey, 2017), I use "queer" as a practice or verb that guides my approach to the continually shifting nature of queerness. Queerness disrupts the historically normalized boundaries of ideologies that govern such relational structures such as dating, sex, marriage, family, and kinship, so that alternative modes of living may be articulated. Queerness further denaturalizes the essentialist illusion of normative timelines of linear progress in life. However, hierarchical relations of power almost always constrain the material realities of queerness as impossible (Eguchi, Files-Thompson, & Calafell, 2018). Thus, the present-ness of queerness paradigmatically ties to the politics of failure (Halberstam, 2011; Muñoz, 2009). The queer politics of failure enable queers to recognize *imperfections* of the present while also pushing them to revisit forgotten possibilities of the past and to reimagine uncertain possibilities of the future. In so doing, queerness interrupts the cisheterosexist arrangement of what the present looks like – that is, straight time (e.g., Chambers-Letson, 2018; Keeling, 2019; Muñoz, 2009), becoming a borderland in which queers remain peculiar and constituting the impossible possibilities of queerness (Abdi & Calafell, 2017). Because queerness operates with cross-border relations between the past, the present, and the future, I closely read *Yellow Fever* and *Front Cover* in relation to one another.

Despite temporal, spatial, and contextual differences between these two films, Yeung's transnational vision of two Asian men falling in love generates a static figuration of sticky rice fixed in the old-new immigrant dynamic. The active forces of White supremacy that normalize a linear growth expectation of immigrants create an *always-alreadyness* of sticky rice. At the same time, a continually shifting racialized gender borderland where queer Asian male immigrants actually meet and relate to one another also shapes the particularities of Yeung's visions of sticky rice that differentiate *Yellow Fever* and *Front Cover*. For example, the production of *Yellow Fever* took place in the late 1990s in London, England. At that time, England was a colonizer of the director Yeung's homeland Hong Kong for almost hundred years and was about to return Hong Kong to China. However, *Front Cover* switched its contextual focus to another space and time: New York in the mid-2010s. Its production took place around the moment that the social institution of same-sex marriage became federally legalized in the U.S. under President Obama's administration. These changing cultural landscapes of present-ness affect the *impossible possibilities* of queerness surrounding sticky rice in both texts. Yet there are still some similarities between *Yellow Fever* and *Front Cover* as the products of Yeung's vision. Thus, I argue that both films educate queers about "something" that is missing from the changing cultural landscapes that they depict. Because the vernacular of sticky rice configures the queerness of Asian male immigrant subjects as dwelling in temporal paradoxes between old and new, the spaces between *Yellow Fever* and *Front Cover* explicate, elucidate, and elaborate on the inner workings of sticky rice that step "out of the linearity of straight time" (Muñoz, 2009, p. 25). Therefore, in this chapter I engage in an intertextual and comparative analysis of these two films.

To the theoretical frameworks of queerness, I also add the concept of intersectionality. Crenshaw (1989, 1991), a woman of color feminist, proposes intersectionality to account for simultaneous and multifarious operations of power differentials, particularly pertaining to the intersections among race and gender.

Intersectionality originated as a means to identify and critique how a legal, political, and cultural system almost always erases institutional experiences of Black/African American women (Chávez, 2012). The institutionalized discourse of race tends to privilege Black men; simultaneously, discourses of gender tend to privilege White women. Borrowing this intersectional argument, queer of color theorists such as Cohen (1997), Johnson (2001), and Muñoz (1999) call for knowledge embedded in the material realities of sexual minoritarians coming from raced, gendered, and classed communities. They emphasize a deeper analysis of nuanced and particular modes of racialized gender queerness. Puar (2007) raises a concern over such use of intersectionality by asserting, "As a tool of diversity management and a mantra of liberal multiculturalism, intersectionality colludes with the disciplinary apparatus of the state…in that 'difference' is encased within a structural container that simply wishes the messiness of identity into a formulaic grid" (p. 212). For Puar, the conceptual use of intersectionality appears to privilege the naming, stabilizing, and essentializing of queerness as identity or positionality politics. However, Chávez (2013) defends the use of intersectionality in relation to queerness. She says that "the work of attending to the multiple vectors of power that create privilege and oppression remains of utmost concern for queer theorists" (p. 90). Queerness can never be ontologically and epistemologically isolated from interwoven forces of power. The simultaneous and multifarious processes of power always complicate productions, constitutions, and performances of queerness.

Accordingly, queer theorists in the Communication discipline regard intersectionality as a way to complicate knowledge productions of racialized gender queerness (e.g., Alexander, 2008; Calafell, 2013; Chávez, 2012; Eguchi, 2015; Johnson, 2013; LeMaster, 2015; Yep, 2013). I further draw on Yep's (2010) proposal of thick intersectionalities as a way to resist the use of intersectionality as a simplistic, formulaic listing of multiple identity variables. Yep (2010) calls for identification and critique of "history and personhood in concrete time and space, and the interplay between individual subjectivity, personal agency, systemic arrangements, and structural forces" (p. 173). Privileging this point, thick intersectionalities require queer of color theorists to analyze multiple, fluid, and unstable particularities of queerness that alter, shape, and/or reinforce hierarchal relations of power in and across historically specific times, spaces, and contexts. Through an emphasis on thick intersectionalities in relation to queerness, I offer a close reading of the concept of sticky rice in and across *Yellow Fever* and *Front Cover*.

My close reading reveals how the films draw on and reinforce the logics of whiteness that structure gay sexual culture to construct the mobility of the "old" immigrant subject. At the same time, the films challenge the racialized gender politics that obscure the diversity among Asian men. Further, Yeung's figuration of sticky rice showcases queer kinship and relational structures that disrupt the present-ness of racialized cisheterosexism. Thus, I organize my reading into the following themes: *The Mobility of the "Old" Immigrant Subject, The Denaturalizing of Racialized Gender,* and *The Queer Kinship and Relational Structures.* The simultaneous workings of these three themes represent constructions of sticky rice that display the *impossible possibilities* of queerness in and across two temporal, spatial, and contextual sites.

The Mobility of the "Old" Immigrant Subject

The territory of whiteness produces and reproduces modalities of sticky rice in and across *Yellow Fever* and *Front Cover.* The strategic workings of whiteness pressure all queer Asian immigrant subjects to perform naturalizations that protect the invisible center historically occupied by Whites, cismales, the able-bodied, and the affluent. Under such discursive and material conditions, Yeung's old-new immigrant dynamic of sticky rice arranges the "old" Asian immigrant subject (Monty in *Yellow Fever* and Ryan in *Front Cover*) as forming a border checkpoint between the West and East. The "old" immigrant subject, who is capable of passing as *almost White*, is visualized as closer to the center than the "new" immigrant subject, who performs inescapable foreignness. This "almost whiteness" suggests a continually shifting racialized medium through which the economic and cultural maintenance of White supremacy enables some "non-threatening" and/or "exceptional" queer Asian immigrant subjects to obtain the mobility enabled by whiteness. Only with performative adaptabilities of whiteness can Monty in *Yellow Fever* and Ryan in *Front Cover* be framed to sustain the centrality of the West as a liberal, modern, and sexually exceptional society. I begin this argument with an example from *Yellow Fever.*

In the beginning when Monty meets Jai Ming, who introduces himself to Monty in Mandarin at the entrance of Monty's apartment, Monty tells Jai Ming, "I am sorry. I do not speak Chinese" (Yeung, 1998, 1:25). Monty's tone showcases his dissatisfaction with Jai Ming, who has switched from speaking English to Mandarin as soon as he sees Monty. Jai Ming's code-switching insinuates Monty's only partial belonging to Britain because of his racialized cisgender body. Simultaneously, Monty's reply – "I do not speak Chinese" (Yeung, 1998, 1:25) – reinforces the historical, colonial, and imperial power of English as a global standard language. As he meets Jai Ming, Monty brings the privilege of his Britishness to the fore. Later in the film, Monty speaks Cantonese, which non-Chinese speakers may mistake as Mandarin, and the film does not mark the linguistic difference between Mandarin and Cantonese, which creates an intercultural encounter between Monty and Jai Ming. Instead, *Yellow Fever* showcases the juxtaposition between Monty's fluent use of English and Jai Ming's accented English, emphasizing the old-new immigrant dynamic of sticky rice between Monty and Ryan. This encounter between the West and the East contextualizes how Monty performs whiteness, bolstering the inferiority of Jai Ming as the "new" immigrant subject.

Similar to his work in *Yellow Fever*, Yeung recycles the old-new immigrant dynamic of sticky rice in *Front Cover*. When the "old" immigrant Ryan first meets the "new" immigrant Ning in a restaurant in New York's Chinatown, Ryan corrects Ning, who mispronounces "Ryan" as "Lyan" (Yeung, 2016, 09:52). Ning responds by describing Ryan as "American Borrow Chinese" (Yeung, 2016, 10:17) and "the pandas borrow from China" (Yeung, 2016, 10:24) Ning's use of the phrase "American Borrow Chinese" (Yeung, 2016, 10:17) adapts the phrase American-born Chinese (ABC), referring to people of Chinese descent born in the U.S. By using *borrow* instead of *born*, Ning critiques Ryan, who performs whiteness as an embodied sign of naturalization. In spite of Ryan's performance, Ning sees Ryan as more Chinese than American. The follow-up insult – "the pandas borrow from China" (Yeung, 2016, 10:24) – further highlights Ning's marking of Ryan as Chinese. Using the metaphor of Panda bears native to south-central China, Ning dismisses American-born Chinese people as U.S. citizens. However, soon the complex borderland of Ryan's in-betweenness becomes hypervisible. When a dish of steamed crabs is served, Ryan uses tea to rinse off the grease. Ning looks at Ryan strangely. This moment alludes to an intercultural encounter between Ning as a northern Chinese subject and Ryan as a southern Chinese subject. Ryan grew up in a first-generation, Cantonese speaking, working-class migrant household. In southern China, it is a Cantonese tradition for people to use tea to rinse off the grease if needed. At the same time, however, Ryan can be read as performing the modern concept of (White) Western diets rooted in healthism, through which anti-Asian racism marks Chinese American dishes as unhealthy fast foods. Growing up in New York, Ryan probably knows how to eat a dish of steamed crabs without rinsing off the grease in a Chinatown restaurant. Still, *Front Cover* does not emphasize Ryan's in-betweenness as challenging the strategic naturalization of the old-new immigrant dynamic in the text. Just like *Yellow Fever*, the premise of *Front Cover* pushes aside a difference between Ning as a northern Chinese subject and Ryan as a southern Chinese subject.

This establishment of the West-East dichotomy contextualizes the way in which both Monty from *Yellow Fever* and Ryan from *Front Cover* act as *Western imperial agents*. The "old" immigrant subjects travel back and forth between multiple spaces in and across *Yellow Fever* and *Front Cover*. Borrowing McBride's

(2005) argument that whiteness structures experiences of sexual and intimate relationships for gay men of color, I posit that this modality of sticky rice operates within the (Western) gay sexual cultural logics of whiteness that organize the hierarchal relations of mobility between/among Asian men. The performative adaptabilities of whiteness act as the social capital of the queer Asian immigrant subject in and across different times, spaces, and contexts.

In *Yellow Fever*, the "old" immigrant subject Monty remains in denial of his sticky rice desire toward the "new" immigrant subject Jai Ming, even after he sleeps with Jai Ming for the first time. He tells his British Chinese female friend Jaclyn Tse that he is not supposed to be in love with a Chinese man. He despises Chinese people as loud and dirty, which further ignores the political possibility of Jai Ming identifying as Taiwanese because of cross-straits (Mainland-Taiwan) relations. Then Jaclyn says, "Marrying a White knight won't make you less Chinese" (Yeung, 1998, 23:51). Realizing his contradiction, Monty goes back to Jai Ming once again to admit his love. This narrative progression draws on the liberal and progressive logics of whiteness that organize rhetorics of individualism, personal choice, responsibility, and merit. In the name of freedom, today's liberalism erases ongoing institutional problems of race and racism as past issues. Under such discursive and material effects, the performance of falling in and out of love with the "new" immigrant becomes the journey of *self-discovery* and *self-fulfillment* for the "old" immigrant. So the "old" immigrant subject overcomes his internalization of anti-Asian racism.

Likewise, *Front Cover* provides more mobility to the "old" Asian immigrant subject Ryan than the "new" immigrant subject Ning. Ryan's boss Francesca assigns Ryan as a stylist for Chinese actor Ning, who pays Francesca everything in cash and requests to work only with "a Chinese person" (Yeung, 2016, 05:52). At first, Ryan despises this job. However, Francesca forces Ryan to work for Ning. Around the same time, Ryan cruises a gay hook-up website, and a White male ignores Ryan when he says he is a top. This moment affirms the gay sexual cultural logics of whiteness that frame Asian men as inferior sexual bottoms. As Nguyen (2014) argues, "In a gay sexual marketplace that valorizes fantasies of 'masc,' 'str8-acting,' 'DL,' 'bi,' 'married,' 'muscle,' and 'hung' – that is, attributes of masculinity – Asian men appear to occupy the most unsexy, undesirable position of all, seen as soft, effeminate, and poorly endowed" (p. 2). This typical narrative of being rejected by a White man becomes Ryan's turning point to become close to Ning. The more Ryan understands Ning, who wants to represent his Chineseness through his fashion, the more Ryan moves toward desiring Ning. Accordingly, Ryan even considers moving to China. This sticky rice narrative re-secures the "old" immigrant subject Ryan as the *Western imperial agent* to whom rice queens – White men exclusively interested in dating Asian men – in particular can also relate. There has been a historical, colonial, and imperial path for men whose Western/U.S. American citizenships reflect mobility, cultural capital, and economic privilege to fall in and out of love with foreign men (Pérez, 2015). The idea of moving abroad for love is nothing new.

Taken together, these textual constructions of Monty from *Yellow Fever* and Ryan from *Front Cover* juxtapose how both Jai Ming and Ning signify inescapable foreignness. The "new" immigrant subjects are framed as barely crossing from somewhere *over there* to *over here*. They symbolize the colonized forms of non-White, non-Western bodies to the "old" immigrant subjects, who are much closer to the invisible center. Here, mobility is used to organize the old-new immigrant dynamic of sticky rice. To demonstrate, *Yellow Fever* confines the "new" immigrant subject Jai Ming to an apartment complex, thereby tethering him to the notion of domesticity and femininity. Jai Ming's career, social life, and queer dating life, which require mobility, remain unexplored. Jai Ming is kept to the mediated space of home, which is a historical and ideological location of domesticity, where "a set of highly conventional social roles [have been] played by family members and guests alike" (Spigel, 2001, p.387). Home is also a contested site of the ideological struggle to reproduce hetero-patriarchal traditions of gender relations. Accordingly, one's mobility to travel away from the home is a form of cultural capital and economic privilege. Thus, *Yellow Fever's* limitation of Jai Ming's mobility reveals the logics of whiteness that organize the feminized and domesticated figurations of Asian immigrant subjects. Jai Ming remains stuck in an ahistorical, unspecified Asia, while the performative adaptabilities of whiteness provide the "old" immigrant subject like Monty the mobility to navigate through historical, colonial, and imperialist contexts of the West-East dichotomy.

Front Cover's framing of the "new" immigrant subject Ning also remakes the inescapable foreignness *Yellow Fever* assigns to Jai Ming. As I mentioned earlier, this film first introduces Ning in New York's Chinatown, through which architectural and performative elements of foreignness are unquestionably signified. Simultaneously, the film visualizes Ning in relational circles where fellow foreign Chinese subjects socialize, but only when Ryan is physically present does Ning step into the White cultural spaces, including high-end restaurants and the famous gay bar *Phoenix* in Manhattan. Such a depiction of Ning is questionable. Considering Ning is a *well-known* Chinese actor visiting New York, it would seem likely for him to have a wider social network. His economic privilege would have likely allowed him to travel to, through, and away from White cultural spaces, regardless of Ryan's presence. However, he is mostly kept to non-White cultural spaces. Thus, Ning is *the foreigner* who remains *somewhere out there*, and Yeung's old-new immigrant framing of sticky rice reasserts the hierarchal relations of mobility be-tween/among Asian men and the logic of linear growth expected of immigrants.

The Denaturalizing of Racialized Gender

Despite the confinements of the sticky rice dynamic described above, both *Yellow Fever* and *Front Cover* trouble the ahistorical, unspecific stereotypes of Asian men as less masculine and more feminine than White men. As Han (2015) has argued before, the whiteness that organizes gay sexual cultures only rewards Asian men for embodying the feminine role. However, the concept of Asian men and their masculinities (and femininities) is never monolithic. Asian men and their masculinities (and femininities) are multiple, fluid, and unstable concepts in and across historically specific times, spaces, and contexts. Accordingly, the vernacular of sticky rice can be used to denaturalize and de-essentialize "Asian" men as a racialized gender category. To showcase this argument, I begin with *Yellow Fever*.

The film bluntly and paradoxically demonstrates anti-Filipino racism to showcase the hierarchal relationship between Filipino men and Chinese men participating in gay sexual cultures. The beginning of the film introduces Monty partying with his friends. A White male friend, Andrew, tells Monty to go to "the Long Yang Club" (Yeung, 1998, 4:19) to find a White partner in response to Monty's complaints that he is still single, to which Monty's British Chinese gay friend Dex replies, "Those places where there's only old White men, you can't pick up anything else" (Yeung, 1998, 4:24). Then another British Chinese gay friend, Ernest, adds, "And Filipino Go-Go boys in search of a sugar daddy" (Yeung, 1998, 4:27). Dex and Ernest look down on Filipino Go-Go boys, or dancers who typi-cally wear only underwear briefs to show off their toned bodies and entertain pa-trons at a gay bar or club, as the symbol of an Asian-White colonial dyad. Filipino Go-Go boys are assumed to seek older White men who provide financial benefits. This narrative implicates a prominent homoerotic fantasy about Asian men as the *houseboy*, or an Asian man fetishized to stay home and undertake domestic duties for a (White) older man who can afford to take care of him financially. Younger and underprivileged Asian men are imagined to be seeking older and more privileged White men (Lim, 2014; Nguyen, 2014). Fung (2005) suggests, "The fantasy is also a reality in many Asian countries where economic imperialism gives foreigners, whatever their race, the pick of handsome men in financial need. The accompanying cultural imperialism grants social status to those Asians with White lovers" (p. 344). Dex and Ernest's lines foreshadow the effacement of anti-Filipino racism. Darker skin colors have been marked as the sign of the field labor associated with lower socioeconomic statuses. Simultaneously, light skin colors signal and affirm racial privilege. Filipino men, who are imaged as having darker skin color than Chinese men, illustrate the disadvantages of racialized (gay) cultural capital. Paradoxically, *Yellow Fever*'s depiction of hierarchal relations of power based on skin color illustrates differences between/among Asian men.

This plotline also implicates the temporal context of *Yellow Fever*, setting the tone for a relationship between a British Chinese man, Monty, and a newly arrived migrant from Taiwan, Jai Ming. In following up what Dex and Ernest have said about the Filipino Go-Go boys, Andrew asks where Asian men go to find a White partner. Monty replies, "B-B-B-But I have been there, and the only White knight there is on the last page of 'Boys Magazine'" (Yeung, 1998, 4:36). Andrew says, "Who is your White knight then?" (Yeung, 1998, 4:43). Dex mentions, "It has to be an [White] American" (Yeung, 1998, 4:44). Monty protests, "No, no, no, no, no, no. Those Yanks have nothing up here [pointing to the brain]" (Yeung, 1998, 4:46). Monty's rejection of an American hints at the particular political, economic, cultural, and historical moment of *Yellow Fever*. The film was released shortly after Britain had transferred Hong Kong to Mainland China in 1997. Yet, under the national policy of "one country, two systems," Hong Kong retained its political separation from Mainland China. However, nostalgia for the British Empire, its occupation, and its rule became visible in Hong Kong and its diaspora to minimize the communist influence from Beijing. This post-colonial discourse is the background of Monty's aspiration toward Britishness as the liberal and progressive symbol of White democracy. Monty's contempt for Americans reflects the particularized product of (British) colonial fantasy associated with being Hong Kongese.

It is also worth noting that this party scene actually follows Monty's first encounter with Jai Ming, who has disclosed that he comes from Taiwan, where the British colonial occupation did not take place. Taiwan had been a Japanese imperial colony between 1895 and 1945. Then, in 1949 the Republic of China (ROC) officially relocated their territory to Taiwan as a result of the Communist Party of China that established the People's Republic of China (PRC) on the mainland. While director Yeung does not address such differences between Hong Kong and Taiwan and relies on the ahistorical, unspecified notion of being Chinese that monolithically organizes the old-new immigrant dynamic of sticky rice, the scene of Monty privileging British men over American ones does further distinguish among Asian men, not unlike the distinctions between Chinese and Filipino men described earlier.

Seventeen years later, *Front Cover* also remakes and slightly alters *Yellow Fever*'s old-new immigrant dynamic of sticky rice in a way that paradoxically denaturalizes a monolithic category of Asian men. When the "old" immigrant subject's (Ryan) parents unexpectedly meet the "new" immigrant subject Ning, Ryan's mother Yen asks Ning if he speaks Cantonese, and Ning replies that he speaks Mandarin. Ryan's father Ba replies to Ning in Mandarin, in which he is barely fluent. So Ryan suggests, "Why don't we speak English?" (Yeung, 2016, 46:03). As they discuss Ning's acting career in China in English, Yen serves a quarter cut of one manju (a Chinese baked sweet pastry) on a disposable paper dish to Ning. In this scene, Yen and Ba's working-class appearances and demeanors are used to mark the *fabulousness* of Ning who is said to come from China's capital, Beijing. Speaking standard Mandarin, Ning symbolizes an elitist and industrialized representation of today's Chinese national. He was also born into and raised in a wealthy family household. However, Yen and Ba, speaking Cantonese as their primary language, are marked as low-skilled migrants from *somewhere* in southern China. As a viewer I assume Yen and Ba are from Hong Kong because of Yeung's background, but Yen and Ba's places of origin actually remain ahistorical, unspecified throughout the film. Thus, except for marking the class privilege of Ning who comes from Beijing, *Front Cover* continues the impulse to cast the rest of China in unspecified or ahistorical ways. Yeung reinforces the ideological assumption of *sameness* that operationally homogenizes the heterogeneous notion of China as a homeland for all the immigrant characters in this scene.

In so doing, *Front Cover* paradoxically reorients the hierarchal relationship between Ryan and Ning for diversifying a monolithic category of "Asian" used in and across gay sexual cultures. Compared to Ryan as the "old" immigrant subject, Ning remains in a non-White, non-Western space in which he lacks cultural capital. Ryan's presence is an ideological default that minimizes Ning's class exceptionalism in China. Ning does not know how to dress stylishly despite being a popular Chinese actor, for instance. This is why Ning hires Ryan to be his fashion stylist to begin with. Ryan *westernizes* (or *whitens*) Ning's Chinese fashion backwardness. Gay sexual cultures organized by whiteness demand the naturalization of non-White, non-Western queer immigrant subjects of color into the market for its capital suitability. Thus, Yeung's old-new immigrant dynamic, which implies a linear growth expectation of immigrants, signals a particular direction away from non-modernized, working-class, and Global South assemblies of migrants like Yen and Ba who comes from *somewhere* in China. By maintaining the ahistorical, unspecified notion of China as a homeland, *Front Cover* represents the old-new immigrant dynamic of sticky rice that can be used to paradoxically and problematically denaturalize Asian men as a monolithic racialized gender category.

At the same time, both *Yellow Fever* and *Front Cover* also challenge the monolithic, essentialist scripts of Asian men as feminine and submissive bottoms. In

Yellow Fever, Monty and Jai Ming have their first sex after Monty rushes into Jai Ming's apartment to kiss him. This sex scene focuses on the "new" immigrant Jai Ming pleasuring the "old" immigrant Monty. Monty's moaning face alludes to being anally penetrated by Jai Ming. In an analysis of U.S.-based gay pornography, Nguyen (2014) maintains that Asian American male actors are given more sexual agency to be both tops and bottoms than foreign Asian male actors. However, *unlike the usual*, the foreign Asian male penis is present here. The "new" immigrant Jai Ming occupies the role of a sexual top, though the foreign Asian male is normally imagined as a bottom. *Front Cover* also introduces a sex scene that counters the gay racial logic of desire. After going to a famous gay bar, Phoenix, in Manhattan's East Village, Ryan and Ning are mutually pleasuring each other in Ryan's apartment. They are both topping and bottoming. This versatility of sticky rice sex illustrates a possibility of queerness in which simultaneous imaginations of the Asian male penis and ass denaturalize the politics of racialized gender essentialize Asian men as feminine and submissive bottoms. However, it is important to recognize the ways in which the sticky rice sex images described above actively reuse the homogenization of queer sexual acts rooted in the White phallic economy of gay sexual desire. The performance of male-to-male anal penetration, as the normative gay sexual formation, marginalizes queer sexual formations. Yet, both *Yellow Fever* and *Front Cover*'s images of sticky rice sex that work within the White phallic economy of gay sexual desire explicitly problematize the racialized gender assumptions about Asian men essentialized as feminine and submissive bottoms.

The Queer Kinship and Relational Structures

In relation to the denaturalizing of racialized gender described above, *Yellow Fever* and *Front Cover* represent queer kinship and relational structures of sticky rice that disrupt ongoing formations of whiteness. The vernacular of sticky rice can never be excised from White gay formations as "homonormative locations that comply with heteronormative protocols" (Ferguson, 2005, p. 53). However, the old-new immigrant dynamic of sticky rice, anchoring *Yellow Fever* and *Front Cover*, exposes "something" that is missing from the present shaped by racialized cisheterosexsim. Next, I unpack this argument as I examine how *Yellow Fever* represents Monty's British Chinese friend Ernest despising homonormative gay anal penetration.

As he is struggling with his sticky rice desire, Monty asks Ernest if he finds Asian men attractive. Ernest replies that all men are unattractive. Then he says that the gay sex culture is boring because all men work hard to look "straight" in order to be sexually desired by other men. In response to Monty's question, "What about sex?" (Yeung, 1998, 8:30). Ernest also says, "Who needs it? Pick up the phone, call up a girlfriend, good gossip. Try it. Lasts a lot longer, and you don't have to deal with a wet patch" (Yeung, 1998, 8:31). Here, Ernest refuses to be a part of gay sexual cultures where men act and behave like straight men. Duggan (2002) suggests that the politics of homonormativity, representing gay men as similar to heterosexual men, is overwhelmingly prevalent in media. The respectability politics of gay male assimilation to nation-state gentrifies representations of queerness to recycle the compulsory logic of White, heterosexual masculinity.

Simultaneously, Ernest's desires to hang out with his "girlfriends," with whom he can gossip, illustrates *queerness*, challenging the homonormative formation of anal penetration that recentralizes the White masculinist phallic power. For Ernest, gossip is more pleasurable than gay anal sex and its "wet patch," or, ejaculate. Ernest's violation of the gay sexual code that disassociates from anal penetration reveals the queerness of sticky rice desire, in which a *sisterly* man chooses to stick with another *sisterly* man. Consequently, Ernest fashions a path to the queerness of same-sex desire that steps out of the present-ness naturalized by racialized cisheterosexism that disciplines Ernest as *improperly gay*. Ernest wanting to embrace his "girlfriend" for "good gossip" destabilizes and denaturalizes the racialized gender scripts of Asian men in need of the White phallus. Thus, Ernest's desire is a sticky rice politics that interrupts top-bottom, masculine-feminine, and White-Asian dichotomies representing the material realities of Asian men participating in gay sexual cultures.

In addition to Ernest's rejection of homonormative gay sex, *Yellow Fever* goes beyond the old-new immigrant dynamic of sticky rice to decenter the superiority of whiteness. For example, a unnamed Black man, wearing a shiny green spandex cut-out suit, is jogging between Monty and Monty's friend Dex, also British Chinese, at the gym. Monty asks Dex in Chinese/Cantonese whether he is attracted to a Chinese man. Dex replies, "Monty, you don't find anyone attractive. You are such a princess. When was the last time you had a shag [British slang for sexual intercourse]?" (Yeung, 1998, 13:23). Monty says, "Four. No. Five months ago" Yeung, 1998, 13:30). Dex code-switches to English and yells, "Five months. Hello! Monty, wake up!" (Yeung, 1998, 13:34). So the Black man between them says, "You tell her, honey" (Yeung, 1998, 13:41). The following scene takes place in the locker room, where Dex tells Monty what to wear to go out to a nightclub. Here, the Black man opens a door and flirts with them by saying, "Hey, Miss Thing!" (Yeung, 1998, 13:57). Dex questions, "Miss Thing?" (Yeung, 1998, 13:59). Making a forceful facial expression, he says, "I do not think so" (Yeung, 1998, 14:00). Then the Black man disappears.

This disappearance of the Black male body demonstrates a gay master narrative, given the racialized gender stereotype that Asian men are not sexually and romantically interested in Black men, no matter how masculine they are (Phua, 2007). The superiority of whiteness as the inner workings of gay sexual cultures triangulates connections between Asians as hyper-feminine Others and Blacks as hyper-masculine Others. Simultaneously, in reality Asian men actually meet, date, and have sex with Black men; Black men actually meet, date, and have sex with Asian men (Eguchi, 2015). However, there has been a lack of representation of queer Asian-Black pairing in mainstream Western gay media. Thus, this interracial pairing implicates a potential path toward decentering the colonialist superiority of whiteness that organizes racialized gender stereotypes of people of color. *Yellow Fever*'s vulgar representation of an Asian man rejecting a Black man is an impossible possibility of queerness associated with sticky rice that decenters whiteness.

However, *Front Cover* marginalizes *Yellow Fever*'s queerness surrounding the vernacular of sticky rice as it reorients the new-old immigrant dynamic of sticky rice in the text. More precisely, *Front Cover* centralizes the heteronormative expectations of family, kinship, and marriage that uphold the institutionalization of same-sex marriage in the U.S. When the "new" immigrant subject Ning joins Ryan's family visit to his grandmother, Ryan's mother Yen pulls Ning aside. Then she asks, "Your parent know you are… [gay]?" (Yeung, 2016, 49:18). Ning says, "No" (Yeung, 2016, 49:23). Yen replies, "Give them time" (Yeung, 2016, 49:25) and later says that "Chinese people very old-fashioned, take long, long time changing" (Yeung, 2016, 50:12). Then Yen shares that Ryan did not talk to her for a year after he had come out. So Yen tells Ning, "You good Chinese son. You no want to tell your parents because you no want to hurt their feeling. You want to give them hope" (Yeung, 2016, 50:48). This scene upends the racist stereotypes of Chinese migrant parents as homophobic. A queer ethnic minority like Ryan symbolizes "a marker of the homophobia (and the claim that homosexuality reflects the taint of the West) of his or her racial/ethnic/immigrant community" (Puar, 2007, p. 28). However, since whiteness actively pressures her naturalization, Yen's understanding of Ryan reveals her futuristic aspiration toward the U.S. as a (homo)sexually exceptional society. Yen being open about Ryan's sexuality is the product of the liberalism supporting White gay formations.

Still, Yen's broken English signifies the confinement of her inescapable foreignness. Yen cannot disembody the past. Yen's past – where she comes from – continues to shape her present-ness of living in the U.S. Ning asks Yen, "What about no grandkids?" (Yeung, 2016, 51:00). Looking a bit teary, Yen tells Ning that "it's fate. Some things are never meant to be" (Yeung, 2016, 51:05). Here, Yen's sense-making mimics the ancient Chinese philosophy of naturalists (also known as the school of yin-yang), orienting human experiences in the realm of nature. Yen's phrase "some things are never meant to be" suggests that she has no control over Ryan's same-sex desire. It is inherently scripted by the embodiment of spiritual fate. So she accepts that she may not witness Ryan's future with his own offspring. However, the blood-based kinship system of heteronormative reproduction determines the prosperity of Chinese families and their legacies. Thus, she looks sad as her sense-making process is caught up within a contradictory tension between her past, present, and future. She remains a part of and is never able to completely escape "very old-fashioned" China.

This scene leads to the shifting moment where the heterosexual matrix of White gay formations begins to unfold in *Front Cover*. After Ning's scene with Ryan and his family, a Chinese tabloid reports that Ning is "an undercover gay," accompanied by a picture of Ning with Ryan. This incident animates a plotline of Ning's acting career being in jeopardy. Angry with the tabloid, Ning tells Ryan that he must stop seeing him. This is not the first time Chinese tabloids have speculated about Ning's sexuality. Following this, Ning's girlfriend Miao from China arrives in New York. As soon as she arrives, Ning's agent sets up a press conference to deny the report about Ning being with Ryan. During the press conference Miao shows off her engagement ring as an indication of her romantic attachment to Ning. Ryan is also invited to sit along with Ning and Miao to tell the press that he is "the best friend" of the couple so Ning's gay gossip can be killed. Immediately after the press conference, Ryan leaves Ning, who privileges his "straight" image over his same-sex desire for Ryan. Ryan's departure from Ning signals how *Front Cover* reinforces the intelligibility of coming out of the closet as a normative lesbian-gay-bisexual-transgender-queer (LGBTQ) cultural expectation.

In fact, *Front Cover* uses Ning's faux-fiancée Miao to (mis)represent Ning's culture-specific performance of same-sex desire as the closet. As McCune (2014) and McRuer (2006) suggest, the closet is constructed as a sexually backward space through which Western science once marked same-sex desire as a medical disorder. The coming out of the closet signifies the individualistic logic of liberation from sexual oppression. This paradigm ignores nuances of non-White, non-Western subjects who perform the intersectional unintelligibility of queer sexualities. Ning shying away from pursuing his same-sex sexual desire reinserts the White, Western stereotype of China as a place/space in/through which national acceptances of LGBTQ rights are way behind. Ning's identity marks China's sexual backwardness. This textual arrangement further ignores the material reality of some well-known U.S. actors remaining in the closet.

In addition, *Front Cover* does not take into account the queerness of Ning and Miao, who perform their marriage of convenience. Huang and Brouwer (2018) demonstrate that Chinese queer subjects are often known to arrange and pursue xinghun (形婚), that is, a contract marriage between a queer woman and man. With such a marriage, Chinese queer subjects not only meet the heteronormative expectations of gender roles to save the public images of their families as culturally significant collective units, they also preserve some private spaces to perform their queer sexual freedoms. However, *Front Cover* does not elaborate the historical, specified expectations of Chinese family tradition. Still, this faux-fiancée representation offers a queer pedagogical moment of sticky rice.

Conclusion(s)

In this chapter, I have attempted to trouble the vernacular of sticky rice in and across *Yellow Fever* and *Front Cover*. Director Yeung's old-new immigrant dynamic of sticky rice is composed of three paradoxical layers of impossible possibilities of queerness. Yeung highlights the mobility of the "old" immigrant subject juxtaposing the "new" immigrant subject, even though neither of them escapes the active pressures of White supremacy that enforce naturalization. Yeung also represents the queerness of sticky rice in ways that denaturalize the racialized gender script of Asian men organized by whiteness. Moreover, Yeung's films offer space for visualizing the queerness of sticky rice that disrupts the present-ness of racialized cisheterosexism. Thus, the vernacular of sticky rice is both politically problematic and powerful. It works *on and against* the whiteness that organizes the inner workings of gay sexual cultures.

Before ending this chapter, I offer another look at the overall implication of the vernacular of sticky rice that *Yellow Fever* and *Front Cover* offer. I maintain that Yeung's old-new immigrant dynamic draws on the underlying logic of *stickiness (or sameness)* in relation to the ahistorical, unspecified notion of China as a homeland. This arrangement marginalizes China as a fluid, unstable, and multiple concept in and across political, economic, and historical contexts. As a Hong Kong-born filmmaker, Yeung assembles the seemingly monolithic notion of being Chinese to assert the *stickiness (or sameness) of thick intersectional differences* between Monty and Jai Ming in *Yellow Fever* and Ryan and Ning in *Front Cover*. Moving to, through, and away from *stickiness (or sameness)* of Chineseness coordinates the old-new immigrant dynamic of sticky rice. This is why Monty and Ryan as the "old" immigrant subjects struggle to fall in love with the "new" immigrant subjects who carry fictive and performative signs of Chineseness read as inescapable foreignness. Thus, I am left questioning what kinds of sexual and romantic relations are socially, culturally, and politically qualified to be *sticky rice*. What constitutes the *stickiness (or sameness)* of sticky rice pairing?

Consequently, I argue that a vernacular of sticky rice as queerness demonstrates a racialized gender borderland, that is, a continually shifting and ambiguous space of in-betweenness where intraracial "Asian" homoeroticism teaches queers "something" that is missing from the present. Displaying an ongoing temporal tension between the past and the future, the present-ness of racialized cisheterosexism represents impossible possibilities of sticky rice as a form of queerness that "rescues and emboldens concepts such as freedom" (Muñoz, 2009, p. 32). Only with such a racialized gender borderland can sticky rice cultivate the *stickiness (or sameness)* of queer Asian immigrant subjects. They may develop political solidarities that resist the superiority of whiteness. This is the only (historical, colonialist and imperialist) context of sticky rice that works, as the racialized gender politics of borderland cultures "are compounded by historic events and social structures and continue to be influenced by the environment in which a person lives" (Han, 2015, p.162). Without such racialized gender politics, the *stickiness (or sameness)* of sticky rice does not really trouble the *normal* and *ordinary*.

I end this chapter by reiterating that the queerness of sticky rice requires one's labor to move to, through, and away from continually shifting, ambiguous borderless (trans)Asia. It is also worth noting that the logics of patriarchy, heteronormativity, and cissexism provide unearned incentives to queer Asian immigrant subjects engaging in sticky rice desires. Nakayama (1994) reminds, "Not only is sexual identity unstable, but gender, 'race,' [and] nationality as well are much more fluid than they might seem" (p. 176). Therefore, I invite other queer theorists in the Communication discipline to join me in critiquing the racialized gender makings and unmakings of sticky rice as impossible possibilities of queerness in and across transnational Asian cultures.

Note

1   Originally published as/in Eguchi, S. (2020). Sticky rice politics: Impossible possibilities of queerness in and across *Yellow Fever* and *Front Cover*. *Women's Studies in Communication*, *43*(1), 67–84. https://doi.org/10.1080/07491409.2019.1696435

References

Abdi, S., & Calafell, B. M. (2017). Queer utopias and a (Feminist) Iranian vampire: A critical analysis of resistive monstrosity in A Girl Walks Home Alone at Night. *Critical Studies in Media Communication, 34* (4), 358–370. http://doi.org/10.1080/15295036.2017.1302092

Alexander, B. K. (2008). Queer(y)ing the postcolonial through the western. In N. K. Denzin, Y. S. Lincoln, & L. T. Smith (Eds.), *Handbook of critical and indigenous methodologies* (pp. 101–133). Sage Publications.

Anzaldúa, G. (2012). *Borderlands/la frontera: The new mestizo* (4th ed.). Aunt Lute Books. *Asian Queer Shorts*. [Collection]. (2009). Frameline.

Calafell, B. M. (2013). (I)dentities: Considering accountability, reflexivity, and intersectionality in the I and the We. *Liminalities: A Journal of Performance Studies, 9*(2), 6–13. http://liminalities.net/9-2/calafell.pdf

Calafell, B. M., & Delgado, F. P. (2004). Reading Latina/o images: Interrogating Americanos. *Critical Studies in Media Communication, 21*(1), 1–24. http://doi.org/10.1080/0739318042000184370

Chambers-Letson, J. (2018). *After the party: A manifesto for queer of color life*. New York University Press.

Chávez, K. R. (2012). Doing intersectionality: Power, privilege, and identities in political activist communities. In N. Bardhan & M. P. Orbe (Eds.), *Identity research and communication: Intercultural reflections and future directions* (pp. 21–32). Lexington Books.

Chávez, K. R. (2013). Pushing boundaries: Queer intercultural communication. *Journal of International and Intercultural Communication, 6*(2), 83–95. http://doi.org/10.1080/17513057.2013.777506

Cohen, C. J. (1997). Punks, bulldaggers, and welfare queens: The real radical potential of queer politics? *GLQ: A Journal of Lesbian and Gay Studies, 3*(4), 437–465. http://doi.org/10.1215/10642684-3-4-437

Crenshaw, K. (1989). Demarginalizing the intersection of race and sex: A black feminist critique of antidiscrimination doctrine, feminist theory, and antiracist policies. *The University of Chicago Legal Forum*, 139–167. https://chicagounbound.uchicago.edu/uclf/vol1989/iss1/8/

Crenshaw, K. (1991). Mapping the margins. *Stanford Law Review, 43*, 1241–1299. https://doi.org/10.2307/1229039

Dee, E. (2016, September 18). Interview: Front Cover director Ray Yeung. *New Bloom*. Retrieved from https://newbloommag.net/2016/09/28/front-cover-director-interview/

Duggan, L. (2002). The new homonormativity: The sexual politics of neoliberalism. In R. Castronovo & D. Nelson (Eds.), *Materializing democracy: Toward a revitalized cultural politics* (pp. 175–194). Duke University Press.

Eguchi, S. (2015). Queer intercultural relationality: An autoethnography of Asian-Black (dis)connections in White gay America. *Journal of International and Intercultural Communication, 8*(1), 27–43. http://doi.org/10.1080/17513057.2015.991077

Eguchi, S., Files-Thompson, N., & Calafell, B. M. (2018). Queer (of color) aesthetics: Fleeting moments of transgression in VH1's *Love & Hip-Hop: Hollywood Season 2. Critical Studies in Media Communication, 35*(2), 180–193. http://doi.org/10.1080/15295036.2017.1385822

Eng, D. L. (2001). *Racial castration: Managing masculinity in Asian America.* Duke University Press.

Eng, D. L. (2010). *The feeling of kinship: Queer liberalism and the racialization of intimacy.* Duke University Press.

Ferguson, R. A. (2005). Race-ing homonormativity: Citizenship, sociology, and gay identity. In E. P. Johnson & M. G. Henderson (Eds.), *Black Queer studies: A critical anthology* (pp. 52–67). Duke University Press.

Fung, R. (2005). Looking for my penis: The eroticized Asian in gay video porn. In R. Guins & O. Z. Cruz (Eds.), *Popular culture: A reader* (pp. 338–348). Sage Publications.

Gutierrez-Perez, R. (2018). Theories in the flesh and flights of the imagination: Embracing the soul and spirit of critical performative writing in communication research. *Women's Studies in Communication, 41*(4), 404–415. http://doi.org/10.1080/07491409.2018.1551695

Halberstam, J. (2011). *The queer art of failure.* Duke University Press.

Han, C. W. (2015). *Geisha of a different kind: Race and sexuality in gaysian America.* New York University Press.

Huang, S., & Brouwer, D. C. (2018). Negotiating performances of "real" marriage in Chinese queer xinghun. *Women's Studies in Communication, 41*(2), 140–158. http://doi.org/10.1080/07491409.2018.1463581

Johnson, E. P. (2001). "Quare" studies or (almost) everything I know about queer studies I learned from my grandmother. *Text and Performance Quarterly, 21*(1), 1–25. http://doi.org/10.1080/10462930128119

Johnson, J. R. (2013). Cisgender privilege, intersectionality, and the criminalization of CeCe McDonald: Why intercultural communication needs transgender studies. *Journal of International and Intercultural Communication, 6*(2), 135–144. http://doi.org/10.1080/17513057.2013.776094

Keeling, K. (2019). *Queer times, Black futures.* New York University Press.

King, C. S. (2016) American queerer: Norman rockwell and the art of queer feminist critique. *Women's Studies in Communication, 39*(2), 157–176. http://doi.org/10.1080/07491409.2016.1165778

LeMaster, L. (Published as B.) (2015). Discontents of being and becoming fabulous on RuPaul's Drag U: Queer criticism in neoliberal times. *Women Studies in Communication, 38*(2), 167–186. http://doi.org/10.1080/07491409.2014.988776

Lim, E.-B. (2014). *Brown boys and rice queens: Spellbinding performances in the Asias.* New York University Press.

McBride, D. A. (2005). *Why I hate Abercrombie & Fitch: Essays on race and sexuality.* New York University Press.

McCune, Jr. J. Q. (2014). *Sexual discretion: Black masculinity and the politics of passing.* University of Chicago Press.

McRuer, R. (2006). *Crip theory: Cultural signs of queerness and disability.* New York University Press.

Morrissey, M. E. (2017) The incongruities of queer decorum: Exploring Gabriel García Román's queer icons. *Women's Studies in Communication, 40*(3), 289–303 http://doi.org/10.1080/07491409.2017.1346532

Muñoz, J. E. (1999). *Disidentifications: Queers of color and the performance of politics.* University of Minnesota Press.

Muñoz, J. E. (2009). *Cruising utopia: The then and there of queer futurity.* New York University Press.

Nakayama, T. K. (1994). Show/down time: "Race," gender, sexuality, and popular culture. *Critical Studies in Media Communication, 11*(2), 162–179. http://doi.org/10.1080/15295039409366893

Nguyen, H. T. (2014). *A view from the bottom: Asian American masculinity and sexual representation.* Duke University Press.

Nishime, L. (2017). Reviving Bruce: Negotiating Asian masculinity through Bruce Lee paratexts in Giant Robot and Angry Asian Man. *Critical Studies in Media Communication, 34*(2), 120–129. http://doi.org/10.1080/15295036.2017.1285420

Pérez, H. (2015). *A taste for brown bodies: Gay modernity and cosmopolitan desire.* New York University Press.

Phua, V. C. (2007). Contesting and maintaining hegemonic masculinities: Gay Asian American men. *Sex Roles, 57,* 909–918. http://doi.org/10.1007/s11199-007-9318-x

Puar, J. K. (2007). *Terrorist assemblages: Homonationalism in queer times.* Duke University Press.

Spigel, L. (2001). Media homes: Then and now. *International Journal of Cultural Studies, 4*(4), 385–411. http://doi.org/10.1177/136787790100400402

Wu, C. (2018). *Sticky rice: A politics of intraracial desire.* Temple University Press.

Yeung, R. (Director). (1998). *Yellow fever.* Sankofa Film Productions.

Yeung, R. (Director). (2015). *Front cover.* NewVoice Productions.

Yep, G. A. (2010). Toward the de-subjugation of racially marked knowledges in communication. *Southern Communication Journal, 75*(2), 171–175. http://doi.org/10.1080/10417941003613263

Yep, G. A. (2013). Queering/quaring/kauering/crippin'/transing "other bodies" in intercultural communication. *Journal of International and Intercultural Communication, 6*(2), 118–126. http://doi.org/10.1080/17513057.2013.777087

Queering Gender Borders of Sticky Rice: On *Koreatown*

Both before and after the liberation of the U.S. immigrant policies beginning in the mid-twentieth century, the assignment of gender based on White cis-hetero-patriarchal ideals has enabled state and societal control of Asian bodies, social relations, and movement for the purposes of socioeconomic extraction and securing racialized Asianness as the external/internal boundary for the settler nation-state --- (Chen, 2019, p. 44).

Asian American men began from a place of dissident queerness – even if their relationship to it is sometimes inadvertent, unappreciated, or anxiety provoking. The operations of U.S. capitalism, imperialism, and militarism indelibly sculptured a social landscape in which inequalities continue to express themselves racially --- (Wu, 2018, p. 163).

As Chapter 1 showcases, sticky rice not only serves as a gay vernacular that describes a racialized Asian man who engages in same-sex sexual and romantic relationships with other racialized Asian men. But its trope also requires continually shifting and ambiguous spaces that produce the *stickiness (or sameness)* of men who fall under a racialized label *Asian*. Indeed, this *stickiness* operates as a racialized gender borderland where Asian male sexual minoritarians meet, date and have sex with one another. In this sense, "[s]tickiness involves a form of relationality, or a 'witness,' in which the elements that are 'with' get bound together" (Ahmed, 2004, p. 91).

Still, this homoeroticism points to the settler colonialist logics of whiteness that (re)organizes the cisheteropatriarchal ideals of gay phallic masculinity materialized as the *buffed out gay Adonis* (BOGA). Its embodied performance can be seen in and across the U.S. gay villages such as Los Angeles's West Hollywood, New York's Chelsea, and San Francisco's Castro (Muñoz, 2009). Consequently, the discourse of oppression rooted in the castration of racialized Asian cisgender men having failed to meet the aesthetic expectations of BOGA characterizes the contextual background of sticky rice politics (e.g., Han, 2015; Nguyen, 2014; Wu, 2018). However, this narrative obfuscates the simultaneous technology of cisgenderism working with masculinism, patriarchy, and phallic hegemony that produces *taken-for-granted* privileges for racialized Asian men in the political economy of settler nation-state (e.g., Shimizu, 2012; Wu, 2018). They are not innocently victims of (gay) racism. The certain dimensions of sticky rice reproduce the *mundane* executions and operations of whiteness that organize the cisheteropatriarchal ideals of gay phallic masculinity.

Directed by Steven Liang and written by Steven J. Kung, Here TV's *Falling for Angeles'* episode *Koreatown* (S1E2) points to the aforementioned landscape of sticky rice as a gay vernacular. The U.S.-based premium cable television network Here TV launched in 2002 programs the lesbian-gay-bisexual-transgender (LGBT) theme contents. The network collaborates with the LGBT community-based events and organizations as well. Created by David Millbern, the series *Falling for Angeles* represents how gay men of color from raced and classed communities experience Los Angeles's dating scene, develop intimacies, and manage everyday personal issues of sex, sexual health, and wellbeing. Writing for a popular LGBT-theme magazine *Adovocate*, Gettingger (2017) praises that this series is a timely and authentic portrayal of gay Los Angeles scene. Each episode of *Falling for Angeles* focuses on a neighborhood of Los Angeles such as Boyle Heights, Koreatown, Leimert Park, Silver Lake, Bel-Air, and Malibu. The 25-minute and 24 second episode, *Koreatown*, represents a *trans-Asian intercultural* encounter between a younger Taiwanese American Kevin (played by Ty Chen) and an older adopted Korean American Gino (played by Dale Song). Similar to *Yellow Fever's* and *Front Cover's* scenarios from Chapter 1, Kevin who look for dating White men begins to fall in love with Gino.

With the storyline of Kevin developing a feeling for Gino, *Koreatown* unsettles the White cisheteropatriarchal ideals of masculinity that reproduces the historically settled depiction of racialized Asian cisgender men having failed to meet the settler colonial branding of manhood. Indeed, *Koreatown* politically works toward disrupting what Han (2015) has argued is a normative path for racialized Asian men to gaze toward desiring the White masculine ideal in gay sexual cultures. In an article from Resonate Team (2017), the director Liang reiterates that *Koreatown* "conveys Asian American men as attractive — not only to other races but to each other." I so appreciate how *Koreatown* offers an alternative space to represent the trope of sticky rice.

At the same time, I also feel the strong urge to take a pose here. The political effort to produce the attractive sticky rice images do not necessarily dismantle the settler colonial power of whiteness that organizes the logic of gay phallic masculinity. The normative U.S. cisgender male attractiveness yet pressures, disciplines, and controls the racialized Asian men to aspire the White masculine ideal. Under the discursive effects of whiteness as a beauty standard, *Koreatown* invisibly reorients the *mundane* executions and operations of gay phallic masculinity without the representation of the White male bodies. Hence, I feel in need of disrupting how the White cisheteropatriarchal ideals of gay phallic masculinity arrange the architecture of sticky rice in *Koreatown*.

Accordingly, I trouble how *Koreatown* recycles a gay phallic economy of desire to narrate a *trans-Asian intercultural* encounter between a Taiwanese American Kevin and an adopted Korean American Gino in this chapter. I am also concerned with how *Koreatown* displays a moment of transgression that pedagogically points to what is missing from the present. The intersectionality of gay and Asian, constrained by White cisheteropatriarchal ideals, implicates vernacular possibilities of queerness around the trope of sticky rice. Here, I follow a Black feminist legal scholar Crenshaw (1989, 1991) and a queer of color performance scholar Muñoz (1999) to conceptualize the intersectionality of gay and Asian as a paradoxical site of resistant knowledge, performance, and politics. By this, I mean the way simultaneous operations of differences (e.g., ethnicity, gender performance, class, nationality, class, language, coloniality, and the body) produce complex contradictions of racialized Asian male subjects who identify and disidentify with the logic of whiteness that organizes gay sexual cultures. As Hill Collins (2019) reminds, "Intersectionality offers a window into thinking about the significance of ideas and social action in fostering social change" (p.286). Keeping this perspective in mind, I interrogate the cisgender, patriarchal, and phallic architecture of *Koreatown* to envision how the trope of sticky rice represents impossible possibilities of queerness as minoritarian resistance politics. The overall goal of this chapter is to gesture toward destabilizing of ongoing colonial histories of a cisgender binary ingrained in social institutions such as media.

In what follows, I first contextualize discourses around the intersectionality of gay and Asian that shape the trope of sticky rice. Following this, I discuss how I mobilize my queer analytic for this chapter that pays close attention to how the simultaneous technology of gender, working with differences, assembles the trope of sticky rice in *Koreatown*. Here, I justify why the intersectionality of gay and Asian that operates within the power and privilege of gay phallic masculinity requires a queer critique on gender. Then, my close reading of *Koreatown* follows. Lastly, I offer my concluding remarks of this chapter.

Intersectionality of Gay and Asian

The settler colonialist logics of whiteness organize gay sexual cultures are known to ignore, erase, and marginalize racialized Asian cisgender men through its popular media and community buildings (e.g., Eguchi, 2015; Han, 2015). The ordinary sets of gay and Asian narratives recenter the power and privilege of the White masculine ideal. The racialized Asian men are mostly imagined as *sexual bottoms* lacking in power and endowment (e.g., Eguchi, 2019; Phua, 2007; Poon 2006; Poon & Ho, 2008). The gay sexual cultural logic that normalizes anal sex penetration stigmatizes *sexual bottoms who get fucked* (Nguyen, 2014). A gay vernacular "getting fucked," signaling a man who is dominated by another man, implicates the subordinated positioning of bottoming as being weak or humiliated (Wu, 2018). This highly gendered construct of bottoming suggests the privileged position of topping known as *fucking*, working with the masculinist logic of cisnormative heteropatriarchy. Because a chauvinistic sign of male authority *the Phallus* is a gay sexual currency, the performance of topping (or fucking) signals a man's power being *sexually active*, *dominant*, and *masculine* (Han, 2015; Nguyen, 2014). Then again, Nakayama (1994) reminds, "In a White society, such as the United States, any relationship to the signification process must incorporate the White phallus. Any 'lack' of a White phallus already marks one as marginal" (p. 167). *The Phallus* cannot be just the Phallus in the settler colonialist nation-state that normalizes the supremacy of whiteness. The White phallic power and privilege relegates racialized Asian men as a second-class citizen.

Consequently, the "lower" phallic hierarchy of Asian men becomes a key narrative that occupies the intersectionality of gay and Asian. The interdisciplinary collection of queer Asian/American studies writers (e.g., Ayres, 1999; Fung, 2005; Lim, 2014; Phua, 2007; Poon, 2006; Poon & Ho, 2008) questions and critiques the gay sexual cultural operation of "Asian" as the subcultural fetish category for the older and masculine White men seeking younger and feminine Asian men. This "Asian" fetish category points to a larger political, economic, and historical context of globalization that maintains the supremacy of whiteness. Some Asian men in foreign countries are assumed to meet, date, and have sex with White men for the purpose of relocating to the west offering the same-sex marriage rights and benefits (e.g., Fung, 2005; Suganuma, 2012; Yue, 2008). So, they may escape from their local politics of cisheterosexism that disadvantage their same-sex desires.

Here, the Western institution of same-sex marriage is constructed as a symbol of sexual liberalism (Puar, 2007). At the same time, the Asian fetish that perpetuates the femininization of Asian men is a major source of conflict that reifies the discourse of sexual unattractiveness and desireability around the intersectionality of gay and Asian (e.g., Eguchi, 2015; Fung, 2005; Han 2015; Lim, 2014). Given gay sexual cultures that religiously worship youthfulness of phallic masculinity marginalize older men, Asian men become to signify someone whom (White) men can start to date when they get older. Dating Asian men can be a sign for (White) men who becomes less attractive and desirable. Such racialized gender stigmatization points to the way Asian men are thought to have a limited selection of sexual and romantic partners in gay sexual cultures that privileges the mundane operations of whiteness.

Despite the "lower" positioning of Asian men who struggle to find sexual and romantic partners, gravitating toward the White masculine is the norm for Asian men. They are known to compete against each other to get attention from the small pool of so-called *rice queens* – White men who are interested in dating Asian men (Han, 2015). However, desires for and attractions toward non-White men, including other Asian men, are often overlooked (Nguyen, 2014; Phua, 2007; Wu, 2018). In my previous work (Eguchi, 2015), I examine the way Japanese cisgender males living in New York City meet, date, and have sex with Black/African American cisgender males. Yet, such interracial relationality is never separated from the settler colonial logics of whiteness. Particularly for these Japanese men, the homoerotic and fetishized images of the U.S. as an imperialist power produce their same-sex sexual and romantic desires for Black/African American men as the *racialized insiders* of a settler nation-state. They are attracted to the hyper-sexualization of Black male bodies that maintains the phallocentric hegemony working with continuing histories of cisgenderism, racism, settler colonialism, and imperialism. Thus, everyday *mundane* performances of racialized Asian men who desire other men of color cannot entirely break free of the settler colonial mechanism of whiteness.

Still, resisting the discourse of oppression rooted in the castration is happening through the remasculinizing of racialized Asian cisgender men (Han, 2015). In another previous work of mine (Eguchi, 2019), I examine the representations of a sexually unidentified Vietnamese-American cisgender male Peter Le largely known as a model for the Los Angeles-based gay male underwear brand called *Andrew Christian*. Peter Le is also a gay porn adult entertainer/producer and personal trainer/body builder who breaks through the historical Asian male stereotypes. Rejecting a feminine Asian bottom stereotype, Peter Le says that "I always felt that Asian models had to push themselves harder...I was told that

I wouldn't go far because I was Asian. So, I wanted to break the Asian stereotypes" (Gremore, 2014). Here, Peter Le is a performer that embodies a brief moment of racialized gender transgression in the current logics of gay sexual cultures that reinforce the feminization of Asian men. However, the performative move does not fully dismantle the settler colonial branding of the White masculine ideal as the normative beauty standard. Indeed, Peter Le becomes like an *almost White* man through his self-fashioning of hypermasculinity (Eguchi, 2019). He is a light-skin Asian American cisgender male spectator who performs the politics of racialized gender transgression and gets benefits from the settler colonialist logics of whiteness. Peter Le's self-fashioning of racialized hypermasculinity implicates how the political effort to counter the historical castration of "Asian" men ironically works within the logic of whiteness.

Queering Cisgender Borders of Gay and Asian

Because the resistant performances of racialized Asian cisgender men do not necessarily dismantle the settler colonialist logics of whiteness, I remain concerned with how the intersectionality of gay and Asian maintains the simultaneous technology of cisgenderism working with masculinism, patriarchy, and phallic hegemony. Accordingly, similar to the Chapter 1, I mobilize "queer" as a practice or verb to interrogate the trope of sticky rice represented in *Koreatown*. Here, the notion of queer(ing) operates as a critical methodology that questions, critiques, and shifts the present moment through which queers are yet stuck in the normalized boundaries of power and ideologies (Muñoz, 2009). At the same time, I highlight that my focal point of this chapter's queer critique is different from the previous chapter that destabilizes and denaturalizes the old-new immigrant dynamic organizing the trope of sticky rice in and across *Yellow Fever* and *Front Cover*. Here, I pay careful attention to gender borders of gay and Asian, sustaining masculinism, patriarchy and phallic hegemony that architect the representation of sticky rice in *Koreatown*. I am concerned with the production and constitution of gender as an assemblage working with historically imbalanced power relations of differences. As Yep, Russo, and Allen (2015) remind, "gender is a critical concern for all individuals inhabiting various positions in a gender system" (p. 70). Hence, similar to Communication scholars such as Alexander (2012), Calafell (2015), Johnson (2014), and LeMaster (2015), I am interested in pushing borders of the *mundane* in order to envision gender beyond existing normative schema. Hence, I "queer" the architecture of gender that orchestrates a *trans-Asian intercultural* encounter between Kevin and Gino in *Koreatown* in this chapter.

My embodied urge to queer the production and constitution of gender in *Koreatown* emerges from my huge frustration with the cisgender, patriarchal, and phallic architecture of gay sexual cultures. I have been and am troubled with how the U.S. gay sexual cultures easily recenters the normative power relations of difference such as race, gender, class, nation, and the body. As Puar (2007) has critiqued before, the contemporary politics of homonationalism that capitalizes the LGBT (Lesbian-Gay-Bisexual-Transgender) rights as a nationalist product of the U.S. exceptionalism almost always privileges the White, cisgender, male, affluent, and able-bodied images of queer subjects. This phenomenon implicates how the origin of gay liberation movement that was concerned with multi-dimensions of queer politics (i.e., racism, sexism, classism, colonization, incarnation, and anti-capitalism) have gradually become only concerned with the issue of (homo)sexuality. As Ferguson (2019) reminds, "In fact, since the late sixties – from the Stonewall uprisings even – the intersectional interest of gay liberation expressed a politics that would try to relate to issues of sexuality, race, class, and gender to one another" (p. 2). Here, it is important to highlight that the 1969 New York's stonewall riots that promoted the gay liberation movement actually involved various transgender people of color who fought with the police on the front line (Calafell, 2019). There has been a clear and concrete alliance between cisgender queers and transgender people on the ground. Still, the contemporary gay liberation movement that marginalizes transgender people strategically preserves ongoing settler colonial histories of cisgender power and privilege. The politics of homonationalism that normalizes the relationship between homosexuality and nationalism rooted in whiteness deploys cisgender queer male subjects to aspire toward becoming and being hetero-masculine (Puar, 2007). Accordingly, anti-women, anti-feminine, and anti-transgender sentiments organize the architecture of gay sexual cultures (Muñoz, 2009). Hence, I call to queer the temporal and spatial specificities of (racialized) gender as an assemblage, designing impossible possibilities of queerness around sticky rice in *Koreatown*.

Centering my queer analytic of gender described above, I engage in my close reading of *Koreatown*. While repeatedly watching *Koreatown*, I observe how the *mundane* executions and operations of gay phallic masculinity that privilege whiteness shape the mediated displays of sticky rice as a vernacular. The gay phallic economy of desire that capitalizes the cisnormativity of sexual competition arranges the architecture of a *trans-Asian intercultural* encounter between Kevin and Gino. By cisnormativity, I mean a social structure that normalizes the power of cisgender privilege (e.g., Johnson, 2013; Spencer, 2015; Yep, Russo, & Allen, 2015). In addition, the relational juxtaposition between Kevin and Gino that mechanically remains unbalanced hints to the settler colonialist logics of whiteness, providing Gino more mobility than Kevin. However, the intersectionality of gay and Asian produces collective pain rooted in the castration establishes the *stickiness* (or *sameness*) of Kevin and Gino. Still, the unknowable future of Kevin and Gino that *Koreatown* ends with provides a temporal space of queer pedagogy that explicates what's missing from the present moment. By queer pedagogy, I mean a method of education that transgresses the normative ways of knowing, being, and acting. Thus, I organize my reading into the following four themes: *Cisnormative Phallic Competition, Relational Juxtaposition, Stickiness of Collective Pain,* and *the Unknowable Future.* Next, I begin showcasing my reading with the first theme *Cisnormative Phallic Competition.*

Cisnormative Phallic Competition

In *Koreatown*, the White cisheteropatriarchal logics of phallic sexual competition that subordinates racialized Asian cisgender men organize an ongoing interplay of tensions between Kevin and Gino. The interpersonal tension that pits an "Asian" man against another "Asian" man sparks from the initial moment when Kevin meets Gino. Kevin knocks the entrance door # 1018 in the hotel as soon as he gets off the elevator. Gino opens the door and says "what's up" (Liang, 2017, 01:48). With his confusing facial expression, Kevin replies to Gino that "I am Kevin" (Liang, 2017, 01:52). Gino follows up saying "umm…surprised?" (Liang, 2017, 01:57). Here, the narrative of Kevin not knowing how Gino looks like becomes obvious. However, Kevin avoids a possible confrontation. He says "just that I am getting laid. It happens less often than I'd like to admit" (Liang, 2017, 02:00). Then, a few seconds after he ponders, Kevin enters into Gino's room. Later in the episode, *Koreatown* evidences a storyline of Gino refusing to send his face photo to Kevin prior to their face-to-face encounter. This scenario suggests the *mundane* of being Asian in online gay sex cruising spaces that privilege the cisnormativity of whiteness as a social capital. Nguyen (2014) showcases that the technique of cropping off of the face is a passing strategy for Asian men to minimize their racialized cisgender disadvantages while maintaining anonymity online. The headless photo provides Asian men *virtual whiteness*. So, they can increase chances to meet other men offline. By virtual whiteness, I mean a digital performance of whiteness without physical presences of the body that carry scent and sensuality. Accordingly, the discriminatory characterizations of the Asian face are the social and performative sites of ideological struggle particularly for Gino who can otherwise pass like *almost White.* Because he grew up in the White, the U.S. adopted family, Gino can perform the whiteness of *buffed out gay Adonis* onto his lighter-skin well-exercised cisgender male able-body. Still, because of his Asian face, Gino struggles to pass like *almost White* offline.

The following sex scene gives an excuse for Gino's refusal to send his face photo to Kevin prior to their meeting. As soon as Kevin enters into Gino's room, he enjoys the 10th floor's view of Los Angeles. Gino says to Kevin that "you're cuter than the picture" (Liang, 2017, 02:26). After Kevin replies "thanks" (Liang, 2017, 02:28), Gino who undresses himself asks to Kevin, "so you wanna do this?" (Liang, 2017, 02:36). Gazing toward Gino's body, Kevin says "sure" (Liang, 2017, 02:46) and then proceeds to kiss Gino. By avoiding to kiss Kevin, Gino guides Kevin to put him on a knee. Kevin says that "it's fucking so hot" (Liang, 2017, 03:20) right after looking at Gino's penis. At this juncture, Kevin sucks Gino's penis. Then, as Gino says "suck it's so good" (Liang, 2017, 03:28), a cut moves to Gino penetrating Kevin from the back. This cisgender phallic sex narrative sequence not only proves how Gino's *headless* Asian body "resembles and conforms to the ideal of body of a young White man" (Nguyen, 2014, p. 198). But it also suggests an additional complexity of being Asian in online gay sex cruising spaces. In this sex scene, Gino is a top. Nothing suggests that Gino is a versatile who both fucks and get fucked. Then Gino refusing to sending the face photo to Kevin prior to meeting is excusable. Because the White cisheteropatriarchal logics of phallic sexual competition that shape gay sexual cultures do not imagine Asians as tops, Asian tops struggle to find their sexual partners (Han, 2015). Then, Gino who possess a "fucking so hot" (Liang, 2017, 03:20) penis may remain anonymous online for his cisgender male advantage. Gino is an Asian man who is *not* supposed to be a top. Gino is competitive in online gay sex cruising spaces that value the *phallus* as long as he counterbalances his *headless* Asianness. The often-invisible logics of cisnormativity, "analogous with respect to gender identity to the relationship between heteronormativity and sexual orientation" (Spencer, 2015, p. xix), reifies the historically racialized gender stereotypes of male endowment for the gay sexual beauty competition.

Simultaneously, Kevin sending out his face photo to Gino prior to their meeting suggests that the White cisheteropatriarchal logics of phallic sexual competition shape Asian bottoms differently from Asian tops. Despite of being born into Taiwanese migrant family household, Kevin learned how to perform whiteness as a cultural and linguistic labor. Kevin grew up in the White neighborhood and went to White schools. He is also a lighter skin just like Gino. Consequently, by cropping off of his Asian face in the photo, Kevin can also maintain the cisnormativity of virtual whiteness in online gay sex cruising spaces similar to Gino. However, by openly sharing his Asian face, Kevin chooses not to hide or neutralize his racialized Asianness while seeking out his sexual partners online. Here, it is possible to read that Kevin is more comfortable with his Asianness than Gino. *Koreatown* uncovers that Taiwanese migrant parents taught Kevin about his cultural heritage. Yet, Gino is a Korean adoptee who had to learn about his heritage by himself when he became an adult. However, Kevin is an Asian bottom getting fucked by Gino. Nothing suggests Kevin as a versatile either. Accordingly, because gay sexual cultures that recycle the White cisheteropatriarchal logics of phallic sexual competition embrace Asian men who play into the racialized gender stereotypes (Han, 2015), Kevin's sexual position helps ease Kevin to be open about his Asianness. While Kevin is not a feminine Asian male, Kevin performs the gay Asian bottomhood through his sexual performance. Consequently, there are both online and offline spaces through which Kevin can market himself as an Asian bottom. The gay sexual marketability of the Asian bottom requires the Asian face as a racialized gender symbol of the fetish category. Nguyen (2014) maintains "for many men, the face photo is the deciding factor, the deal maker or deal breaker....Not surprisingly, most people will not agree to meet offline for sex without seeing at least one face picture" (p. 198). Thus, Gino refusing to share his face photo online creates competing interpersonal tensions between Kevin as an Asian bottom and Gino as an Asian top even prior to their offline meeting for sex.

In addition, the climax of Gino penetrating Kevin crystalizes how the cisheteropatriarchal mechanism of phallic sexual competition organizes a top/bottom positioning in *Koreatown*. When Gino ejaculates inside of Kevin, Gino's condom breaks. So, Kevin gets upset with Gino by saying "while you were inside of me?" (Liang, 2017, 03:58). Kevin immediately goes to the bathroom. Gino shouts "you have nothing to worry about. I'm clean. The Cedars-Siani emergency room has PEP [post-exposure prophylaxis]. I'll call you an Uber" (Liang, 2017, 04:01). As soon as Kevin comes out of the bathroom, he abruptly leaves for the emergency room. Later, Gino finds out that Kevin left his keys in the hotel room. So, Gino calls Kevin and leaves his voicemail. This phone call scene leads to the following scene where Kevin comes to a Koreatown's Karaoke bar to pick up his keys from Gino. This narrative progression is quite puzzling.

Taking pre-exposure prophylaxis known as PrEP is becoming a common practice for HIV prevention nowadays (Dieffenbach & Fauci, 2011). While PrEP requires one's financial resources to access health care (Spieldenner, 2016), it is also known to protect people from transmitting HIV when they are exposed to bodily fluids during sex. Also, the gay media programming often features the PrEP advertisements for the HIV prevention. So, this could have been an interest of Here TV's *Falling for Angeles* series who requires advertising sponsorship. Still *Koreatown* does not advertise the increasing health practice of PrEP in representing Gino penetrating Kevin. And *Koreatown* recenters the magnitude of a male condom in HIV prevention practice.

At the same time, Kung's depiction of Gino's condom break reorients the controlling power of semen that sustains the *phallocentric cisnormativity*. When Gino's condom breaks, Gino instantly becomes *a suspect* who might have transmitted HIV to Kevin. There is no consideration of Kevin as a bottom possibly transmitting HIV to Gino. The normative understanding of receptive anal sex is a high risk for getting HIV. However, this illustration of Kevin at risk points to the controlling power of Gino. Kevin has no control over Gino's condom break. Gino's semen determines Kevin's health status even though one-time semen exposure does not necessarily lead to contract HIV. In addition, this cisnormative phallic narrative recenters what Cruz (2016) reminds is that a cumshot of a cisgender man ejaculating is an essential profit-making in the pornographic industry. Because *Koreatown* is not a pornographic episode, it cannot represent a graphic image of a cisgender man's ejaculation. However, through a condom break narrative, *Koreatown* invisibly normalizes the performance of a (top) cisgender man's ejaculation as a normative climax of gay sex that privileges the Phallus. This is a temporal spatiality of cisnormative phallic sexual competition where a man fucks has more controlling power of semen than a man who gets fucked, even when they may flexibly switch their sexual positions.

Furthermore, Kevin's strong reaction to Gino's condom break goes back to Gino refusing to send the face photo. Even though Kevin has no idea of Gino as an "Asian" top up until when Gino opens his hotel room door, Kevin still has sex with Gino. As I have mentioned earlier, Kevin is indeed attracted to Gino's headless body that replicates the cisnormativity of virtual whiteness. However, later in the episode *Koreatown* exposes that Kevin is normally a *potato queen* – a racialized Asian man interested in hooking up with and dating White men. So, for Kevin, Gino is not someone whom he usually looks to have sex. Simultaneously, in the beginning of their sex, Gino avoids kissing Kevin when Kevin wants to kiss Gino. These two frustrations add up to a temporal moment of Kevin's rage when he receives an unwanted semen expose. This is why Kevin says that "no, you've done enough" (Liang, 2017, 04:36) in response to Gino offering a company to the emergency room. At this point, Gino signifies *a headless Asian top suspect*.

Relational Juxtaposition

Simultaneously, the White cisheteropatriarchal logic of phallic competition rearranges the politics of naturalization that produce the social hierarchy of mobility. By this means, *Koreatown* provides much more spatial mobility to Gino than Kevin. Gino is framed to be closer to the cisnormativity of whiteness than Kevin. After he has gone to the emergency room, Kevin again meets Gino at the Koreatown's Karaoke bar to pick up his keys he has left at Gino's. While Kevin wants to leave as soon as he meets Gino, Gino persuades Kevin to stay. He says "I've been in your situation before. The last thing you wanna do is be alone, especially with your thoughts right now" (Liang, 2017, 07:21). A next cut is Kevin eating food with Gino at the bar. Then Gino's cisgender female friend, another Korean adoptee Lisa comes to remind Gino of a party happening at another side of the bar. She then invites Kevin to join them. Because the Karaoke party is for Los Angeles's Korean adoptees' support group, both Kevin and Gino begin to share their "Asian" heritages to one another. After Gino discloses that he is about to leave for Seoul to find his birth parents in next six hours, Kevin tells Gino "I'm not used to hanging out with so many Asians. I mean I went to a Chinese Baptist church when I was a kind and all that. But as an adult, I'm just not used to it" (Liang, 2017, 10:21). This is where Gino who refuses to send his face photo online asks Kevin "you didn't think I was gonna be an Asian" (Liang, 2017, 10:31). Then, after leaving the karaoke party, they discuss their heritages. Kevin shares that growing up in the White neighborhood where he was called "Ching Chong" (Liang, 2017, 12:14) and "Chinese boy or Karate Kid" (Liang, 2017, 12:17) at the school shaped him to act *(almost) White* to make friends with White people. Here, Kevin uncritically re-centers the language of assimilation that measures people of color's performative and spatial proximity to whiteness. So, Gino asks if Kevin feels connected to his Taiwanese heritage. Kevin replies that he speaks Mandarin and has visited Taiwan a few times with his migrant parents. Here, Gino shares the lack of connection to his heritage due to the absence of his birth parents. This narrative sequence builds an illusion of Kevin and Gino having in common. Both of them appear to lack embodied connections to their heritages. They are *almost White*.

However, a relational juxtaposition between Kevin and Gino mechanically remains unbalanced. The illusion of both Kevin and Gino being disconnected from their heritages does not operate as the *stickiness* (or *sameness*) of their sticky rice duo. According to the cisheteropatriarchal ideals of biological family and kinship, Gino who is an adoptee signals his inauthentic connection to his Korean heritage. Because of the migrant parents raising Kevin, Kevin is framed as more authentically "Asian" than Gino who learns about his heritage by his own. Consequently, Gino is symbolically tied to his adopted family household that represents whiteness. However, the household in which Kevin was raised by his migrant parents signals a racialized gender space of foreignness. Thus, while Gino who was born in

Korea is indeed a first-generation immigrant subject, Gino is much more spatially constructed as *almost White* than Kevin because of the White household he grew up in. Here, the cisnormative notion of household is a major social institution of whiteness as a territory.

Consequently, *Koreatown* maintains the language of *connection* to describe Kevin's negotiation with his heritage while using the language of *reclaiming* to describe Gino who learns about his heritage by his own. In the aforementioned narrative sequence, Gino asks, "Do you connect to your heritage at all?" (Liang, 2017, 12:28). Then, Kevin shares his ability to speak Mandarin and his previous visits to Taiwan. However, when Gino shares his lack of connection to his heritage, Kevin asks Gino "So, how did you reclaim your heritage?" (Liang, 2017, 13:19). The implication of *reclaiming* points to how Gino is temporarily cut off from his Korean heritage because of the transnational adoption. However, just like children of migrant parents, adopted parents may try to have their children to stay connected to their heritages through socialization processes. Yet, *Koreatown* does not take into account the alternative storyline of Gino learning about his heritage with his White adopted parents. Here, Gino's adopted parents are (invisibly) assumed to be cisgender and heterosexual as well. Still, without considering any alternative storylines, *Koreatown* reorganizes Gino as more (*almost) White* than Kevin. Doing so strategically redefines the cisnormativity of whiteness that provides more mobility to Gino than Kevin.

In addition, the following dialog between Gino and Kevin evidences my argument further. In response to Kevin's saying of "how did you reclaim your heritage?" (Liang, 2017, 13:19), Gino replies "well, my first Asian boyfriend was Japanese. He told me to just go to Koreatown and eat. So that's what I did" (Liang, 2017, 13:23). Because of his Japanese boyfriend's encouragement, Gino learns Korean food and then Korean language. In so doing, Gino ends up hanging out with Koreans. He says "being in Koreatown, it's just centered me" (Liang, 2017, 13:41). Accordingly, Gino follows up to celebrate Koreatown as a space that presents a magic. To support Gino's statement, Kevin also brings up about a Los Angeles' neighborhood SGV known as San Gabriel Valley. It is where early Chinese migrant labors first settled and then different kinds of Asians continue to reside. Here, both Gino and Kevin embrace "Asia" as a unified notion that mingles *different ethnicities and races* shored under. While this narrative sequence sounds like empowering for Asian/America, Gino's reclaiming of his heritage not only ignores political tensions, economic hierarchies, and historical struggles in (transnational, intercultural) Asia. But it also re-centers the uncritical paradigm of being "Asian" in the White settler colonial nation that strategically pits racial ethnic minorities against each other.

The culturally unspecific introduction of Gino's first Asian/Japanese boyfriend Chris demonstrates the problem. Had Chris been a Japanese American whose ancestors went through the internment camps, he might not have encouraged Gino to reclaim his heritage. Because of the internment camps as a symbolic legacy of racial and xenophobic oppression, Japanese Americans as the collective have minimized claiming their Japanese heritages for the survival purpose (Nakayama, 2012; Wu, 2014). At the same time, if he originally comes from Japan, he brings different kinds of politics to the fore. The contemporary Korea-Japan relations through which Japan brutally colonized Korea between 1907 and 1945 are on-going histories of struggle that contextualize its social interactions and processes. Had Chris strongly carried out Japan's anti-Korean sentiment rooted in its ethnocentrism, he might have wished Gino to remain being an *almost White* who may be cut off from his Korean heritage. So, Gino's Japanese boyfriend could have felt he was dating *an American who just looks like him* in the historical and contemporary context of Japan where tries to westernize/U.S. Americanize its social institution. However, Chris could have been a mixed-race and/or mixed-ethnic Japanese man who reclaims his heritage just like Gino. This would have denaturalized the racially homogenized assumption of Gino's first Asian/Japanese boyfriend. Still *Koreatown* that reifies the cisnormativity of whiteness does not account the historically specific and culturally saturated possibilities of Gino's Japanese boyfriend Chris, which entirely change the narrative of Gino reclaiming his heritage.

More troublingly, *Koreatown* uncritically promotes the unified notion of being *Asian*. While the historical continuum of anti-Asian racism that essentializes differences is always already present, the logics of whiteness capitalize political, economic, and historical tensions among Asians to maintain its power and privilege. For example, the social discourses around the health crisis of COVID-19, circulated the media, specifically reinsert the logics of anti-Chinese sentiment. Since the disease is assumed to originate from Wuhan, China, the media targets China as a major source of problem. At the same time, the media represents China's neighboring nations such as Japan and South Korea as the U.S. allies whom China also troubles. This framing of China hints to how a White settler nation-state capitalizes intraregional tensions for its advantage. So, the U.S. continues to be global and imperial power. Yet, *Koreatown* uncritically orients his first Asian/Japanese boyfriend Chris as a gateway for Gino to reclaim his Asian/Korean heritage.

At the same time, this *Koreatown*'s uncritical, uncultural paradigm of *being Asian* is meant to regenerate an emphasis of Gino's mobility promoted by the cisnormativity of whiteness. The next cut Kevin discloses his romantic interest for Gino leads to a storyline of Gino being able to meet, date, and have sex with different kinds of men. In the middle of night after walking out of the karaoke bar, Kevin tells Gino that a hook up turning into a date that lasts all night is his romantic fantasy. Because Kevin is having a good time despite of the traumatic condom break, he says "there's just something about you [Gino] that makes me feel safe" (Liang, 2017, 15:00). Then Kevin tries to kiss Gino who avoids kissing Kevin again. So, Kevin interrogates why Gino refuses to kiss. Gino tells to Kevin that it is because of him going to Seoul for a few weeks. Kevin replies "that's fine by me. I'll still be single when you come back" (Liang, 2017, 15:22). So, Gino discloses that he is not looking for a relationship. Gino likes "to have sex. No commitment. No attachment" (Liang, 2017, 15:50). He follows up that he not only has failed to be in the open relationship but also has cheated on all of his ex-boyfriends. Then, this interaction gradually progresses to a heated argument to the point where Kevin tries to leave Gino. He abruptly cuts off the interaction by saying it is late at night. Here, despite of Gino having refused to send his face photos originally, Gino who does not want to be in a relationship appears to have opportunities to have sex with men as he likes. Gino breaks through a glass ceiling implicates his currency as an *almost White gay Adonis* with a "fucking so hot" (Liang, 2017, 03:20) penis. This is Gino's cisgender male privilege.

However, from the beginning of *Koreatown*, Kevin tells that he rarely gets laid. Kevin saying of "I'll still be single when you come back" (Liang, 2017, 15:25) is not something Kevin would easily say to Gino whom he has just met. While reading Kevin as someone looking for a sexually monogamous romance is possible, Kevin's line is an embodied product of Kevin who can't break through a glass ceiling created for racialized Asian cisgender men. Kevin saying he will be still single when Gino comes back is his vulnerability of wanting to find a cisgender boyfriend whom he can't find. In the following scene at the Korean restaurant, Kevin says he thought he would have an easy time to date someone in Los Angeles because it is known as a city where gay men date gay Asian men. But Kevin is now having a difficult time to find someone special. This narrative progression points to how the cisnormative whiteness of gay phallic masculinity that unbalances a relational juxtaposition between Kevin and Gino privileges Gino and disadvantages Kevin.

Stickiness of Collective Pain

Then and there, *Koreatown* orients the *stickiness* of Kevin and Gino's sticky rice duo. At the juncture where Kevin who tries to leave Gino looks back and says "hey, Gino. You hungry?" (Liang, 2017, 17:41), the politics of collective pain that reproduces the intersectionality of gay and Asian organizes a meeting point of trans-Asian connectivity between Kevin and Gino. The racialized cisgender pains they embody to carry out help them contextualize and constitute the *stickiness* of Kevin and Gino. Next, I take some time to unpack what I mean by this.

As soon as Gino gazes toward Kevin saying "you hungry?" (Liang, 2017, 17:41), *Koreatown* presents Gino and Kevin eating the Korean foods at late night. Gino sharing the history of Sundae Wichitage as a dish originated from Los Angeles's Koreatown turns to Kevin's sharing of being unable to find a boyfriend. Kevin tells that he cannot still find someone special despite of having lived in Los Angeles for three years even when he heard that "the gays here [Los Angeles] actually date Asians" (Liang, 2017, 18:59). This leads to Kevin problematizing how his male co-worker says "Daniel Dae Kim [Korean-American male actor] was attractive for an Asian guy" (Liang, 2017, 19:10). Gino agrees with Kevin by characterizing Kevin's co-worker's comment as "fucked up" (Liang, 2017, 19:13). Then Kevin challenges Gino as he begins that "you are acutely aware of racism. That is the real reason why you didn't send a face pic. Not for privacy" (Liang, 2017, 19:33). Kevin continues that most men who drive their cars across town to meet up with Gino "*might as well*" (Liang, 2017, 19:47), have sex with him regardless of Gino's Asian face. So, Gino asks, "Is that why you slept with me? Cause, might as well?" (Liang, 2017, 19:56). This opens up a heated debate between Kevin and Gino. Kevin calls out Gino's unavailability to date even when Gino flirts with Kevin. So, Gino calls out Kevin as a "self-loathing Taiwanese-American that isn't attracted to other Asians" (Liang, 2017, 20:39). Then, Gino reiterates that being with his Japanese boyfriend Chris has changed his racial dating preference. Prior to Chris, all the Gino's ex-boyfriends and ex-girlfriends used to be White. So, Gino argues that being able to love someone who looks like himself is the potential to love himself. Then, Kevin tells Gino that "well, now you know why I wanted to kiss you" (Liang, 2017, 21:45). As soon as Gino hears this, he holds Kevin's hand as Kevin looks teary. This leads into the *Koreatown's* ending scene where Gino kisses Kevin in the early morning that is before Gino departs for Seoul.

Similar to *Yellow Fever* and *Front Cover* analyzed in Chapter I, *Koreatown* articulates the way gay racism that normalizes the supremacy of the White Phallus is the *stickiness* (or *sameness*) of Kevin and Gino's sticky rice duo. Kevin and Gino mutually develop an affective connection to one another over the collective pain produced by the politics of racialized gender. At the same time, gay Asian pain ignores how the *stickiness* (or *sameness*) of Kevin and Gino's sticky rice duo reinserts the power and privilege of cisnormativity that organizes gay sexual cultures. The aforementioned dialog between Kevin and Gino taking place in the Korean restaurant marginalizes multi-dimensional politics of anti-Asian racism working with differences such as gender, class, ethnicity, nationality, language and the body.

Scholars (e.g., Eguchi & Long, 2019; Han, 2015; Nguyen, 2014) have already articulated how the common phrase of *No Fats, No Femmes, No Asians*, prevalent in and across online gay sex cruising spaces, re-centers the whiteness of *buffed out gay Adonis (BOGA)* as an inviable and universal power. The phrase, which is intersectional by nature, normalizes heteropatriarchal ideals of gay phallic masculinity as the normative cisgender male gender attractiveness. The sexual minoritarian subjects who fall under all of fats, femmes, and Asians are highly stigmatized as sexually unattractive. However, in *Koreatown* both Kevin and Gino do not occupy the temporal spaces of fats and femmes even when they are racialized as Asian. They are both well-toned, masculine-presenting cisgender male subjects who may be only disadvantaged because of their Asianness.

Accordingly, the *stickiness* (or sameness) of Kevin and Gino's sticky rice duo more or less supports the *mundane* executions and operations of gay phallic masculinity that produce sexual cultures of *No Fats, No Femmes, No Asians*. The logic of fatphobia that creates a hatred against overweight people is a gay sexual cultural norm that shapes male sexual minoritarians to physically work out (Whitesel, 2014). So, they can present their well-toned, gym-going, muscular bodies to be sexually desirable and attractive in online gay sex cruising spaces that normalizes *buffed out gay Adonis*. At the same time, sissyphobia that is an irrational fear of effeminacies correct, discipline, and surveil male sexual minoritarians' gender presentations (Eguchi, 2011). This disdain of sissy-ness that sustains the normativity of phallic masculine patriarchy ultimately plays into gay anti-Asian racism. The castration of Asian men as *feminine Others* is the major source of gay anti-Asian racism (e.g., Han 2015; Lim, 2014; Nguyen, 2014; Wu, 2018). Still, *Koreatown* does not problematize, disrupt, and shift the intersectional technologies of anti-Asian racism working with fatphobia and sissyphobia. One-dimensional politics of gay anti-Asian racism, disconnected from fatphobia and sissyphobia, shapes Kevin and Gino's racialized cisgender pain.

In addition, Kevin and Gino's *stickiness* (or *sameness*) erases other intersectional issues and concerns of being gay and Asian. The logics of cisheteronormativity that organize various Asian-American communities such as Taiwanese-American and Korean-American are known to marginalize sexual and gender minoritarians in such racialized spaces (Han, 2015). However, *Koreatown* does not pay attention to how Kevin and Gino negotiate the logics of homophobia – and irrational fear of homosexuality – in and across their social interactions with family, friends, colleagues, and more. Only when Kevin meets up again with Gino after he has gone to the emergency room due to the condom break incident, Kevin mentions that he fears of a possibility to come out as gay to his parents. This storyline has the potential to be developed further. Still, the storyline disappears as the narrative progresses. The entire 25-minute and 24-second episode of *Koreatown* does not articulate how intersectional dimensions of being gay and Asian constitute Kevin and Gino's *stickiness* (or *sameness*) rooted in their collective pain.

Simultaneously, Kevin and Gino's *stickiness* (or *sameness*) of being Asian that questions the White Phallus works only within the homoeroticism of a West-East encounter coded as a White-Asian encounter. Similar to *Yellow Fever* and *Front Cover* from Chapter I, *Koreatown* does not elaborate any possibilities of Kevin and Gino meeting, having sex, dating with male sexual minoritarians of color such as Blacks and Latinos. However, the rhetoric of Kevin and Gino meeting, having sex, dating with *either* Whites *or* Asians is unrealistic in Los Angeles. *Koreatown* forgets to politicize, historicize, and contextualize the architecture of Los Angeles's Koreatown as an interracially contingent space. Take for example, the 1992's Los Angeles riots that involved the physical damages of stores and surroundings in Koreatown point to ongoing political, economic, and historical tensions between Blacks, Koreans, and Latinixs. As Delgado and Stefancic (2012) have suggested, the settler colonial logics of whiteness that organize the U.S. social institutions pit racial minority groups against one another for the purposing of maintaining the White supremacy. The legacy of the 1992's Los Angeles riots is still seen almost three decades later. According to Lah (2017), Blacks, Koreans, and mostly Latinixs continue to reside Koreatown today. Still, *Koreatown* marginalizes the Koreatown's legacy of non-White interracial relations between Blacks, Koreans, and Latinixs. In so doing, *Koreatown* represents its sticky rice narrative as an *alternative* to the stereotypical gay narrative of a White-Asian encounter.

The Unknowable Future

Thus far, I have attempted to queer the architecture of gender as an assemblage, representing the trope of sticky rice in *Koreatown*. The three following themes; *cisnormative phallic competition*, *relational juxtaposition*, and *stickiness of collective pain* chronologically point to the cisnormative whiteness of gay phallic masculinity as an exceptional power. It shapes the intersectionality of gay and Asian through which racialized Asian male sexual minoritarians meet, have sex, and date with other "Asian men." Kevin falling in love with Gino works on and against the *mundane* executions and operations of gay phallic masculinity. The simultaneous workings of the aforementioned three themes that architect *Koreatown* recenters the logic of cisnormativity, restricting the emergence of gender possibilities for normalizing "Asianness" of Asian American men and masculinities.

The discursive practice of cisnormativity described above resembles the functionality of whiteness. Since whiteness is an invisible and universal power, whiteness strategically maneuvers in and across times, spaces, and contexts (e.g., Jackson, 1999; McIntosh, Moon, & Nakayama, 2019; Nakayama, 1994; Nakayama & Krizek, 1995). The settler colonial logic of whiteness adapts social, cultural, and political changes to appear something new. However, new appearance of whiteness functions "the same old" that maintains the settler nation-state. Hence, in *Koreatown*, the cisnormativity of gay phallic masculinity strategically maneuvers under the language of empowering Asianness of Asian American men. The "empowered" masculine presentation of sticky rice narrative reiterates how racialized Asian male subjects embody the whiteness of gay phallic masculinity to seek the approval from queer peers. Hence, the queering of gender architecting *Koreatown*'s sticky rice narrative showcases the functionality of cisnormativity similar to whiteness.

At the same time, the simultaneous workings of the aforementioned three themes do not conclude any future plots of Kevin and Gino. *Koreatown* ends with Gino kissing Kevin before leaving for Seoul leaves a space of queer transtemporal imagination where the future of Kevin and Gino remains unknowable. Drawing Gopinath (2018), I define queer transtemporal imagination as an anti-normative conduit for disorienting the present in relationships with the past and present providing "a glimpse of alternative social orders and political imaginaries" (p. 175). Next I unpack how the unknowable future of Kevin and Gino operates as a queer pedagogy that questions what's missing from the present.

In the early morning ending scene of *Koreatown* when Gino says he wishes he would have met Kevin in a different timing, Gino finally kisses Kevin. Since Gino has previously mentioned that kissing is a sign of intimacy, Gino kissing Kevin right before going to Seoul signifies how Gino has also started to fall for Kevin. The collective pain of being gay and Asian cultivates a temporal space of Kevin and Gino's sticky rice intimacy. Still *Koreatown* that ends with this kiss scene does not suggest the concrete future of Kevin and Gino. However, both Kevin and Gino return to an episode six *Malibu* of *Falling for Angeles* which another gay couple is getting married. Right after the wedding, Kevin approaches to Gino and asks "what are you doing here?" (Clift & Millbern, 2017, 10:30) at the venue near by the beach in Malibu. In this conversation scene, Gino mentions that going to South Korea changes everything for him. Gino describes, "It's like in a way I find myself" (Clift & Millbern, 2017, 11:01). Then, both Kevin and Gino talk about the last gathering when they went to eat corn cheese late night and then have kissed. This leads to both of them admiring another couple getting married. At this juncture where Kevin says "I'd like to have that [referring to another couple getting married] someday" (Clift & Millbern, 2017, 11:32), Gino holds Kevin's hand and walks out toward a reception. Then, later Gino and Kevin end up dancing together at the reception. Still *Falling for Angeles*, which *Koreatown* is a part of, concludes its series without suggesting the future of Kevin and Gino as a sticky rice duo.

Here, I celebrate the unknowable future of Kevin and Gino that *Koreatown* offers. The ending storyline of Kevin and Gino points to a space of queer transtemporal imagination through which a sticky rice duo suspends the cisheteropatriarchal logics of linear growth model for intimacy. Conforming to the current landscape of a mainstream U.S. gay rights movement that normalizes a same-sex marriage, Kevin and Gino may get into a romantic relationship, get married, and have children in the future. It is also possible that Kevin and Gino never meet up again after the wedding. Or they may continue to casually hook up. As a viewer of *Koreatown*, I will never know the future of Kevin and Gino. However, this unknowability of Kevin and Gino is a queerness of sticky rice as "a state of being out of place and disoriented in the landscape of [cis]heteronormativity" (Gopinath, 2018, p. 61). Queerness provides a temporal space of (im)possibility through which alternative ways of knowing, being, and acting can be imagined (e.g., Chambers-Letson, 2018; Chávez, 2013; Keeling, 2019). In *Koreatown*, queerness of sticky rice offers a moment of transgression against the cisheteropatriarchal logics of linear growth model for intimacy embraced in the U.S. settler nation-state.

Still, the queer transtemporal imagination of Kevin and Gino struggles to dismantle how the cisheteronormative productions of biological family and kinship shape *Koreatown*'s narrative of being Asian in Los Angeles's gay sexual cultures. *Koreatown* ends with Gino leaving for Seoul to find his birth parents. Then, in the last episode of *Falling for Angles, Malibu*, Gino comes back from Seoul and tells Kevin that having visited South Korea helps him find who he really is. This Gino's self-discovery and self-fulfillment of returning to South Korea where he was born may be empowering on the surface. Simultaneously, this storyline suggests how *Koreatown* conceptualizes a homeland that privilege the cisheteropatriarchal structures of biological family and kinship. Here, a homeland is a space and place of origin where the racialized Asian subjects can only claim and reclaim their "Asian" heritages. This conceptualizing of homeland reinserts the White settler colonial cartography of "Asia" that essentializes Asian Americans as permanently foreigners. However, *Koreatown*'s conceptualization of homeland ignores a possible way the adopted sexual minoritarian subjects continue to be disconnected from their birth places even after their returning visits. The homeland can be a space and place that disciplines and repudiates queerness of the adopted sexual minoritarian subjects like Gino. Accordingly, the adopted Asian sexual minoritarian subjects may continue to live in an in-between, liminal space that continually disrupts the normative upward directionality of linear growth. They may not magically claim and reclaim their "Asian" heritages rooted in the cisheteropatriarchal productions of biological family and kinship. Still, *Koreatown* does not account such impossible possibility in representing Gino.

Yet, this *Koreatown's* failure rooted in the logics of cisheteropatriarchy points to the way the unknowable future of Kevin and Gino implicates the significance of queer diaspora in theorizing the trope of sticky rice. Gopinath (2018) reminds of queer diaspora as "both a spatial and a temporal category" (p. 6). More precisely, queer diaspora not only "challenges the heteronormative and patrilineal underpinnings of conventional articulations of diaspora and nation" (p. 5). But it also "reorients traditionally backward glance of conventional articulations of diaspora, often predicated on a desire for a return to lost origins" (p. 5). Queer diaspora provides an alternative cartography of desire, intimacy, and relationality that questions, critiques, and shifts the normative articulations of national and cultural borders (Yue, 2011). From this line of theorizing, I borrow Otalvaro-Hormillosa (1999) to argue that *homelessness* of racialized Asian sexual minoritarians, challenging the conventional articulations of diaspora, nation, and (homo)sexuality, is a queerness of sticky rice, alternatively producing the *stickiness* (or *sameness*).

For example, both a Taiwanese-American cisgender male Kevin and an adopted Korean-American cisgender male Gino struggle with whiteness of gay sexual cultures that relegates their embodiments of being racialized as Asian. At the same time, both of them struggle with cisheteronormative intersections of homeland, hostland, and diaspora that regulate, control, and discipline their queerness. Still, they receive unearned cisgender male privileges. However, the complex and messy intersections of power, privilege, and oppression are a continually shifting and ambiguous space from which both Kevin and Gino negotiate the unknowable future of their sticky rice desire, intimacy, and relationality. It remains invisible and unintelligible within the conventional logics of present-ness.

Consequently, a temporal space of *homelessness* where racialized Asian men meet, date, and have sex with other racialized Asian men is indeed a *queer diaspora*. It provides "alternative ways of seeing and knowing capable of challenging the scopic and sensorial regimes of colonial modernity" (Gopinath, 2018, p. 7). In this fashion, I take a further step to call for attending sticky rice as one of the many aesthetical practices of queer diaspora. To showcase my call, I propose the following questions; *how do the conventional logics of present-ness constraint possibilities of sticky rice for the future? How do impossible possibilities of sticky rice require revisitations of the past as forgotten possibilities that transgress the normative cartography of the present-ness? What can be gain and can be lost in impossible possibilities of sticky rice as an aesthetical practice of queer diaspora? How does the stickiness (or sameness) of sticky rice connect disconnected fragmentations of bodies and landscapes and histories and temporalities to archive the alternative cartographies of desire, intimacy, and relationality? At what point does stickiness (or sameness) of sticky rice fall away?* These questions require historically specific and cultural-saturated examinations of sticky rice as a relational connectivity of queer diaspora(s).

Concluding Remarks

To further build on my analysis of *Yellow Fever* and *Front Over* in the previous chapter, I have attempted to interrogate how *Koreatown* recycles the *mundane* executions and operations of gay phallic masculinity to construct the performative displays of sticky rice in this chapter. In particular, I have centralized a queer analytic to denaturalize the architecture of (racialized) gender as an assemblage, representing the trope of sticky rice in *Koreatown*. The gay phallic economy of desire that capitalizes sexual competition arranges the relational background of Kevin and Gino. At the same time, a relational juxtaposition between Kevin and Gino that remains unbalanced hints to the settler colonial logics of whiteness that produces one's social capital. *Koreatown* suggests how the cisnormativity of whiteness that shapes social institutions gives more mobility to Gino who was raised in the White household than Kevin who was raised in the migrants' household. However, the politics of collective pain, emerged from the intersectionality of gay and Asian, generates the *stickiness* (or *sameness*) of Kevin and Gino as a sticky rice duo. Still, *Koreatown* that ends with the unknowable future of Kevin and Gino offers a space of queer transtemporal imagination through which the cisheteropatriarchal logics of linear growth model for intimacy are problematized. The operation of sticky rice as an aesthetical practice of queer diaspora is possible. Yet, the overall representation of sticky rice in *Koreatown* is politically problematic and powerful just like *Yellow Fever* and *Front Cover*.

References

Ahmed, S. (2004). *The cultural politics of emotion*. Edinburgh University Press.

Alexander, B. K. (2012). The performative sustainability of race: Reflections on Black culture and the politics of identity. Peter Lang.

Ayres, T. (1999). China doll -the experience of being a gay Chinese Australian. In P. A. Jackson & G. Sullivan (Eds.), *Multicultural queer: Australian narratives* (pp. 87–97). Harrington Park Press.

Calafell, B. M. (2015). *Monstrosity, performance, and race in contemporary culture*. Peter Lang.

Calafell, B. M. (2019). Narrative authority, theory in the flesh, and the fight over the death and life of Marsha P. Johnson. *QED: A Journal in GLBTQ Worldmaking, 6*(2), 26–39.

Chambers-Letson, J. (2018). *After the party: A manifesto for queer of color life*. New York University Press.

Chávez, K. R. (2013). *Queer migration politics: Activist rhetoric and coalitional possibilities*. University of Illinois Press.

Chen, J. N. (2019). *Trans exploits: Trans of color cultures & technologies in movement*. Duke University Press.

Clift, W., & Millbern, D. (Directors). (2017). Malibu. [Television series episode]. In D. Millbern (Creator), *Falling for Angles*. HereTV.

Crenshaw, K. (1989). Demarginalizing the intersection of race and sex: A black feminist critique of antidiscrimination doctrine, feminist theory, and antiracist policies. *The University of Chicago Legal Forum*, 139–167. https://chicagounbound.uchicago.edu/uclf/vol1989/iss1/8/

Crenshaw, K. (1991). Mapping the margins. *Stanford Law Review, 43*, 1241–1299. https://doi.org/10.2307/1229039

Cruz, A. (2016). *The color of kink: Black women, BDSM, and pornography*. New York University Press.

Delgado, R., & Stefancic, J. (2012). *Critical race theory: An introduction* (2nd ed.). New York University Press.

Dieffenbach, C. W., & Fauci, A. S. (2011). Thirty years of HIV and AIDS: Future challenges and opportunities. *Annals of Internal Medicine, 154*, 766–771. http://doi.org/10.7326/0003-4819-154-11-201106070-00345

Eguchi, S. (2011). Negotiating sissyphobia: A critical/interpretive analysis of one 'femme' gay Asian body in the heteronormative world. *Journal of Men's Studies, 19*(1), 37–56. http://doi.org/10.3149/jms.1901.37

Eguchi, S. (2015). Queer intercultural relationality: An autoethnography of Asian-Black (dis)connections in White gay America. *Journal of International and Intercultural Communication, 8*(1), 27–43. http://doi.org/10.1080/17513057.2015.991077

Eguchi, S. (2019). Queerness as strategic whiteness: A queer Asian American critique of Peter Le. In D. M. D. McIntosh, D. G. Moon, & T. K. Nakayama (Eds.), *Interrogating communicative power of whiteness* (pp. 29–44). Routledge.

Eguchi, S., & Long, H. (2019). Queer relationality as family: Yas fats! yas femmes! yas Asians! *Journal of Homosexuality, 66*(11), 1589–1606. http://doi.org/10.1080/00918369.2018.1505756

Ferguson, R. A. (2019). *One-dimentional queer*. Polity.

Fung, R. (2005). Looking for my penis: The eroticized Asian in gay video porn. In R. Guins & O. Z. Cruz (Eds.), *Popular culture: A reader* (pp. 338–348). Sage Publications.

Gettingger, A. (2017, December 4). Falling for Angeles is a timely depiction of gay L.A. *Advocate*. https://www.advocate.com/television/2017/12/04/falling-angels-timely-depiction-gay-la

Gopinath, G. (2018). *Unruly visions: The aesthetic practices of queer diaspora*. Duke University Press.

Gremore, G. (2014, January 10). Adult film star Peter Le redefines the Asian male as a dominant sexual force to be reckoned with. *Queerty*. http://www.queerty.com/adult-film-star-peter-le-redefines-the-asian-male-as-a-dominate-sexual-force-to-be-reckoned-with-20140110

Han, C. W. (2015). *Geisha of a different kind: Race and sexuality in gaysian America*. New York University Press.

Hill Collins, P. (2019). *Intersectionality as critical social theory*. Duke University Press.

Jackson II, R. L. (1999). White space, white privilege: Mapping discursive inquiry into the self. *Quarterly Journal of Speech, 85*(1), 38–54. http://doi.org/10.1080/00335639909384240

Johnson, A. (2014). Confessions of a video vixen: My autocritography of sexuality, desire, and memory. *Text and Performance Quarterly, 34*(2), 182–200. https://doi.org/10.1080/10462937.2013.879991

Johnson, J. R. (2013). Cisgender privilege, intersectionality, and the criminalization of CeCe McDonald: Why intercultural communication needs transgender studies. *Journal of International and Intercultural Communication, 6*(2), 135–144. http://doi.org/10.1080/17513057.2013.776094

Keeling, K. (2019). *Queer times, black futures*. New York University Press.

Lah, K. (2017, April 29). The LA riots were a rude awakening for Korean-Americans. *CNN*. https://www.cnn.com/2017/04/28/us/la-riots-korean-americans/index.html

LeMaster, L. (Published as B.) (2015). Discontents of being and becoming fabulous on RuPaul's Drag U: Queer criticism in neoliberal times. *Women Studies in Communication, 38*(2), 167–186. http://doi.org/10.1080/07491409.2014.988776

Liang, S. (Director). (2017). Koreatown. [Television series episode]. In D. Millbern (Creator), *Falling for Angles*. HereTV.

Lim, E.-B. (2014). *Brown boys and rice queens: Spellbinding performances in the Asias*. New York University Press.

McIntosh, D. M. D., Moon, D. G., & Nakayama, T. K. (2019). Introduction: Introducing twenty-first century whiteness or 'everything old is new again.' In D. M. D. McIntosh, D. G. Moon, & T. K. Nakayama (Eds.), *Interrogating the communicative power of whiteness* (pp. 1–12). Routledge.

Muñoz, J. E. (1999). *Disidentifications: Queers of color and the performance of politics*. University of Minnesota Press.

Muñoz, J. E. (2009). *Cruising utopia: The then and there of queer futurity*. New York University Press.

Nakayama, T. K. (1994). Show/down time: "Race," gender, sexuality, and popular culture. *Critical Studies in Media Communication, 11*(2), 162–179. http://doi.org/10.1080/15295039409366893

Nakayama, T. K. (2012). Dis/orienting identities: Asian Americans, history, and intercultural communication. In A. Gonzalez, M. Houston, & V. Chen (Eds.), *Our voices: Essays in culture, essay, and communication* (5th ed., pp. 20–25). Oxford University Press.

Nakayama, T. K., & Krizek, R. L. (1995). Whiteness: A strategic rhetoric. *Quarterly Journal of Speech, 81*(3), 291–309. http://doi.org/10.1080/00335639509384117

Nguyen, H. T. (2014). *A view from the bottom: Asian American masculinity and sexual representation*. Duke University Press.

Otalvaro-Hormillosa, S. (1999). The homeless diaspora of queer Asian Americans. *Social Justice, 26*(3), 103–122.

Phua, V. C. (2007). Contesting and maintaining hegemonic masculinities: Gay Asian American men. *Sex Roles, 57,* 909–918. http://doi.org/10.1007/s11199-007-9318-x

Poon, M. K.-L. (2006). The discourse if oppression in contemporary gay Asian diasporal literature: Liberation or limitation? *Sexuality and Culture, 10*(3), 29–58. http://doi.org/10.1007/s12119-006-1019-z

Poon, M. K.-L., & Ho, P. T.-T. (2008). Negotiating social stigma among gay Asian men. *Sexualities, 11*(1/2), 245–268. http://doi.org/10.1177/1363460707085472

Puar, J. K. (2007). *Terrorist assemblages: Homonationalism in queer times*. Duke University Press.

Resonate Team (2017, December 11). New TV series Falling for Angeles: Koreatown's explores Asian men tacking gay racism. *Resonate: Global voices on East Asian issues*. https://www.weareresonate.com/2017/12/new-tv-series-falling-angels-koreatown-explores-asian-men-tackling-gay-racism/

Shimizu, C. P. (2012). *Straight sexualities: Unbinding Asian American manhoods in the movies*. Stanford University Press.

Spencer, L. G. (2015). Introduction. Centering transgender studies and gender identity in communication scholarship. In L. G. Spencer & J. C. Capuzza (Eds.), *Transgender communication studies: Histories, trends, and trajectories* (pp. ix–xxii). Lexington Press.

Spieldenner, A. R. (2016). PrEP whores and HIV prevention: The queer communication of HIV Pre-Exposure Prophylaxis (PrEP). *Journal of Homosexuality, 63*(12), 1685–1697. http://doi.org/10.1080/00918369.2016.1158012

Suganuma, K. (2012). *Contact moments: The politics of intercultural desire in Japanese male-queer cultures*. Hong Kong University Press.

Whitesel, J. (2014). *Fat gay men: Girth, mirth, and the politics of stigma*. New York University Press.

Wu, C. (2018). *Sticky rice: A politics of intraracial desire*. Temple University Press.

Wu, E. D. (2014). *The color of success: Asian Americans and the origins of the model minority*. Princeton University Press.

Yep, G. A., Russo, S. E., & Allen, J. (2015). Pushing boundaries: Toward the development of a model for transing communication in (inter)cultural contexts. In L. G. Spencer & J. C. Capuzza (Eds.), *Transgender communication studies: Histories, trends, and trajectories* (pp. 69–89). Lexington Press.

Yue, A. (2008). Same-sex migration in Australia. From Interdependency to Intimacy *GLQ: A Journal of Lesbian and Gay Studies, 14*(2–3), 239–262. https://doi.org/10.1215/10642684-2007-032

Yue, A. (2011). Critical regionalities in Inter-Asia and the Queer diaspora. *Feminist Media Studies, 11*(1), 131–138. https://doi.org/10.1080/14680777.2011.537042

SPEAKING WITH RACIALIZED ASIAN QUEER MALE SUBJECTS

CHAPTER THREE

Living in Paradox: Seeing "Alternative Cartographies" through Sticky Rice

[Q]ueerness and diaspora should be used not only to reevaluate the past but to orient the future development of Asian American political projects and strategies whose claims on a politics of social transformation can be acknowledged as such. This moment should be marked by a definitive shift away from a politics of cultural nationalism to a politics of transnational culturalism --- (Eng, 2001, p.219– 220).

Framing queerness through the region, and the region through queerness, provides us with an alternative mapping of sexual geographies that links disparate transitional locations and allows new models of sexual subjectivity to come into focus --- (Gopinath, 2018, p.30).

The first two chapters of *Asians loving Asians: Sticky Rice Homoeroticism and Queer Politics* have analyzed the media texts that represent a gay vernacular sticky rice, signifying a racialized Asian male subject falling in love with another racialized Asian male subject. While performing sticky rice desires can be empowering for the racialized Asian queer subjects participating in gay sexual cultures, it can also reinsert the *mundane* executions and operations of gay phallic masculinity working with the logics of cisnormativity, patriarchy, whiteness, capitalism, and more. Hence, sticky rice is *a queer of color politics* that simultaneously works on and against gay sexual cultural norms. With this grasp in mind, I shift my attention to social interactions and processes through which the racialized Asian queer male subjects negotiate vernacular discourses around sticky rice to perform their impossible possibilities of queerness every day.

My reason to conduct a meso-level analysis of sticky rice is because I landscape relational and communal ties as major cultural sites where the subjects perform who they are, what they do, and how they make sense of what they do in relation to people around them. The relational and communal ties alter, shape, and reinforce how the macro structures and conditions of power relations arrange and rearrange connections among identity, culture, and power (e.g., Halualani & Nakayama, 2010; Martin & Nakayama, 1999). As a matter of fact, queer of color scholars (e.g., Anzaldúa, 2012; Cohen, 1997; Johnson, 2001; McCune, 2014; Snorton, 2014) have already showcased how relational and communal ties shape and reshape historically specific and culturally saturated modes of queerness in and across the lines of differences (i.e., race, gender, class, nation, coloniality, language, the body, and more). No one can be magically queer in the present moment terrorized by historical and existing power relations (Muñoz, 2009). Impossible possibilities of queerness that demonstrate futurity are in constant flux with ongoing histories of power producing the dynamics of social interactions and processes (e.g., Chamber-Letson, 2018; Keeling, 2019). Hence, I am committed to pay close attention to the relational and communal processes of sticky rice as a gay vernacular, elaborating the connections and disconnections among identity, performance, culture, and power.

Simultaneously, I am reminded of what Communication scholars (e.g., Calafell & Delgado, 2004; Lechuga, 2020; Morrissey, 2013; Ono & Sloop, 1995) have argued that vernacular discourses are indicative of specialized and resistant knowledge(s) emerged from lived experiences of minoritized subjects. For this reason, I am concerned with how vernacular discourses around sticky rice explicate, elucidate, and elaborate lived experiences of racialized Asian male subjects who participate in the U.S. gay sexual cultures. Here, I return to Moraga and Anzaldúa's (1983) *theories in flesh* in the lives of sexual and gender minoritarians of color. Specifically, theories in flesh privileges the material realities of everyday minoritized experiences generating the embodied politics of resistance as a necessary survival (e.g., Calafell, 2015; Johnson, 2001; Madison, 1993). What sexual and gender minoritarians of color do and how they make sense of what they do around people are the embodied means of navigating around the normative sets of historical and existing power relations. Thus, in this chapter, I listen to voices on sticky rice uttered by the racialized Asian queer male subjects. So, I can take a step toward fully, carefully unpacking cultural nuances of racialized Asian queer male subjects who embody the minoritarian politics of resistance through everyday social interactions and processes.

To do so, I orient queer diasporas to examine vernacular discourses around sticky rice emerged from my in-depth interviews with racialized Asian queer male subjects. By queer diasporas, I mean *a border-crossing analytic* "for bringing other worlds into view that attest to our conjoined pasts, presents, and potential futures" (Gopinath, 2018, p. 175). Through this analytic, I am interested in mapping out alternative cartographies of the social orders which the racialized Asian queer male subjects see through their negotiations with vernacular discourses around sticky rice. To actualize my interest, I examine how they struggle with and resist images associated with the gay sexual category of "Asian" that sustains the settler colonialist logics of whiteness as the normative beauty standard. Simultaneously, I look into how they fail to transgress the "settled" boundaries of whiteness that organizes the hierarchies of differences in and across the U.S. gay sexual cultures. By paying attention to the paradox, I draw how vernacular discourses around sticky rice emerged from my in-depth interviews with the co-researchers implicate impossible possibilities of queerness that "names a state of being out of place and disoriented in the landscape of [cis]heteronormativity" (Gopinath, 2018, p. 61). In so doing, I take advantage of this chapter as an additional platform to unpack the everyday lived experiences of racialized Asian queer male subjects.

Mobilizing Queer Diasporas as an Analytic

Before showcasing the analysis, I take a moment to conceptualize my mobilization of queer diasporas as a border-crossing analytic. As queer scholars of color (e.g., Anzaldúa, 2012; Chamber-Letson, 2018; Eng, 2010; Keeling, 2019; Muñoz, 2009) have showcased, minoritized sexual and gender subjects who negotiate with simultaneous workings of power exist in and across constantly shifting and ambiguous spaces of borderlands that are often unintelligible. Put simply, *queerness is location-less* (Gopinath, 2018). Hence, I approach the concept of queer diasporas "as an alternative to the biological kinship structure of the nation" (Velasco, 2020, p. 99). Accordingly, I reject the conventional, rigid, and narrow-minded conceptualizations of diasporas that reinsert the triangulated relationship between hostland, homeland, and diaspora rooted in the cisheteronormative logic of biological family, kinship, and reproduction. However, by tracing back to the historical development of diaspora as a concept, Communication scholars Drzewiecka and Halualani (2002) remind the following: "Although the dispersions of peoples lead to the fragmentation of culture and to fluid notions of identity, diasporic identities are often built on claims to 'natural' or 'original' identities with the homeland" (p. 344). The conceptualizing of diaspora that transgresses the normative cartography of a border between hostland and homeland resecures a location of origin(ality) where the diasporic subjects belong to or come from. The idea of where one "originally" comes from reinserts the cisheteronormative logic of family, kinship, and reproduction.

For example, Safran (1991) privileges both symbolic and material notions of homeland in defining the parameters of diaspora. Diasporic subjects are assumed to hold nostalgia and/or fantasy about returning to homelands eventually even though they do not really have "choices" to return there. Because of this thought, Safran (1991) exemplifies the Jewish diasporas as the ideal constructs of diasporas. Israel, founded in 1948 after the British conquest of Palestine, represents a symbol of the Jewish homeland. However, many Jewish diasporic subjects actually come from diverse and multiple locations of origin. They remain disconnected from Israel as a homeland. Accordingly, the idea of returning to Israel serves a symbol for many Jewish diasporic subjects. This conceptualizing of diaspora can be also seen in and across Black/African diasporas. Because of the institutions of chattel slavery that trafficked the Black bodies from (West) Africa to Americas and Caribbean Islands, the culturally unspecific locations of Africa signify the homelands for Black/African diasporic subjects whose ties are involuntarily cut off from the continent (e.g., Keeling, 2019; Snorton, 2017).

According to the parameters of diaspora suggested by Safran (1991), most Asian Americans would not be classified as diasporic subjects. Because the migrations from Asia largely took place for economic reasons, most of the migrants from Asia voluntarily settle in the U.S. settler colonial nation-state and may not desire to return to their homelands (Otálvaro-Hormillosa, 1999). Simultaneously, there have been calls to locate the spatial politics of globalization in theorizing the concept of diasporas beyond the populations mentioned in the previous paragraph (e.g., Eng, 2001; Lowe, 1996; Okamura, 1995; Rouse, 1991). The contemporary landscape of globalization that promotes the transnational circuits of people, cultures, labors, goods, and technologies complicates the parameters of diaspora (e.g., Drzewiecka & Halualani, 2002; Halualani, 2008). The social, cultural, political, and economic dimensions of diasporas are in a constant flux with the politics of transnationalism that complicate issues and concerns of race, gender, class, citizenship, and migration. As Eng (2001) articulates, "global flows of capital not only give rise to new Asian American identities but also reinforce, renew, and recreate the historical disfranchising of Asian Americans from the U.S. nation-state" (p. 214). The politics of transnationalism working with diaspora messes up the settler colonial configurations of power that sustain normative borders and citizenships (Lowes, 1996). Here, I pay attention to what queer Colombian and Filipina American artist Otálvaro-Hormillosa said about transnationalism and diaspora in the following:

I refer to concepts that have been used to destabilize traditional models of migration in which the transition from the old country to the new country was assumed to involve assimilation to a new order in which ethnicity dropped out. Transnationalism is a process whereby social links between the country of origin and the host country may be maintained to resist this supposed homogenization of assimilation. (p.104)

Indeed, the connections among transnationalism and diaspora trouble a linear growth expectation of immigration that assumes the normalization of assimilation as an end goal. The ongoing transnational circuits of labor, capital, and communication that make the maintenance of a monolithic identity difficult reproduce complex and contradictory productions of hybrid identities (e.g., Lowe, 1996; Rouse, 1996). In addition, ongoing histories of race, ethnicity, nationality, and international relations that hierarchize the social capital do not equally position all migrants in relation to the U.S. settler colonial nation-state (Okamura, 1995; Shome, 2003). Accordingly, "transnationalism becomes a function of diaspora in the sense that within any diaspora, multiple nationalisms can exist that resist monolithic national identities" (Otálvaro-Hormillosa, 1999, p. 104). Hence, the politics of transnationalism that challenges the triangulated relationship between hostland, homeland, and diaspora redirects the attention to reconceptualize the parameters of diasporas as multiple, unstable, and dynamic constructs.

This is where I believe queer diasporas significantly come into play. The intersection between queer(ness) and diasporas hints to the multiple potentiality of border-crossing that radically transgresses the normative arrangements of power. As Gopinath (2018) warns the following:

Imperial, settler colonialism, and racial regimes of power work through spatial practices that order the bodies and landscapes in precise ways; these regimes of power also instantiate regimes of vision that determine what we see, how we see, and how we are seen. (p. 7)

As I have discussed in Chapters 1 and 2, impossible possibilities of queerness offer continually shifting borderlands to interrupt the cisheterosexist configurations of the present moment that reinsert the logic of whiteness, patriarchy, capitalism, and colonialism (e.g., Chambers-Letson, 2018; Keeling, 2019; Muñoz, 2009). Accordingly, impossible possibilities of queerness redirect the attention to temporal and spatial relationships between the past, the present, and the future to rearrange and reconfigure the present-ness of queers as peculiar. The past provides a site of possibility through which queers can pedagogically learn from something "forgotten" in order to differently act toward and envision the future as a utopia (Muñoz, 2009). The present that is missing out something is almost always *depressive* and *toxic* for queers. Here, queerness represents "both the production and regulation of nonheteronormative bodies, desires, and practices, as well as alternative modes of seeing and sensing" (p. 92). Hence, the methodology of queer diasporas is to trouble the cisheteronormative visions of assimilation that organize the forward and upward directionality of diasporic subjects.

Queer diasporas challenge how the cisheteronormative logic of biological family, kinship, and reproduction reorganize the triangulated relationship between hostland, homeland, and diaspora. For example, Eng (2010) calls the attention to the issue of postwar transnational adoption from Asia as an operation of queer diasporas. As a result of Korean War (1950–1953), large numbers of South Korean orphanages were adopted by mostly White American families through the support of Western-based religions and social service organizations (Park Nelson, 2016). According to Eng (2010), the transnational adoptees from South Korea who were involuntarily forced to migrate to the U.S. at the earlier stages of their lives are caught in-between and in-betwixt two motherlands. While they may have some memories about where they were born, they are mostly raised in the American households where they develop and negotiate their social and cultural capital. Yet, just like Gino in *Koreatown* from Chapter 2, the transnational adoptees from South Korea may hold their desires to visit South Korea. Still, because they were involuntarily cut off from South Korea when they were little, they may experience difficulties to develop social links as they reenter into South Korea. However, because of the racialized Otherness signified by their bodies, they may also remain isolated from where they are raised in the U.S. Accordingly, the transnational adoptees may be stuck in continually shifting and ambivalent sites of borderlands where cannot be neatly and easily intelligible. They may not be fully assimilated into one or another. Hence, Eng (2010) politicizes the transnational adoptees from South Korea as queer diasporic subjects who disrupt the logic of biological family, kinship, and reproduction defining the triangulated relationship between hostland, homeland, and diaspora. The transnational adoption challenges the naturalization of heterosexuality as a location of national "origin."

At the same time, Velasco (2020) mobilizes queer diasporas to interrogate the popular cultural representations of Filipina women as mail order brides, domestic laborers sex workers, and caregivers. Discourses around the Filipina body hint to the way the politics of nationalism working with the heteronormative family model of the nation take place in and across Filipina/o diasporas. The gendered and sexualized labor stigmatizations of the Filipina body signify the politically and economically disadvantaged conditions of the Philippine nation implicating ongoing histories of U.S. colonization, imperialism, and empire. Hence, there has been diasporic disdains of the popular cultural representation of Filipina women as the *failed* sign of the Philippine nation. However, Velasco (2020) conducts a queer and feminist critique of the diasporic nationalism as the form of anti-capitalist and anti-imperialist resistance, reconciling with the gendered and sexualized trope of the Filipina body. By orienting a queer diasporic approach to the figures of the Filipina body, Velasco denaturalizes not only the heteropatriachal construction of the nation but also the conception of a diaspora itself. The queer diasporic reimaginings of the Filipina body trouble how the politics of nationalism rooted in the cisheteronormative logic of biological family, kinship, and reproduction almost always triangulates a relationship between hostland, homeland, and diaspora.

Modeling the scholarly examples described above, I mobilize queer diasporas as a border-crossing analytic to look into the way multidirectional and multidimensional operations of power shape continually shifting and ambivalent sites of borderlands for racialized Asian queer male subjects. Specifically, I draw Otalvaro-Hormillosa's (1999) metaphorical reference of the *homeless* diaspora of queer Asian Americans. By this means, the cisheteropatriarchal constructions of the host, homeland, and diaspora simultaneously push queer Asian American subjects to the margin. For example, the U.S. dominant culture that reifies the logic of whiteness working with cisheteropatriarchy marginalizes racialized Asian queer subjects in general (e.g., Han, 2015; Nguyen, 2014). At the same time, diasporic ethnic cultures that normalize the power of cisheteropatriarchy disadvantage racialized Asian queer subjects because of their minoritized sexualities and genders (e.g., Eng, 2001; Wu, 2018). Still, as Chapters 1 and 2 have showcased, the logic of whiteness marginalizes racialized Asian queer subjects who participate in the mainstream gay sexual cultures. Hence, racialized Asian queer subjects who dwell in and across multiply minoritized positions experience intersectional layers of marginalization that produce the affective labors of *homeless-ness*.

However, my mobilization of queer diasporas does not essentially pile all racialized Asian queer subjects under a single queer diasporic category. I recognize the way each of racialized Asian queer subjects who represent different ethnicities, gender performances, migration status, and citizenships has a unique and particular relationship to nation-state, homeland, and diaspora. Still, Eng (2001) reminds of queerness that "gains its very meaning and discursive consistency as a critical terrain on which overlapping histories of sexuality, experiences of racialization and gendering, narratives of immigrant trauma and displacement, and strategies of class oppression and resistance are mobilized" (p.225). Queerness that challenges the cisheteropatriarchal constructions of triangulated relationships between hostland, homeland, and diaspora may hint to coalitional possibilities of shared dissatisfactions that renew and render the heterogeneous constructions of "Asian" and "Asian American." Hence, by mobilizing queer diasporas as the border-crossing analytic, I draw alternative cartographies of the social orders which racialized Asian queer male subjects see through their negotiations with vernacular discourses around sticky rice.

Speaking with Racialized Asian Queer Male Subjects: Auto/Ethnographic Methodology

To actualize the goal of this chapter described above, I speak *with* the racialized Asian queer male co-researchers as interview participants. I describe my methodology as an auto/ethnographic approach to interviewing. By auto/ethnographic, I mean a methodological orientation of my body as a major platform of knowledge and analysis to perform the critical cultural analysis (e.g., Alexander, 2012; Boylorn & Orbe, 2014; Calafell, 2015; Holman Jones, Adams, & Ellis, 2013; McIntosh & Eguchi, 2020). As I have unapologetically mentioned in the introductory chapter, my everyday participations in gay sexual cultures that have exposed me to vernacular discourses around sticky rice prompt my personal, intellectual, and political investment in *Asians loving Asians: Sticky Rice Homoeroticism and Queer Politics*. This book emerges from my lived experiences as a racialized Asian queer male subject. Thus, I am undeniably an active part of the methodological processes through which interview participants co-produce and co-create the knowledge(s). Therefore, as a part of the integrity of ethnical research that values honesty and sincerity, I explicitly orient my body as a major site where co-researchers narrate their temporal and spatial relationships with vernacular discourses around sticky rice.

To better engage with an auto/ethnographic approach to interviewing, I centralize the notion of speaking *with* Others. As Alcoff (1991) argues, there has been a major problem of speaking *for* others in representing minoritized experiences. She says, "The practice of privileged persons speaking for or on behalf of less privileged persons has actually resulted (in many cases) in increasing or reinforcing the oppression of the group spoken for" (p.7). This Alcoff's statement directs my attention to how ongoing histories of power that politicize differences (i.e., race, ethnicity, gender, sexuality, class, nation, coloniality, language, the body, and more) organize tensions between privileges and disadvantages in interpersonal intercultural interactions (e.g, Halulani & Nakayama, 2010; Martin & Nakayama, 1999). While the labels such as "Asian," "Asian American," and "queer" politically hint to the collective shared dissatisfactions between the co-researchers and myself, we do not necessarily own the exactly same group memberships. These political identity labels are very heterogenous. So, I must be critically reflexive of my body that carries the particular sets of power, privileges, and disadvantages into the interview contexts. Simultaneously, Alcoff (1991) reminds, "No easy solution to this problem can be found by simply restricting the practice of speaking for others to speaking for groups of which one is a member" (p. 8). Thus, by grounding racialized Asian queerness as an entry point, I work with how the politics of differences shape my social interactions with the co-researchers who speak *with* me. Boylorn and Orbe (2014) highlight that "difference influence our lives and how our relationship with intimate and unknown others serve as opportunities for communicative enlightenment" (p. 20). Therefore, my auto/ethnographic approach to interviewing is less focused on fashioning commonalities in our lived experiences. Instead, I analyze personal narratives that showcase the outlooks of divergence and contestation as I speak with the co-researchers.

From the methodological standpoint mentioned above, I perform my auto/ethnographic approach to interviewing.[1] To locate co-researchers who are willing to speak with me on vernacular discourses around sticky rice, I depend on my social networks and meet up with the seven racialized Asian subjects participating in the U.S. gay sexual cultures.[2] Here, I am not concerned with the numbers of co-researchers. Instead, my goal is to *detail, document,* and *archieve* the spectrums of personal narratives about sticky rice as a gay vernacular. To create safe spaces where the co-researchers articulate the socially stigmatized issues and concerns of queerness, I strategically capitalize an online medium of telecommunication technology *Skype*. It allows the co-researchers to pick their own private spaces to virtually meet up and speak with me. I believe the most readers of this book who experience the social distancing as a result of the COVID-19 pandemic agree with me for the effectiveness of virtual communication technology. Through this online capacity, I separately speak each of the seven co-researchers for about one hour. Hence, it is important to highlight that, since I am an interlocker of all the co-researchers, this is a collaborative study of the eight racialized Asian queer male subjects including me. After the completion of all the interviews, I transcribe and analyze personal narratives emerged from my speaking with the co-researchers. Then, I organize my descriptions and analyses of personal narratives into the two following large spectrums; *ideality/reality* and *fragmentations*. So, I can best represent alternative cartographies of the social orders which the co-researchers and I see through our negotiations with the trope of sticky rice. Next, I showcase the outlooks of divergence and contestation on sticky rice as I start with the first spectrum named *ideality/reality*.

Ideality/Reality

Our embodied reactions to sticky rice as a gay vernacular showcase that we are the racialized Asian subjects spatially caught up in-between and in-betwixt the paradoxes of queerness. Muñoz (2009) describes that queerness "rescues and emboldens concepts such as freedom that have been withered by the touch of neoliberal thought and gay assimilationist politics" (p. 32). We are still the active participants of the current U.S. settler colonial institutions that capitalize the political economy of sexual liberalism. The social institutions such as family, education, workplace and media often redirect our attentions to liberal conceptions of individualism, freedom, merit, responsibility, and choice that can obfuscate ongoing histories of identity-based inequalities (Eng, 2010). We are (mis)taught to believe that everyone is equal regardless of difference materialized through the socio-historical continuum of identity formation. Joseph (2017) warns, "If we embrace difference without striving for equity, we re-create inequality through forces that pretend sameness, such as, for example, in All Lives Matter" (p. 3319). Here it is important to keep in mind that we are also subjected to the lesbian-gay-bisexual-transgender-queer (LGBTQ) politics work with the liberal, color-blinded notions of self-discovery and self-actualization that normalize the individualistic paradigm of coming out (e.g., Eguchi, Files-Thompson, & Calafell, 2018; McCune, 2014; Snorton, 2014). Hence, we want to believe we should be able to freely desire what we desire.

For example, an Indian American Tayo residing in Washington, DC expresses his hesitation to me as he thinks of dating men who look like him. He says in the following:

> It feels like it's too close to home….It's a weird thing to me where it's like dating another Indian would [be] too weird…especially if like we spoke the same language, like … I don't know. It just seems like kind of weird, almost like incest or something.

Tayo's perception of dating men who look like him reinforces what Nguyen (2014) has said that most racialized Asian queer male subjects find sticky rice as *too incestuous*. In addition, I notice his nuanced emphasis on the subjects who look like him. By this, he means brown-skin men whose cultural backgrounds are Indian. So, I challenge him to think if he would be open to different kinds of Asian and Asian American men. Then, he firmly responds to me that he would be open to them. Then, he clarifies that "if I go online to date or to hookup, it tends to be more White men or Black men who are interested in me or try to talk to me…. Not so much Asian, like Chinese, Japanese, [and] Indian." At this moment, I recognize how Tayo shifts the attention to the logic of whiteness that organizes the racialized architectures of gay sexual cultures. Tayo's saying of "White men or Black men" reinserts the normative U.S. racial paradigm of a White-Black binary that ignores, erases, and marginalizes non-Black people of color, including indigenous people. In so doing, he rhetorically moves away from checking his queer sexual desire that may exclude attractions toward racialized Asian queer male subjects.

Here, Tayo is spatially caught up in-between and in-betwixt the paradoxes of racialized queerness. On the one hand, Tayo is not interested in dating the racialized Asian men who look like him because sticky rice is too incestuous. His queer desire is about moving away from his home. Because the spatial construction of home is almost always feminine (Eng, 2001), Tayo's queerness represents his mobility toward the U.S. settler colonial brandings of masculinity that exclude the racialized Asian men who look like him. On the other hand, going along with the politics of liberalism embracing individualism and sexual freedom, Tayo ideally wants to be open to date other racialized Asian men who may not look like him. However, *in reality* he rarely interacts with any racialized Asian queer subjects as he participates in gay sexual cultures reinforcing a White-Black racial paradigm. In addition to interacting with White and Black men, Tayo says "I actually am attracted to Latinos. I will like kind of approach them or like start talking to them." As Chapters 1 and 2 have showcased, the White masculine ideal is the gay aesthetic norm. Simultaneously, Black and Latino masculinities are historically sexualized, eroticized and fetishized in and across gay sexual cultures where the cisgender patriarchal forms of masculinity are worshiped (e.g., McCune, 2014; Pérez, 2015; Snorton, 2014). Hence, there are some racialized gender spaces where masculinized Black and Latino men are more desirable than feminized Asian men. And Tayo resecures the gay sexual cultural hierarchy of racialized gender desirability though his performance of queerness. Thus, speaking with Tayo, I am reminded of the way the historical stigmatization of racialized Asian queer male subjects as *undesirable Others* is almost always the contextual background generating the vernacular discourse of sticky rice.

Simultaneously, as Eng (2001) has argued before, the historical stigmatization of racialized Asian men as *feminine Others* mostly operates with the East/South East Asian male phonotype in the U.S. Therefore, some may exclusively apply the trope of sticky rice to the phenomenon of racialized East/South East Asian looking queer subjects who date other East/South East Asian looking queer subjects. However, because the U.S. settler colonial institutions racialize South Asians as Asians, Tayo still references South Asian queer male subjects in his utterance of sticky rice. Still, in the moment of speaking with Tayo, I am left questioning if South Asian queer male subjects are racialized (and femininized) similar to East/South East Asian queer male subjects. Here, Puar (2007) reminds me of the way Brown male bodies stereotyped as a sign of Muslimness are threats to the U.S. especially in the post-9/11 age. Hence, the trope of sticky rice rooted in the feminization of racialized Asian queer male subjects may not fully characterize South Asian queer male subjects meeting, dating with, and having sex with South Asian queer male subjects. Yet, what Tayo illustrates through his utterance of sticky rice is a continually shifting and ambivalent site of borderland where he negotiates his racialized queer desire to move away from "Asian" men who look like him. This implicates a rhetorical architecture of sticky rice as *too incestuous*.

At the same time, an Atlanta-based Vietnamese male Lala differently manifests how he is caught up in-between and in-betwixt the paradoxes of racialized queerness. For instance, Lala has been involved with other Vietnamese men in Atlanta over the years. Hence, he has actually performed the trope of sticky rice unlike Tayo. However, Lala still says "Well I don't usually date Asian[s] myself. So far, I've been dating more Caucasian[s], but I've dated a few African American[s]." So, I ask him, "why do you think that is?" Then, Lala details his feeling of dating other Vietnamese men. He says that "I feel like Asian [Vietnamese] people kind of know each other [in Atlanta]....Like if I were to date a Vietnamese guy, basically everyone would know within the community. And there's really no privacy." Lala feels that, when Lala dates a Vietnamese/American queer male subject, this person will "automatically" participate in Lala's social interactions occurring in his ethnic diaspora. At the same time, dating someone who is neither Vietnamese nor Asian provides Lala's mobility to temporally distance from his ethnic diaspora. In such queer interracial spaces, he feels he can do whatever he wants without any relational pressures from his community and family. Here, Lala reminds me of the way performing queerness through sticky rice can reinsert the cisheteronormative logic of "home" or "originality."

Still, Lala idealizes the *stickiness* of sticky rice even though performing sticky rice can make him feel spatially restricted to his ethnic diaspora. He values sticky rice politics that challenges what we as the racialized Asian queer male subjects feel comfortable with or get used to. Lala believes that the feminized stereotypes of racialized Asian men dating with White or Black masculine men should never limit what we actually desire. So, Lala suggests that "just try dating outside your comfort zone at least once." This statement originates from how Lala refuses the colonial logic of racial desirability pitting racialized Asian men against one another to receive the attentions from non-Asian men. According to Han, (2015), the competition drives from the limited numbers of White men desiring the racialized Asian men. However, as I have argued elsewhere (Eguchi, 2015), Lala observes that some racialized Asian men seek after White or Black men. Because of this situation, Lala believes that the *stickiness* of sticky rice troubles a structural path for the racialized Asian men to desire White or Black men. Lala says "[White or Black] Americans see us as Asian, period...... When they see an Asian, they just think Asian....And, we need to stick together." Still, the racialized Asian queer male subjects may not practice Lala's idealization of sticky rice politics. Lala says, "We [are] just so separated [in the gay community.]" Hence, similar to what Tayo sees, Lala points out how the racialized Asian queer male subjects may not interact with one another when they seek out sex and romance. Here, it is important to mention that Lala has never dated different kinds of Asian and Asian American men other than Vietnamese men either. Even so, Lala remains idealizing the *stickiness* of sticky rice as queer Asian American politics that troubles the racialized landscape of gay sexual cultural spaces.

In addition to Tayo and Lala, I keep encountering how vernacular discourses around sticky rice implicate a complex interplay of tensions between ideality and reality while speaking with other co-researchers. No one has negatively described about sticky rice couplings to me. They are "open" to meet, date, and have sex with racialized Asian queer male subjects *if* such opportunities arise. At the same time, I learn how some co-researchers distance from the trope of sticky rice much more ambiguously and strategically than Tayo who says sticky rice as too incestuous. To answer my question "how do you see sticky rice?," a New York-based Chinese/Vietnamese American male Lee states the following:

> I don't see much of [sticky rice couples] on the East Coast ... it's not very common to me to see. Occasionally, you'll see them when you go out to clubs and bars, but again, it's a rare thing to see, that it's not common for me. But again, when I went out to the West Coast, it was ... there was plenty of Asian guys that were holding hands, making out, and it was ... to me, it was a little uncomfortable, but it was surprising. I was like, "Really?" Because it just doesn't occur, and I think here, it's much more common to see Asian person with a White person, Asian person with a Black person, or Asian person with another race. So it doesn't ... at least to my exposure, which is very limited.... I think in many ways, I think it's kind of cool. More power to both of them, to being able to find common ground and identity, and feel comfortable with that. I think it's awesome. I just haven't had exposure.

Lee rhetorically empowers the trope of sticky rice as "kind of cool" and "awesome" even though he was uncomfortable to see intraracial Asian couples at first. He reasons his initial uncomfortable feeling through his lacking of having been previously exposed to racialized Asian men meeting, dating, and having sex with other racialized Asian men around him. Here, Lee brings the notion of location to excuse his initial reaction to sticky rice. Given large numbers of Asian and Asian

Americans are historically known to occupy the major cities in the West Coast such as Los Angeles, San Francisco, and Seattle, Lee associates the intraracial phenomenon of sticky rice with the "West Coast" thing.

However, a Los Angeles-based Filipino American male Polo counters Lee's sense-making of sticky rice grounded in a particular region. Similar to Lee, Polo has also seen sticky rice couplings in California and thinks sticky rice is cool. Then again, by bringing up a gay Asian club event known as GAMeBoi occasionally taking place in West Hollywood, Polo suggests that the racialized Asian men who attend the event are not really looking to hook up with and date other racialized Asian men. He says:

> I feel like the Asian guys at GAMeBoi, because I remember going there a couple times back in the day, it was more like if the Asian guys went, they would go as a group of friends. They don't date each other. They're like, "We're friends, and we're all super close, and we're super silly with each other." Then of course you'll have all the other guys who are not Asian but really want to date an Asian guy. That's their preference.

With the statements described above, Polo explains that the racialized Asian men are likely to look for something different from them in their same-sex sexual and romantic relationships. Polo's view of performing Asian queerness is to move away from Asianness working with cisheterosexism and diasporic nationalism. Hence, Polo does not find the region as salient as Lee. Instead, Polo individualizes one's racial preference to make sense of whether or not the racialized Asian men meet, date and have sex with other racialized Asian men.

Learning more about the way an ongoing interplay of tensions between ideality and reality represents the trope of sticky rice from Lee and Polo, I also begin to question if any racialized Asian queer co-researchers will ever say to me that they are not interested in other racialized Asian men at all. In particular, it was my first time to meet Lee and Polo. My personal friends introduced them to me for the purpose of this study. Hence, there is no doubt that the politics of politeness undeniably plays into our interactions via Skype. In addition, the co-researchers may not openly and frankly refuse the trope of sticky rice in speaking with me. Doing so makes them look as if they are racists against other Asians given it is a heterogenous racial construct. As Han (2015) has previously argued, the major reason why the racialized Asian queer male subjects stay away from meeting, dating, and having sex with other racialized Asian queer male subjects is their embodiment and performance of anti-Asian racism. At the time of my writing of this chapter, the deadly insurrections of the capital took place on January 6, 2021 directs our attention to the issues and concerns of White nationalism suggesting ongoing histories of racism against people of color. So, there seems to be more emerging spaces of dialog through which we can openly and frankly discuss the historical continuum of race and racism. Still, I highly doubt if we as the racialized Asian queer male subjects will feel comfortable to openly and frankly discuss our racial preferences for sex and romance especially when the conversations are being recorded. In addition, the U.S. sexual liberalism that normalizes the idea of open-mindedness may politically correct us to move away from performing the racial preferences for sex and romance. Hence, my co-researchers may downplay their preferences to avoid appearing as the racial fetishists because the logic of heteronormativity stigmatizes, disciplines, and surveils sexual fetishes. Thus, I am concerned with how the politically corrected dynamic of communication obscures possibilities of queerness through which we can actually work toward deconstructing our embodiments and performances of racial preferences.

At the same time, my aforementioned question emerged from speaking with the co-researchers about sticky rice hints to continually shifting and ambivalent sites of borderlands where the racialized Asian queer subjects may be temporally caught up. Because of our queerness, we distance from the constructions of ethnic diasporas that normalize the compulsory heterosexuality. So, we can get to temporal spaces where we can hopefully embrace our queer desires. Still, the politics of homonationalism working with whiteness minoritize our racialized bodies. We will not perfectly fit into gay sexual cultures that idealize the White masculine ideal either. Yet, when we turn our attentions to the U.S. mainstream cultures, we navigate into and around the multiply marginalized positions through which our queerness is corrected, disciplined, and surveilled. Hence, we are continually subjected to the fragmentations of (un)belongings (e.g., Han, 2015; Lim, 2014; Nguyen, 2014). We can be what Otalvaro-Hormillosa (1999) said is homeless. This is why a Chinese/Vietnamese American male Lee reminds me of how the racialized Asian queer subjects experience intersectional layers of depression and anxiety that cultivate some temporal connections or commonalities among one another. The ongoing negotiations of queerness, working with Asianness, reproduce the shared identifications and affiliations (Han, 2015). Indeed, these affective labor spaces that have no "motherland" or "originalities" are queer diasporas, transgressing the cisheteronormative modes of diasporas requiring homelands and hostlands.

Fragmentations

Still, queer diasporas are never free from the hierarchal politics of difference (i.e., race, gender, class, nation, coloniality, language, the body, and more) that terrorizes the present moment. Nguyen (2014) warns that "both queer and diaspora possess the potential to be harnessed for the heteronormative projects of the nation-state" (p. 168). The hierarchal politics of difference that work with the present-ness maintains the emblems of scatterings and fragmentations of diasporic Asian queers. The scattered and fragmented codes of (un)belonging generate *impossible* possibilities of queerness as "a way to challenge the nationalist ideologies by restoring the impure, inauthentic, and non-reproductive potential of the notion of diasporas" (Gopinath, 2005, p. 11). Hence, I recapitalize queerness of sticky rice to carefully dig into the scattered and fragmented landscapes of queer diasporas where the racialized Asian subjects are temporally (un)situated.

A New York-based Japanese male Taro who claims "I, for one, admit being one as a sticky rice" reasons how the U.S. settler colonial scripts of being gay and Asian that produce *common traits* shape him feel more attracted to Asians than non-Asian others. He states:

> I had dated different races…and backgrounds since I've been old enough to sort of go around the block more than once. My conclusion is that after spending enough time here and growing up here, experiencing what it's like to be a minority here, and double minority; gay, Asian, or triple if you count being an immigrant. I just found Asians, fellow Asians to be generally and aesthetically pleasing to me, and sexually as well.

Because I was not sure who are counted as Asians through his articulation of sticky rice, I ask Taro to clarify what he means by he is attracted to Asian guys. He responses that he has never dated Japanese men. Then, Taro tell me that "my ideal date or partner will be an Asian person, not necessarily Japanese, but Asian guy who grew up here." At this juncture, I feel in need of unpacking Taro's utterance of his ideal sticky rice coupling that hints to the hierarchal productions and negotiations of diasporic Asian queers.

Being a U.S. permanent resident, Taro sees himself as much more Americanized than other Japanese people living in the U.S as he came to attend the high school in a small town in Michigan. During the initial stage of getting used to the majoritarian U.S. cultures, values, and customs, he only encountered three or four Asians out of about between 800 and 1000 students at total. This mostly White cultural setting led Taro to identify himself as *Asian*. As he states, this is because of the "community that you automatically belong because you're Asian." This racialized experience is a root of Taro idealizing other racialized Asian queer male subjects who grew up in the U.S. At the same time, Taro's conceptions of common traits among Asians growing up in the U.S. come from the politically shared experiences, identifications, and affiliations as outcomes of un/naturalization of the racialized Asian queer male subject. Hence, Taro's sticky rice ideality reveals his aspiration toward the Americanization of the diasporic and immigrant queers, including himself. In addition, Taro's aspiration implicates an onward and upward directionality of Japaneseness adapting the Americanization. There is a normalized structural path for Japanese people becoming like Americans in the Post-WWII context of Japan where the Americanization of Japan's social institutions intensified (e.g., Eguchi & Kimura, 2021; Sekimoto, 2014; Toyosaki, 2011). Consequently, Taro's idealization of sticky rice that emphasizes the sharing of common traits among Asians who grew up in the U.S. can be read as the embodied product of Japaneseness through which Taro distances himself from.

Simultaneously, Taro's aspiration toward the Americanization of the racialized Asian queer male subject reestablishes how the settler colonial logics of whiteness normalizes a linear growth model expectation of the migrants. The common vernacular phrase, *Fresh off the Boat* (FOB), is the pejorative expression used to represent immigrants whose everyday cultural performances are read as very foreign. As Nguyen (2014) has showcased before, the gay sexual cultural industry utilizes this discursive dynamic of FOB in producing pornographic narratives. The performances of "Asian actors with heavy accents and FOB (fresh-off-the-boat) appearance and demeanor" (Nguyen, 2014, pp. 40–41) are specifically used to produce the poor and immigrant status images of the foreign Asian bottom. Still, Asian actors who can perform the Americanization are given flexibility to play characters beyond the foreign Asian bottom (Nguyen, 2014). Parallel to this, while Taro does not disclose his preference of sexual penetration to me, he is a foreign-born Japanese queer male subject who could be easily positioned as the FOB. However, Taro does not have heavy accents at all. And Taro knows how to culturally perform the naturalized appearance and demeanor on to his racialized body. Taro describes, "I've basically ... grown up here and ... I have more Americanized personality, although I speak fluent Japanese...I relate to people in more American way than Japanese counterpart." From this standpoint, Taro is sexually and romantically interested in Asians who grew up in the U.S. This directionality points to the way the logics of whiteness expect immigrants to assimilate into the settler colonial nation. By desiring the Americanized Asian queer male subject, he both moves away from the poor and immigrant status position of queer diasporas and maintains his privilege, cultural capital, and social mobility. He does not want to step down to the FOB space through his performing of sticky rice. Here, I observe the way "the forward and upward directionality of normative visions of aspirational success" (Gopinath, 2018, p. 82) produces impossible possibilities of queerness around the political economy of sticky rice.

Unlike Taro, a New York-based Taiwanese male Chun states how the normative codes of belonging that produces the feelings of comfort intensify the scatterings and fragmentations of the racialized Asian queer male subjects. As I ask Chun to clarify what kinds of Asian men he is attracted to, he asserts the following:

> I think it's easier to talk to people who were born in the United States, because I think the term or a lot of cultural things that you talk about, it's easier to talk to them. They will be easier to understand what we were talking about. For people who came here or were not born here but came here later to study or work, it really depends. [Coming from other countries,] we [Chun and me] probably had that experience, like the first few years is kind of weird. It's hard to merge into what this society, the culture is about. They probably have to be living here for a few years....

Here, speaking with Chun, I am reminded of how I struggled to embody the U.S. gay sexual cultural codes of communication when I first moved to Orange County, California in 2001. There have been so many linguistic and cultural norms I had to learn from. Even today, as I participate in gay sexual cultures including online dating websites, I have to google idioms and phrases I do not know about. However, since I have been here for two decades, I am socially and culturally equipped enough to navigate around the cartography of whiteness that organizes gay sexual cultures. Through my own learning experience, I can relate to Chun feeling comfortable with the racialized Asian queer male subjects who master navigating around the U.S. society and culture. In the present moment, we do not want to rehash our past as the FOB subjects where we encountered various moments of cultural shocks. However, similar to Taro, this is where we must check how the settler colonial logic of whiteness that produces our linguistic and cultural capital directs our attentions to move away from poor and immigrant status spaces marked as FOB. Both of us are apparently the foreign-born Asian queer subjects who carry out FOB appearances and demeanors. Yet, our everyday participations in the higher education advance our foreign, transnational queerness. Our occupational privileges allow us to distance ourselves from the FOB spaces. Still, regardless of what Chun and I see, a Los Angeles-based Filipino American male Polo observes a clear division "between those who were foreign born, immigrated here versus those who were born here or at least grew up for a good amount of time here." Hence, it is possible that some U.S.-born Asian American queer subjects may not comfortable with Chun as much as he feels comfortable with them. Still, Chun's utterance points to the political economy of sticky rice desire that restrains possibilities of queerness. It fails to dismantle the hierarchal productions and negotiations of queer diasporic subjects.

In addition to the linguistic and cultural capital, Chun brings forth how intraregional international relations play into the vernacular discourses of sticky rice. For example, there is a tendency for Chun's Taiwanese friends to desire Japanese and South Korean men. He reasons that the global consumptions of Japanese and South Korean popular cultures cultivate their sexual and romantic attentions. However, Chun expresses the political complexity that shapes the personal when he thinks to date the racialized Asian queer male subjects who come from the continent China promoting One-China policy. By this, the continent China demands Taiwan to be a part of the People's Republic of China. However, in the 2020's Taiwanese presidential election most Taiwanese citizens voted for Tsai Ing-wen who advocates for sustaining Taiwan's independency. Hence, Chun says "If I'm going to date Chinese guy in the United States, and then I would say, 'Yeah, we talk.' But also it really depends on if that Chinese guy is Chinese American-born or local Chinese-born and came to United States." This concern of a location of birth when Chun thinks of dating a Chinese man is an embodied product of his Taiwaneseness implicating today's politics of Taiwan-China relation. Chun's articulation points out how the *stickiness* of sticky rice can fall way because of the intraregional international politics in and across Asia.

Listening to Chun, I am also reminded of the historical tensions between Korea and Japan that can shape vernacular discourses around sticky rice. Quite honestly, I have never met a Korean-Japanese sticky rice couple around me. Here, I want to clarify that I am not saying that such sticky rice coupling never take place. Still, born and raised in Japan, I recognize how anti-Korean sentiment is strategically used to define the historical continuum of Japan's ethnocentrism. And it is important for Japanese and Japanese American queers to be reflexive of their Japaneseness operating with anti-Korean sentiment that shapes their sexual and romantic desires as we participate in gay sexual cultures. Thus, I cannot deny some political obstacles for Korean-Japanese sticky rice couplings to occur. Therefore, vernacular discourses around sticky rice that suggest impossible possibilities of queerness hint to the influence of intraregional political rivalries in fragmenting queer diasporas. *The politics of sticky rice is always already transnational.*

Simultaneously, the economic structures and systems that normalize the hierarchy of nations in Asia complicate the trope of sticky rice. For instance, Lala states "there's a hierarchy or some kind of invisible social tier to Asian culture where one Asian might feel like they're more superior than another kind of Asian." So, I ask Lala to exemplify his ethnographic observation. Then, he clarifies that "I heard this [in] where I live [Atlanta]. Korean[s] tend to date within Korean[s] only. They don't branch out much. And sometimes they refer to Vietnamese as the potato Asian." At this juncture, my foreignness kicks in. I am confused with what Lala means by "potato Asian." So, Lala restates that Korean people look down on Vietnamese people as "basically farmers" implicating that South Korean society and culture are more urban and economically advanced than Vietnamese society and culture. Here, Lala expresses his concern with how the intraregional economic divisiveness further scatters the fragmentations of the racialized Asian queer subjects marginalized by both whiteness that organizing gay sexual cultures and cisheteropartriarchy that organizing ethnic diasporas.

On the contrast to Lala, Taro refuses to see the scattered and fragmented landscapes of queer diasporas where the racialized Asian subjects are temporally (un)situated. Taro tells me, "I personally never encountered any problems amongst queer Asians.....what's important is more about visibility of Asian and queer." Taro privileges the intersectional significance of being Asian and queer that produces the politically shared experiences, identifications, and affiliations. To exemplify his perspective on sticky rice desire, He brings up his previous involvement in an all-volunteer organization called Gay Asian Pacific Islander Men of New York (GAPIMNY). He states:

> Throughout six years that I was part of the organization, I really got to know and made close friends, which shared the same experiences. And we can be really close to each other. We all speak the same language about the social justice movement, about the politics.

While his statement sounds empowering for racialized Asian queer subjects who are especially drawn to the trope of sticky rice, I immediately question if the organization actually represents the issues and concerns of Pacific Islanders. So, I look at their website. Then, I notice the overwhelming representations of cisgender males who phenotypically look like East/South East Asian. The images of Pacific Islanders are absented from the GAPIMNY's website. This realization reminds me of Taro saying "I personally feel that I've always be counted amongst this Whiter Asian category than Asian category" at one point during the interview. While Taro does not carefully unpack "this Whiter Asian category" with me, what he says subtly hints to the hierarchal productions and negotiations of diasporic Asian queer subjects. Just like the GAPIMNY's website suggests, there is a hierarchy of who gets to be represented and who does not. This representational hierarchy is a political and economic product of global capitalism that privileges some Asian countries like Hong Kong, Japan, South Korea, Singapore, and Taiwan. Indeed, Taro's mentioning of "this Whiter Asian category" that reinserts the U.S. racial paradigm of a Black-White binary implicates the economic capital associated with his Japaneseness.

In the end, these emblems of scatterings and fragmentations mentioned above suggest how the racialized Asian queer subjects perform diasporic tensions of moving toward and/or away from the trope of sticky rice reinforcing stickiness (or sameness). For example, another New York-based Japanese male Yoshi is dating a mixed-race (Asian + White) Japanese American male. And Yoshi expresses his sticky rice preference by saying "it's natural." He goes on to describe:

> His [partner's] mom is Japanese. And he went [to] a Japanese school....so he can speak fluent[ly] in Japanese. He know[s] Japanese culture. He watch[es] Japanese TV. So, he understand[s] Japanese culture. I'm very comfortable with [him]...

Here, Yoshi emphasizes on the cultural significance of Japaneseness that operates as a stickiness between him and his partner. Being with the racialized Asian queer male subject who is linguistically and culturally familiar with where Yoshi comes from creates a temporal feeling of being at home. Having lived in the U.S. more than two decades, Yoshi recognize how being able to speak in his own first language with his partner makes him feel comfortable. He tells me:

> I didn't know he could speak Japanese when I first saw him. But I feel really connected [after having learned he can speak Japanese]. So that's why we are dating now, I guess.....We mostly speak [in] Japanese. It's very comfortable [for] both of us to communicate each other [in Japanese].

Here, Yoshi's perspective also reinforces what Lala tells me about the hierarchies of the racialized Asian queer subjects described earlier. Because of the intra-Asia political and economic hierarchies, Lala says to me that dating with racialized Asian queer subjects coming from the same ethnic background feels like much more equal and long lasting than racialized Asian queer subjects coming from different ethnic backgrounds. So, I also ask Yoshi to consider how he feels about dating non-Japanese, Asian subjects. Then, Yoshi tells me that, while he is open to such sticky rice couplings, he prefers not to talk about the historical issues in his relationship. His life goal right now is to have a family that provides him feel emotionally supported. Here, the U.S. politics of homonationalism that values how gays and lesbians adapt the heteronormative logic of family and kinship as a healthy sign of assimilation shapes Yoshi's queer desire. Because Yoshi envisions his family through the building of commonalities with his partner, Yoshi prefers to eliminate differences as much as possible before getting into his relational commitment. So, he can avoid potential conflicts that stress him out. Accordingly, Yoshi feels ease at leaning toward the trope of sticky rice in materializing *the stickiness* between him and his partner through their shared co-performances of Japaneseness.

Simultaneously, some co-researchers see that the trope of sticky rice, reinforcing *stickiness* (or sameness), restraints possibilities of queerness around them to have (queer) freedom or feel free. A New York-based Taiwanese male Chun also tells me why he is not as comfortable to date Taiwanese men in addition to continent Chinese men I have described earlier. He reasons:

> We can talk in the same language. But, [for] certain things [such as sexual and romantic matters], I am comfortable to talk about [them] in English. When it switch[es] back to Mandarin or Taiwanese, I'm just like "Okay, that's little bit weird to talk about in my native language."

This Chun's perspective juxtaposes to Yoshi's feeling of comfort to speak with his partner in his first language. Here, as an ESL (English as a Second Language) speaker, I am reminded of the way each foreign-born racialized Asian queer subject develops their relationships to their native and foreign languages differently. Because Chun is much more comfortable to talk about sexual and romantic matters in English than Mandarin or Taiwanese, he has had intimate relationships with the racialized Asian queer subjects who speak neither Mandarin nor Taiwanese. So, he says to me, "I hang out with the guys from Southeast Asian area or Indian people." This is similar to what Tayo feels awkward to date men who look like him. Here, the concept of being queer is a mobility to move away from the cisheteronormative logic of family and kinship that constitutes what home is and what isn't. Yet, Chun's sexual and romantic attention implicates intraregional economic hierarchies of power that produce a global and transnational flow of colonial fantasy for queer male subjects from Global North to desire queer male subjects from Global South. For example, an inbound queer sex tourism to Thailand from East Asian countries such as Japan, South Korea, and Taiwan has been popular (Kang, 2017). There is a structural path of privilege for queer male subjects from Global North to desire queer male subjects from Global South. Hence, vernacular discourses around sticky rice implicate how the racialized Asian queer male subjects negotiate ongoing interplays of diasporic tensions between sameness and differences that implicate social, political, economic, and historical contexts.

Concluding Remarks

In this chapter, I have oriented queer diasporas as a border-crossing analytic to showcase the social orders through which the racialized Asian queer male coresearchers negotiate vernacular discourses around sticky rice. The racialized Asian queer male subjects idealize the trope of sticky rice as we should be able to meet, date, and have sex with anyone. Still, in reality there are contestations for us to perform queerness through the trope of sticky rice stigmatized as too incestuous. Yet, the racialized Asian queer male subjects are subjected to the fragmentations of (un) belongings because of being marginalized from the U.S. mainstream cultures, gay sexual cultures, and ethnic diasporas simultaneously. These continually shifting and ambivalent spaces of (un)belongings that have no "motherland" or "originalities" are indeed queer diasporas. Still, the hierarchal politics of difference that terrorizes the present moment further scatter the fragmentations of queer diasporas where the racialized Asian queer male subjects are (un)situated. The ongoing interplays of diasporic tensions between sameness and differences shape and reshape political rivalries, economic competitions, and historical struggles organizing the trope of sticky rice. Hence, the vernacular discourses around sticky rice point to impossible possibilities of queerness through which the racialized Asian queer subjects struggle to break free from the past and the present for the future as an ideal destination where we can be whom we want to be.

Before moving on to next chapter that continues my auto/ethnographic approach to interviewing, I return my attention to the *disjunctions* of queer diasporas where the racialized Asian male subjects are temporally (un)situated. A New York-based Chinese/Vietnamese American male Lee expresses his observation of lacking the sense of "a community" among the racialized Asian queer male subjects who are supposed to experience "similar" marginalization processes. By this means, Lee says "I don't know that they're willing to take the step to form a group, or to be active, or to have a cause." While acknowledging the visibilities of the subjects identifying with "Asian" and "queer," Lee's observation comes from having participated in organizations such as *AQUA* (Asian/Pacific Islander Queers United for Action) and *Asians & Friends*. Lee expresses the following:

> Whenever I attended those meetings it made me feel uncomfortable, because it was no longer about just being gay and being Asian. It was ... gay [because of White men that are involved in the organizations]. And then there was competition [among Asians], and then not only competition, but then you're put on display for these, quote-unquote, "friends," or whatever it was. And you're subjected or objectified, and it wasn't celebratory.

Here, Lee suggests how the racialized Asian queer spaces that are framed to cater the social and political needs of Asians getting to know one another are not really created for them. Instead, the supposedly Asian queer coalitional building spaces facilitate the gay sexual cultural dynamics of older White men meeting up younger Asian men. Since more foreign-born than U.S-born Asian subjects occupy these Asian queer spaces, Lee also feels *foreign* around foreign-born Asian subjects whose cultural rituals and performances are marked differently from him. At the same time, Lee brings up his younger biological brother's experience of being a U.S.- born racialized Asian queer male subject in California. Lee says, "he has a network of both gay Asian friends and a mixed groups of different people.....he actually had a boyfriend who was Filipino for three or four years." This statement reinforces what I have said earlier about Lee's imagining of sticky rice with the "West Coast" thing. Lee's vision implicates hyper visibilities of Asian and Asian American communities in the region. Still, Lee's observation of "a community" ironically reminds me of multiple disjunctions of queer diasporas through which the racialized Asian male subjects interact with one another. In reality, multiple axes of differences that have no commonalities are essentially shored under queer and Asian.

Simultaneously, the disjunctions of queer diasporas are indeed possibilities of queerness as an alternative optic that troubles how the logic of cisheteropatriarhcy organizes the majoritarian codes of belonging working with the politics of nation-building. Listening to Lee who expresses the lack of a community among the racialized Asian queer male subjects, I begin to question how we are supposed to feel, embody, and perform the sense of a community. Put simply, *what is a community anyway?* The building of a community is to connect people with each other. A community building that requires the shared commonalities can be dangerous for queers. It can easily reinsert the majoritarian rules and systems that discipline, correct, and surveil possibilities of queerness through social interactions and processes. At the same time, as *Asians loving Asians: Sticky Rice Homoeroticism and Queer Politics* has thus far showcased, there is no single way to connect disjunctions of the racialized Asian male subjects through queerness of sticky rice. The vernacular discourses around sticky rice, uttered by my co-researchers, hint to the scatterings and fragmentations of queer diasporic (un)belongings through which the racialized Asian male subjects are socially, culturally, politically, economically, and historically disconnected from one another. Hence, in next chapter I examine how vernacular discourses around sticky rice display moments of coalitional possibilities for the racialized Asian male subjects.

Notes

1   My current affiliation's IRB office granted me approval to interview co-researchers.
2   See, Appendix I for Co-Researchers' Demographic Information.

References

Alcoff, L. (1991). The problem of speaking for others. *Cultural Critique, 20*(1), 5–32. https://doi.org/10.2307/1354221

Alexander, B. K. (2012). *The performative sustainability of race: Reflections on Black culture and the politics of identity*. Peter Lang.

Anzaldúa, G. (2012). *Borderlands/La Frontera: The New Mestiza*. Aunt Lute Books.

Boylorn, R. M., & Orbe, M. P. (2014). Introduction: Critical autoethnograohy as method of choice. In R. M. Boylorn & M. P. Orbe (Eds.), *Critical autoethnography: Intersecting cultural identities as everyday life* (pp. 13–26). Left Coast Press.

Calafell, B. M. (2015). *Monstrosity, performance, and race in contemporary culture*. Peter Lang.

Calafell, B. M., & Delgado, F. P. (2004). Reading Latina/o images: Interrogating Americanos. *Critical Studies in Media Communication, 21*(1), 1–24. https://doi.org/10.1080/0739318042000184370

Chambers-Letson, J. (2018). *After the party: A manifesto for queer of color life*. New York University Press.

Cohen, C. J. (1997). Punks, bulldaggers, and welfare queens: The real radical potential of queer politics? *GLQ: A Journal of Lesbian and Gay Studies, 3*(4), 437–465. https://doi.org/10.1215/10642684-3-4-437

Drzewiecka, J. A., & Halualani, R. T. (2002). The structural-cultural dialectic of diasporic politics. *Communication Theory, 12*(3), 340–366. https://doi.org/10.1111/j.1468-2885.2002.tb00273.x

Eguchi, S. (2015). Queer intercultural relationality: An autoethnography of Asian-Black (dis)connections in White gay America. *Journal of International and Intercultural Communication, 8*(1), 27–43. https://doi.org/10.1080/17513057.2015.991077

Eguchi, S., & Kimura, K. (2021). Racialized im/possibilities: Intersectional queer-of-color critique on Japaneseness in Netflix's *Queer Eye: We're in Japan! Journal of International and Intercultural Communication, 14*(3), 221–239. https://doi.org/10.1080/17513057.2020.1829675

Eguchi, S., Files-Thompson, N., & Calafell, B. M. (2018). Queer (of color) aesthetics: Fleeting moments of transgression in VH1's *Love & Hip-Hop: Hollywood Season 2. Critical Studies in Media Communication, 35*(2), 180–193. https://doi.org/10.1080/15295036.2017.1385822

Eng, D. L. (2001). *Racial castration: Managing masculinity in Asian America*. Duke University Press.

Eng, D. L. (2010). *The feeling of kinship: Queer liberalism and the racialization of intimacy*. Duke University Press.

Gopinath, G. (2005). *Impossible desires: Queer diasporas and South Asian public cultures*. Duke University Press.

Gopinath, G. (2018). *Unruly visions: The aesthetic practices of queer diaspora*. Duke University Press.

Halualani, R. T. (2008). "Where exactly is the pacific?": Global migrations, diasporic movements, and intercultural communication. *Journal of International and Intercultural Communication, 1*(1), 3–22. https://doi.org/10.1080/17513050701739509

Halualani, R. T., & Nakayama, T. K. (2010). Critical intercultural communication studies: At a crossroads. In T. K. Nakayama & R. T. Halualani (Eds.), *The handbook of critical intercultural communication* (pp. 1–16). Wiley-Blackwell.

Han, C. W. (2015). *Geisha of a different kind: Race and sexuality in gaysian America.* New York University Press.

Holman Jones, S., Adams, T. E., & Ellis, C. (Eds.). (2013) *Handbook of autoethnography.* Left Coast Press.

Johnson, E. P. (2001). "Quare" studies or (almost) everything I know about Queer studies I learned from my grandmother. *Text and Performance Quarterly, 21*(1), 1–25. https://doi.org/10.1080/10462930128119

Joseph, R. (2017). What's the difference with "difference"?: Equity, communication, and the politics of differences. *International Journal of Communication, 11,* 3306–3326. https://ijoc.org/index.php/ijoc/article/viewFile/6443/2112

Kang, D. B. (2017). Eastern orientations: Thai middle- class gay desire for 'white Asians'. *Culture, Theory and Critique, 58*(2), 182–208. https://doi.org/10.1080/14735784.2017.1288580

Keeling, K. (2019). *Queer times, black futures.* New York University Press.

LeChuga, M. (2020). Mapping migrant vernacular discourses: Mestiza consciousness, nomad thought, and Latina/o/x migrant movement politics in the United States. *Journal of International and Intercultural Communication, 13*(3), 257–273. https://doi.org/10.1080/17513057.2019.1617332

Lim, E.-B. (2014). *Brown boys and rice queens: Spellbinding performances in the Asias.* New York University Press.

Lowe, L. (1996). *Immigrant acts: On Asian American cultural politics.* Duke University Press.

Madison, S. D. (1993). "That was my occupation": Oral narrative, performance, and black feminist thought. *Text and Performance Quarterly, 13*(3), 213–232. https://doi.org/10.1080/10462939309366051

Martin, J. N., & Nakayama, T. K. (1999). Thinking dialectically about culture and communication. *Communication Theory, 9*(1), 1–25. https://doi.org/10.1111/j.1468-2885.1999.tb00160.x

McCune Jr., J. Q. (2014). *Sexual discretion: Black masculinity and the politics of passing.* University of Chicago Press.

McIntosh, D. M. D., & Eguchi, S. (2020). The troubled past, present disjunctures, and possible futures: Intercultural performance communication. *Journal of Intercultural Communication Research, 49*(5), 395–409. https://doi.org/10.1080/17475759.2020.1811996

Moraga, C., & Anzaldúa, G. (Eds.). (1983). *This bridge called my back: Writing by radical women of color.* Kitchen Table.

Morrissey, M. E. (2013). A DREAM disrupted: Undocumented migrant youth disidentifications with U.S. citizenship. *Journal of International and Intercultural Communication, 6*(2), 145–162. https://doi.org/10.1080/17513057.2013.774041

Muñoz, J. E. (2009). *Cruising utopia: The then and there of queer futurity.* New York University Press.

Nguyen, H. T. (2014). *A view from the bottom: Asian American masculinity and sexual representation.* Duke University Press.

Okamura, J. (1995). The Filipino American diaspora; Sites of space, time, and ethnicity. In G. Y. Okihiro., M. Alquizola, D. Fujita Rony., & K. S. Wong (Eds.), *Privileging positions: The sites of Asian American studies* (pp. 387–400). Washington State University Press.

Ono, K. A., & Sloop, J. M. (1995) The critique of vernacular discourse. *Communication Monographs, 62*(1), 19–46. https://doi.org/10.1080/03637759509376346

Otalvaro-Hormillosa, S. (1999). The homeless diasporas of queer Asian Americans. *Social Justice, 26*(3), 103–122.

Park Nelson, K. (2016). *Invisible Asians: Korean American adoptees, Asian American experiences, and Racial exceptionalism.* Rutgers University Press.

Pérez, H. (2015). *A taste for brown bodies: Gay modernity and cosmopolitan desire.* New York University Press.

Puar, J. K. (2007). *Terrorist assemblages: Homonationalism in queer times.* Duke University Press.

Rouse, R. (1991). Mexican migration and the social space of postmodernism. *Diaspora: A Journal of Transnational Studies, 1*(1), 8–23. https://doi.org/10.1353/dsp.1991.0011

Safran, W. (1991). Diasporas in modern societies: Myths of homeland and return. *Diaspora: A Journal of Transnational Studies, 1*(1), 83–99. https://doi.org/10.1353/dsp.1991.0004

Sekimoto, S. (2014). Transnational Asia: Dis/orienting identity in the globalized world. *Communication Quarterly, 62*(4), 381–398. https://doi.org/10.1080/01463373.2014.922485

Shome, R. (2003). Space matters: The power and practice of space. *Communication Theory, 13*(1), 39–56. https://doi.org/10.1111/j.1468-2885.2003.tb00281.x

Snorton, C. R. (2014). *Nobody is supposed to know: Black sexuality on the down low.* University of Minnesota Press.

Snorton, C. R. (2017). *Black on both sides: A racial history of trans identity.* University of Minnesota Press.

Toyosaki, S. (2011). Critical complete-member ethnography: Theorizing dialectics of consensus and conflict in intercultural communication. *Journal of International and Intercultural Communication, 4*(1), 62–80. https://doi.org/10.1080/17513057.2010.533786Velasco, G. K. (2020). *Queering the global Filipina body: Contested nationalisms in the Filipina/o diaspora.* University of Illinois Press.

Wu, C. (2018). *Sticky rice: A politics of intraracial desire.* Temple University Press.

CHAPTER FOUR

Pedagogy of Unfreedom: Building Queer Relationalities through Sticky Rice

Queer of color critique approaches culture as one site that compels identification with and antagonisms to the normative ideals promoted by state and capital. Queer of color analysis must examine how culture as a site of identification produces such odd bedfellows and how it – as the location of antagonisms – fosters unimagined alliances. --- (Alexander, 2021, p. 23)

What is Asia? What is Asian? I frequently question about my racial classification as *Asian*, referencing to the largely vague region called *Asia* constructed by the White, Western, cisheteronormative, and colonized cartography. Born and raised in Japan during the 80's and 90's, I was taught to embody the performative logic of Japan's ethnocentrism that distinguishes my Japaneseness differently from the rest of Asia. I was subjected to the homogenized myth of Japaneseness through which the superiority of Japan is historically (mis)understood as a monocultural and monoethnic nation. By Japaneseness, I mean a social and performative condition of being Japanese in and across historical and ideological contexts (Toyosaki & Eguchi, 2017). Consequently, as I crossed the Pacific Ocean to the U.S., I became immediately confused to be racialized as *Asian*. This racial label includes different cultures, ethnicities, languages, histories, politics, and more. So, I, as the racialized "Asian" subject, do not necessarily have in common with various racialized "Asian" subjects. Yet, I was shocked to encounter with some Americans asking me about Chinese cultures and languages which I did not grow up with, for example.

Simultaneously, the more I have participated in the U.S. gay sexual cultures, the more I have also developed my racialized identification as Asian. Because the settler colonial logic of whiteness organizes gay sexual cultures (McBride, 2005), I can never get away from the global gay racial logics that subordinate my body marked as Asian. The historical racialization of my queerness becomes an everyday anchoring point to make sense of who I am and what I do as I interact with queer subjects around me. Hence, while I do not always have in common with my co-researchers who participate in this study's interview, I can also relate to the way the settler colonial logic of whiteness collectively disadvantages us. Hence, there are some kinds of *sameness* between them and me. Here, Calafell and Moreman (2010) remind me of the following: "As we repetitively answer the discursive call, our racial identity becomes naturalized for ourselves and for others" (p. 403). Thus, I am resonated with *somethings* about queer Asia as a continually shifting space of borderland even when all differences are essentially shored under. Therefore, my following questions always stuck in my mind: *What are somethings about queer Asia that bridge differences? How do I/we reclaim queer Asia for my/our own advantages?*

While thinking about the aforementioned questions emerged from my lived experiences, I once again recognize how the intersections among queer and Asia that assemble various modes of difference neglect historically saturated and culturally specific nuances of the racialized Asian sexual and gender minoritarians in and across local, national, and global contexts. Both queer and Asia together operate as an intersecting site of borderland through which the specialized and resistant knowledge(s) embedded in the material realities of the racialized Asian sexual and gender minoritarians are (re)produced (Gopinath, 2018; Nguyen, 2014; Wu, 2018). Indeed, queer Asia is a temporal space where the racialized Asian sexual and gender minoritarians develop ongoing interplays of connections and disconnections among one another. Hence, the cultural production of queer Asia that identifies, counters, and disidentifies with the White, Western colonialism and imperialism of gender, sexuality, and the body cannot be easily dismissed (Chiang & Wong, 2017). The reclaiming of queer Asia as an account of disjunctive modernities requires the sustained attention (e.g., Yue, 2017; Yu, 2020).

To consider the reclaiming of queer Asia as disjunctive modernities, I return my attention to vernacular discourses around sticky rice – Asian men loving Asian men – emerged from my auto/ethnographic approaches to in-depth interviews with the seven racialized Asian queer male co-researchers demonstrated in the previous chapter. In this chapter, I pay specific attention to the way sticky rice offers alternative and additional spaces of intellectualism and geopolitics through which the racialized Asian male subjects perform queer relationalities displaying "shared critical dissatisfactions" (Muñoz, 2009, p. 189) with the constraints and restraints of (queer) freedom. Elaborating scholars such as Gopinath (2018), McCune (2014), Snorton (2014), and Yep, Alaoui, and Lescure (2020), by queer relationalities, I mean multiple, dynamic, and unstable conditions of relating that antagonize and shuffle the inner-workings of cisheteronormativity with whiteness, patriarchy, capitalism, and more. Queer relationalities are every so often unintelligible and unnamable in the present moment, privileging the cisheteronormative paradigms of relating such as marriage, family, and kinship (Eguchi & Long, 2019). Hence, queer relationalities suggest possible pathways to cultivate *the collective* for the future as an ideal destination. Muñoz (2009) reminds:

> [Q]ueerness is primarily about futurity and hope. That is to say that queerness is always in the horizon. I contend that if queerness is only to have any value whatsoever, it must be viewed as being visible only in the horizon. (p. 11)

Thus, I examine how queerness of sticky rice generate and regenerate possible pathways to develop *the collective* among the racialized Asian queer male subjects. In so doing, I take an additional step toward marginalizing the constraints and restraints of (queer) freedom in the present moment.

To actualize my goal, I introduce the way I capitalize queer Asia as an anchoring point of this chapter. At this juncture, I also elaborate the notion of a coalitional possibility in orienting my use of queer Asia. Then, I demonstrate two critical points of sticky rice displaying emblems of queer relationalities emerged from my speaking with the seven racialized Asian queer male co-researchers. I name these two critical points as *Pedagogy of Unfreedom* and *Toward Building Queer Relationalities*. Lastly, I end this chapter by discussing the implications of sticky rice to the intellectual and geopolitical project of queer Asia.

Capitalizing Queer Asia as an Anchoring Point

Queer Asia as critique is meant to trouble the U.S.-centric queer studies as a global and transcultural influencer. Chiang and Wong (2017) reiterate that "queer Asia names the desire of practicing intellectual perversity, which invents new objects of study and rethinks the received knowledge of area, scale, geopolitics, and queerness itself" (p. 125). The queering of Asia aims to marginalize the colonial and imperialist logics of the U.S.-centric queer studies normalizing the White, Western paradigms of minoritized sexualities and genders in and across various global localities (e.g., Chiang & Wong, 2016; Martin et al., 2008). The genealogy of queer Asia interrupts and suspends the transnational and transcultural circulation of queer studies, emerging from and depending on the U.S. queer formations such as Lesbian-Gay-Bisexual-Transgender-Queer (LGBTQ) human rights rooted in the logic of individualism, freedom, personal responsibility and merit (Yue, 2017). Put simply, queer Asia troubles the whiteness of queerness as the power, privilege, and supremacy of Western modernity. In doing so, queer Asia opens up alternative and additional spaces of intellectualism and geopolitics to bring forth the historically saturated and culturally specific nuances of minoritized sexualities and genders that often remain unintelligible and unnamable (e.g., Yue & Leung, 2017; Yu, 2020).

Simultaneously, queer Asia recapitalizes alternative and additional spaces of intellectualism and geopolitics to promote the self-fashioning of queerness while taking into account intraregional flows of power in and across Asia. By self-fashioning of queerness, I mean contested and dynamic processes of deconstructing and reconstructing queerness. The processes of self-fashioning queerness that works with intraregional flows of power regenerate alternative cartographies of Asia as disjunctive modernities, rebelling against the White, Western, and US American paradigms of queerness (e.g., Yue, 2017; Yue & Leung, 2017; Yu, 2020). The intraregional rearrangements and reconfigurations of queerness create possible pathways in which ignored, erased, and marginalized narratives that amend and ratify the geopolitical archives of minoritized sexualities and genders resurface and reemerge. As Chiang and Wong (2017) advocate, "Both terms [queer Asia] are caught in endless chains of signification without fixed referents and predetermined signifiers, thus demanding new historical and geopolitical realignment and assemblage" (p.122). Hence, the self-fashioning of queer Asia as disjunctive modernities revise ongoing histories of the colonial past and present (Yue, 2017).

To take further steps to study queer Asia, some scholars (e.g., Baudinette, 2016; Kan, 2017) examine the trope of Asian men loving Asian men that suggest both the multidirectional effects of queer globalization and intraregional flows of power. For example, Baudinette (2016) engages in an ethnographic study of Tokyo's queer district Shinjuku Ni-chome through which Chinese and South Korean patrons who frequently travel to Tokyo meet, date, and have sex with Japanese patrons. However, Japanese patrons who meet, date, and have sex with foreigners called as Gaijin (外人) are mostly known to seek after the White men coming from the Western nations such as Australia, the U.K., and U.S. The White, Western, and U.S. queer lifestyle as a liberal symbol of sexual advancement and progressivity cultivates their localized sexual and romantic aspirations toward the White men (e.g., Eguchi, 2015; Mackintosh, 2010; Suganuma, 2012). Accordingly, some Japanese patrons see that Chinese and South Korean patrons who phenotypically look like them are ongoing threats who possibly "steal" available White men from them (Baudinette, 2016). At the same time, given the ongoing histories of Japan's xenophobia intertwining with anti-Chinese and anti-Korean sentiments (Kawai, 2015), the architecture of Tokyo's queer district marginalizes Chinese and South Korean patrons (Baudinette, 2016). Still, the Chinese and South Korean patrons who frequently visit Tokyo are less likely interested in the White men as they resist global and transnational circuits of the White, Western, and U.S. queer life-style (Baudinette, 2016). How they consume Japanese literature, popular culture, and gay pornography as superior materials of "Asian" modernities cultivate their aspirations to Japanese men (Baudinette, 2016). Hence, when the Chinese and South Korean patrons meet, date, and have sex with Japanese patrons, such inter-personal intraregional relations may provide a path to produce *the collective* that resists the global and transnational circuits of the White, Western, and U.S. queer lifestyle. Still, the *collective* points to the political economy of global inequality that hierarchizes the intraregional flows of power and capital in and across Asia.

By the same token, Kang (2017) analyzes cultural nuances of everyday life performances associated with middle-class Thai gay male preferences for meeting, dating, and having sex with "White" Asians in Bangkok. By "White" Asians, he means men from South Korea, Japan, Taiwan, Hong Kong, Singapore, or an equiv-alent nation where plays as the financial tigers in the contemporary age of glob-alization. As Kang (2017) details, "'White Asian' here encapsulates a cluster of associations including skin colour, advanced economic development (as a nation or as a minority), cultural proximity and Thai imaginings of what 'Asia' and cos-mopolitan 'Asians' look like" (p. 189). Here, it is important to maintain that such middle-class local Thai gay male preferences are the embodied products of both queer globalization and intraregional flows of power. On the one hand, they re-sist the political, economic, and historical landscape of Thailand as a global queer sex tourist destination through which older and larder-bodied White men seek after younger and fitted-bodied Thai men (Kang, 2017). The middle-class Thai gay men who stigmatize being seen as sex workers purposely stay away from the White men. While sex works should not be condemned at all, the middle-class Thai gay men struggle with the racialized, gendered, and classed stereotypes of Thais as sexually available for the tourists from the West. On the other hand, the middle-class local Thai gay men still lean toward "White" Asians to subtly fashion and maintain their class privileges and cultural capitals. The couplings of Thai men being with "White" Asians passing like friends in public are not as stigmatized as the couplings of Thai men being with White men (Kang, 2017). However, the middle-class Thai gay male preferences for meeting, dating, and having sex with "White" Asians suggests the complex paradox of desire as a political, economic, and historical product. While the couplings of Thai men being with "White" Asians resist privileges given to White men, the relational tropes ironically reinsert the intraregional flows of power that hierarchize differences in and across Asia. The couplings of Thai men being with "White" Asians yet maintain the lower political economic status of Thai men (Kang, 2017).

The intraregional studies on "Asian" men meeting, dating, and having sex with "Asian" men described above suggest potential parallels to my argument presented in the previous chapter. As I have demonstrated, my co-researchers and I observe the way intraregional flows of power circulated in and across Asia and Asian diasporas shape and reshape interpersonal intercultural relations through which racialized Asian men meet racialized Asian men in the U.S. Queer diasporas that provide alternative cartographies cannot entirely break free of ongoing ideological tensions in-between and in-betwixt homeland, diaspora, and hostland in the present moment (e.g., Eng, 2001; Gopinath, 2018). The politics of homeland alters, shapes, and reinforces the politics of diaspora; simultaneously the politics of diasporas alters shapes, and reinforces the politics of homeland (Velasco, 2020). Hence, I bring queer Asia as critique to analyze vernacular discourses around sticky rice emerged from my in-depth interviews with the seven co-researchers. The genealogy of queer Asia cannot ignore, erase, and marginalize how transnational connectivities, produced and reproduced by migrations and diasporas, make and remake impossible possibilities of queerness as disjunctive modernities. Rebuilding queer Asia does not take place exclusively in and across the geographical boundary of Asia as a region.

Consequently, I capitalize queer Asia as an anchoring point to rebuild disjunctive modernities of sticky rice as a temporal moment of coalitional possibility. The way a coalition functions as a collective group of people coming together around a specific political issue to achieve a particular goal is always already temporal and spatial (Chávez, 2013). Because an ongoing interplay between stability and change shapes the manifestation of culture, a coalition requires constant amendments and revisions in and across time, space, and context. As Chávez (2013) asserts, "A coalitional moment occurs when political issues coincide or merge in the public sphere in ways that create space to reenvision and potentially reconstruct rhetorical imaginaries" (p. 8). Here I appreciate Chávez's (2013) emphasis on moment in approaching a coalitional possibility. This coincides with Muñoz (2009) theorizing of queerness as a utopian ideality that requires constant revisions of the present. Queerness is an impossibly possibility (e.g., Chambers-Leston, 2018; Keeling, 2019). Hence, from this notion of coalitional possibility working with queerness, I return to the trope of sticky rice as emblems of queer relationalities that antagonize and shuffle the constraints and restraints of (queer) freedom.

Now, I reenter into the moments of my speaking with the seven racialized Asian queer male co-researchers in this chapter.[1] Compared to the previous chapter that showcases alternative cartographies of the social orders the co-researchers see through, I focus on their personal narratives that hint to the trope of sticky rice as a moment of coalitional possibility. To be precise, I am interested in documenting how the co-researchers articulate and rearticulate vernacular discourses around sticky rice that suggest emblems of queer relationalities implicating possible pathways to develop *the collective*. Here, once again I am not focused on patterning commonalities in our lived experiences as I speak with the co-researchers. I am much more concerned with personal narratives that showcase the spectrums of divergence and contestation on sticky rice as a moment of coalitional possibility. Working with this technique, I arrange my descriptions and analyses of my speaking with the co-researchers into the two spectrums; *pedagogy of unfreedom* and *building queer relationalities*. Next, I detail the first spectrum pedagogy of unfreedom.

Pedagogy of Unfreedom

Reentering into the moments of speaking with my co-researchers, I recognize how each co-researcher and I utter sticky rice as a pedagogy of unfreedom that suggests the constraints and restraints of our sexual and romantic desires implicating the political, economic, and historical conditions of where we socialize. By a pedagogy of unfreedom, I mean a performative method of learning and relearning that points to the social limits of who we are, what we do, and how we make sense of what we do that hinder our freedom of our desires. More specifically, each co-researcher and I negotiate the vernacular discourses around sticky rice to learn and relearn the boundaries of who/what we are attracted to and who/what we are not attracted to. Sticky rice teaches us to acknowledge and do somethings about what we are missing from performing our desires.

An Atlanta-based Vietnamese male Lala expresses to me about the way trying to understand the stigmatization of sticky rice *as inadequately gay* pedagogically allows him to be critically aware of the racialized Asian queer male subjects desiring certain kinds of men. As Han (2015) suggested, the certain kinds of men tend to be White, masculine, cisgender, able-bodied, and dominant. Here, the stigmatization of sticky rice suggests a racialized, gendered, and classed condition of Asian men loving Asian men that fails to meet the White gay sexual cultural expectations of sexual and romantic couplings. Here, Lala articulates:

> They [racialized Asian queer male subjects] are attracted to masculine men usually....I think we should dab into the culture of war and how [White] Americans view Asians as sexual[ly] submissive and how we [as Asians] react to that [White Americans' perception].... 'Cause apparently a lot of Asian guys do like the dominance type. And I feel like a lot of them do like White guys specifically because it [the world] is such a White culture.

As mentioned in the previous chapter, when Lala is around Asians and Asian Americans, they tend to be Vietnamese people sharing the communal ties with Lala. Lala's social network largely takes place in his ethnic diasporas. Hence, when Lala talks about racialized Asian queer male subjects being attracted to White masculine men, he geopolitically speaks from his relational capital through which he interacts with Vietnamese people in Atlanta. Lala demonstrates this contextual particularity.

Specifically, while speaking with me as a Japanese queer subject, Lala refers to the histories of "Vietnam War and the war with Japan" as contextual enablers for White Americans fantasizing submissive Asians and for Asians chasing dominant White Americans. While temporal, spatial, and contextual differences between the Vietnam War and the Pacific War with Japan should not be ignored, the U.S. military and its occupation have structurally shaped both Vietnam's and Japan's social institutions. And the contemporary globalization that forces the transnational practices of a liberal market economy stimulates the Americanization of their local cultures, values, and customs. Hence, the U.S. imperialism cultivates the upward directionality of local "Asians" being aspired to meet, date, and have sex with White Americans as the embodied symbols of power.

Accordingly, Lala reasons that the historical continuum of the U.S. wars with Asia that produces the politics of desire structures the way the racialized Asian queer male subjects desire the White masculine ideal as they participate in and across the U.S. gay sexual cultures. Here, Communication scholars such as Nakayama (1994) and Ono (2005) remind that Asian American identity, performance, and politics are always already transnational. Asian Americans cannot be separated from political, economic, and historical happenings in and across Asia. The U.S. militarism in Asia plays a key role in constructing particular Asians and Asian Americans as the *model minorities* and other Asians ans Asian Americans as *threats* (Wu, 2018). Hence, the stigmatization of sticky rice as inadequately gay implicates how the U.S. empire orchestrates the racialized Asian queer male subjects to desire the White masculine ideal as the model minority stamp of assimilation. Being with the White masculine men is the relational capital for the racialized Asian queer male subjects to navigate the U.S. settler colonial nation-state, in general, and the U.S. gay sexual cultures, in particular. Rodriguez (2014) reiterates that "economic and social power is firmly attached to White masculinity" (p. 59). This is why sticky rice can pejoratively insult some racialized Asian queer male subjects who strategically turn away from loving someone who look like them. They are framed to aspire and obtain the upward mobility of desire materialized by the global and transnational politics of race, migration, and the U.S. patriotism. For them, performing sticky rice that does not involve the White masculine ideal is *un-American*.

By rearticulating the stigmatization of sticky rice as un-American, Lala also distinguishes the relational capital of the racialized Asian queer male subjects aspiring the White masculine ideal from the rest of us who meet, date, and have sex with various men of color. Lala finds that the racialized Asian queer male subjects he encounters in Atlanta are more sexually and romantically interested in *non-Asians* than *Asians*. By saying "I think because they do like that masculine entity," Lala points to how racialized Asian queer male subjects are attracted to hypermasculine images of Black and Latino men perpetuated in and across the U.S. media and popular culture. Here, Lala reinforces a cisgendered binary paradigm of the racialized Asian queer men as feminized and submissive subjects seeking after non-Asian masculine male subjects. The alternative possibilities of racialized Asian queer desire and relationality are erased, ignored, or forgotten. At the same time, Lala's perspective points to the problematic way the settler colonial logics of whiteness reorganize the racialized and cisgendered framings of Black and Brown male sexualities as *excessive*. The racialized Asian queer male subjects actively participate in the U.S. sexual economies of racial fetish that commodify the Black and Brown hypermasculinities (Eguchi, 2015). Yet, Lala clarifies that the racialized Asian queer male subjects meeting, dating, and having sex with Black and Latino men is secondary to those meeting, dating, and having sex with White men who represent the often-invisible cultural norms. The historical continuum of the U.S. racial formation culturally, politically, and economically accents various men of color as the *non-White Others*.

More precisely, the stigmatization of sticky rice as un-American highlights how the White masculine ideal creates and recreates the relational, cultural, and political hierarchies of the racialized Asian queer male subjects based on their sexual and romantic partners' races. The relational proximity to the White masculine ideal is the most desirable capital. At the same time, the proximity to *American* men of color can be an alternative relational capital for the racialized Asian queer male subjects who distance themselves from performing sticky rice desires. A New York-based Japanese male Yoshi tells me in the following:

> Why I liked the Black guy[s] was [that] I [had been] listening to a lot of Black music when I was in Japan, and I kind of longed for ... I want to know what [the] culture is...because it's totally different. It's like a totally different kind of music. And a lot of even Japanese artists [are] really interested [in] them [meaning the music genre and culture]....It's like opposite attraction, maybe? That's what I felt first time. And I have dated two, three [Black] guy[s]. It was kind of hard, because totally different culture, totally different thought sometimes, but it was fun.

Here, Yoshi admits that the global consumption of hip-hop he encountered in Japan prior to moving to the U.S. has cultivated his gaze toward Black/ African American men. Yoshi's utterance of his desire that is politically un-corrected hints to the larger global and transnational problem of racialized gender politics. The U.S. capitalist commodification of hip-hop perpetuates the historically excessive stereotypes of Black men as hypermasculine and hypersexual (e.g., McCune 2014; Morris, 2013; Snorton, 2014). Accordingly, Yoshi fetishizes Black men. At the same time, Yoshi born and raised in Japan is framed to aspire the U.S. as a socially progressive nation (e.g., Eguchi & Kimura, 2021; Sekimoto, 2014; Toyosaki, 2011). Considering the normative, upward progression of LGBTQ human rights in Japan is seen as behind the U.S. (e.g., Suganuma 2012; Welker, 2017), Yoshi moves to the U.S as a sexually exceptional state where he assumes he can be freely queer. Hence, for Yoshi as a Japanese queer male migrant subject, the proximity to Black/African American men is indeed his relational, cultural, and political capital that represents his belonging to the U.S. settler colonial nation-state. From the mainstreamed Japanese point of view, Black/African Americans are *Americans* in the histor-ical continuum of the U.S. militarism taking place in Japan. A New York-based Taiwanese male Chun reminds me that "in Japan it's like you have U.S. mil-itary bases there. The culture [is] still influenced by that." Thus, depending on the political, economic, and historical conditions of where they are from, some racialized Asian queer male subjects aspire the embodied products of Americanness also performed by men of color.

Here, it is important to highlight the way the global and transnational circula-tion of U.S. popular culture as a symbol of American exceptionalism contextualizes vernacular discourses around sticky rice as *un-American*. The lack of the U.S. media and popular cultural representation of Asian American men exacerbates the mate-rial condition through which the normative imagination of masculine ideal excludes Asian American men as Americans. As Nakayama (1994) argued almost three decades ago, Asian Americans are almost always constructed as foreigners in the U.S. media and popular culture. Because of this historical continuity, the racialized Asian queer male subjects who seek to gain the proximity to the embodied sign of

Americanness turn away their attentions from other racialized Asian queer male subjects marked as forever foreign.

Consequently, the relational rivalry and competition among the racialized Asian queer male subjects can emerge especially in and across the U.S. cultural contexts where unearned White privileges are materialized. A New York-based Chinese/Vietnamese American male Lee says to me:

> I think we [Asians] are a very small group of that minority group. But even that minority group, because of all the stigma that comes with being Asian, our cultural backgrounds, family backgrounds, I think it inhibits a lot of [Asian] people from being less inclined to be more free about their coming out, if you will....... I think it also makes it very difficult for the Asian community or Asian gay community to engage or interact or be supportive of each other. Because again, it's that stigma.......Being a gay Asian male, even when just walking down the street, and you see another person who is also gay or Asian, there's naturally this eye contact, and you acknowledge each other, but not in the kindest of ways. You acknowledge each other as almost a little competitive, or whatever it is. There's almost a little bit of discrimination there, too...... So again, it just makes it even much more different for, say, a collective Asian community to kind of come together.

Here, Lee alludes to the way the settler colonial logics of whiteness normalizing the upward directionality of assimilation cultivates the relational rivalry and competition among Asians. Because the foreignization of Asian Americans is historically inevitable, the intraracial rivalry and competition stems from the idea of *who is more American than another.* They fight against one another to prove, evidence and authenticate their embodied performances of assimilation. This is similar to an everyday life situation where people of color are structurally framed to fight against other people of color in order to secure their "diversity" spots in and across workplace organizations such as the University (Calafell, 2015). Hence, the historical supremacy of whiteness that advances ongoing stigmatizations of sticky rice as un-American contextualizes the politics of divisiveness among racialized Asian queer male subjects meeting, dating, and having sex with men.

A Los Angeles-based Filipino American male Polo also elaborate this kind of relational rivalry and competition Lee has uttered above by answering to my question asking why he thinks he rarely sees sticky rice couples in his social environments. Polo says:

> I don't know if you [meaning, the author of this book] feel this way, but sometimes there's this sense of competition, like oh, there's two of us [meaning, two racialized Asian queer male subjects] here; we can't both be here, what are you doing here? There's that element in a way where it's not about connecting but competing.......I wish I could say that it's like ..... I know that the typical answer is like, "Well, we

just never really saw ourselves represented, so we don't really acknowledge ourselves as sexy."

While speaking with me, Polo verbalizes how the sexual and romantic aspiration toward (White) masculine ideal pits the racialized Asian queer male subjects against one another. They are framed to compete with one another to become and be the *only Asian* being around sexy (White) *Americans*. This directionality toward the (White) masculine ideal makes the racialized Asian queer male subjects feel as if they cannot be intimate with one another because of their perceived lack of masculinity. The settler colonial logics of whiteness discount and devalue any masculine emblems of the racialized Asian queer male subjects because they are simply racialized as Asians (Han, 2015). Here, I am once again reminded of how *the body matters*.

Accordingly, the vernacular discourses around sticky rice as un-American point to public safety issues that represent ongoing histories of anti-Asian racism. In response to my question why Lee feels little uncomfortable with the trope of sticky rice, Lee tells me in the following:

> The stigma that I grew up with in terms of being openly gay, holding hands with somebody in public, PDAs, just was a no-no......So again, [sticky rice is] new. And then once I process it [sticky rice], and I can say, "Wow, that's pretty awesome. Here there are not one person, but two Asian guys that are holding hands, and they're comfortable in their relationship when they're together." And again, I think from my experience, already being one, Asian; two, gay; three ... in some moments, more flamboyant or effeminate than others; and four, I have a smaller size frame, so it makes me a target. Like, automatically, I'm a target, and I've been a target wherever we've traveled around the world. Even in the US, I've always been a target. And, so, to have two guys similar to my build, personality or style, or even demeanor or masculinity, hold hands in public ... Again, that's where I get taken aback by it. It's the courage and the ability to feel comfortable to be able to do that, and feel that they are safe to do that, I think it's amazing.

At this juncture, I appreciate Lee's open, frank, and honest sharing of vulnerability and resilience around public safety with me. Being a smaller-built effeminate gay Asian male, Lee is conscious of the potential danger through which strangers could easily target him for hate crimes. Living in New York City, Lee who walks around and use the public transportation to navigate the city is at risk of encountering intersectional hate crimes that suggest the Asian, gay, and effeminate.

At the time of writing this chapter, I observe that the pandemic of COVID-19, which the 45th president Trump named it as "China Virus," has tremendously increased anti-Asian racist hate crimes in and across the U.S. This includes the

2021's Atlanta spa shootings took place on March 16th where six Asian female workers have been shot to death. Correspondingly, the Stop Asian Hate movement that calls to end anti-Asian racism becomes sensationally circulated in the U.S. media and popular culture. This situation highlights ongoing histories of Asians and Asian Americans as the targets of hate crimes. The White supremacy that reinserts the logic of racism working with xenophobia has a major psychological and physical effect on Asians and Asian Americans participating in the public.

Simultaneously, Lee feels he may be less of a target when he is with his non-Asian cisgender partner who is a bigger-built masculine man. Here, Lee does not deny the occurrences of hate crimes against various queer men and queer men of color. What Lee means is that the rhetorical manifestations of hate crimes against "feminized" Asians are often different from hate crimes against various "masculinized" queer men and queer men of color. For example, Asians are historically stereotyped to be weak, timid, and quiet (e.g., Eng, 2001; Sun, 2007; Wu, 2002). Hence, Asians are assumed not to fight back. Under such effect of the anti-Asian racism, Lee is also subjected to the way the logics of homophobia and anti-effeminacy that architect the majoritarian codes of the public intensify his potential danger. Although the politics of homonationalism capitalizes the LGBTQ human rights as the U.S. nationalist ideology to promote the U.S. liberal exceptionalism (e.g., Eng, 2010; Puar, 2007), hate crimes against LGBTQ people continue to take place. As Morris and Sloop (2006) reminded before, the public that reconstitutes the cisgender norm of heterosexuality as moral is a hostile environment for the subjects performing their queer intimacies. Hence, Lee's uncomfortable feeling toward sticky rice redirects the attention to the historical feminization of his racialized gender body being disciplined, controlled, and surveilled by the White masculinist supremacy.

At the same time, sticky rice pedagogically implicates how the racialized gender body working with the public creates a glass ceiling for the racialized Asian queer male subjects in the gay dating and hookup scene. Here, by glass ceiling, I specifically mean an invisible social barrier territorialized by the gay sexual cultural logic of the White masculine ideal maintaining racialized gender segregations. As I ask Lee to clarify his uncomfortable feeling toward sticky rice, he brings up how the gay sexual constructs of Asians as undesirable shapes and reshapes his experiences. Lee says "I don't fall into their [all-American-looking males'] sexual desires, and when you're not objectified, or you're not sexualized, or they don't see you or perceive you in that way, you're basically dismissed." So, I raise an additional question to Lee if the sexually undesirable images around Asian men are changing in recent years. Lee details in the following:

I think there are many guys that will sleep with you [implying, the racialized Asian queer male subjects]. They'll hook up with you, but they'll never take you out in public. You'll never meet them or their friends or socialize with you, and they'll never tell their friends that they've hooked up with you. For whatever reason that is, but it happens, and it's happened to me I can't tell you how many times. But immediately, if they want a booty call, they'll call you. You know what I mean? So you'll hook up there, but in terms of meeting or socializing, or engaging with their community or their friends, won't occur.

At this phase, Lee rearticulates the complex paradoxes of desire that implicate the contextual values of the racialized Asian queer male subjects.

On the one hand, the racialized Asian queer male subjects are indeed valued for hookups. As a number of scholars (e.g., Fung, 2005; Han, 2015; Lim, 2014; Nguyen, 2014; Wu, 2018) have suggested before, the gay sexual subcultural category of "Asian" indeed works as the racial fetish. Because some men fetishize Asian people, cultures and languages, they want to hook up with the racialized Asian queer male subjects. At the same time, some men may be also turned on by the stigmatization of the racialized Asian queer male subjects. As Bailey (2016) reiterates, "sexual pleasure is experienced through our apparent contradictions. These contradictions of sexuality are about the difference between what we say – sometime who we say we are – and what we actually do" (p. 239). Hence, the sexual stigmatization of the racialized Asian queer male subjects is not simply undesirable; it is highly complex and contested.

On the other hand, the racialized Asian queer male subjects may not be valued for dating as much as hookups. By this, I mean some men prefer to keep sexual pleasures with the racialized Asian queer male subjects inside "the bedroom." They do not want to come out of "the bedroom" with the racialized Asian queer male subjects who may be vulnerable to hate in the public. Here, I am reminded of Lee verbalizing that some men sleep with Asians *on the down low* like "their friends may not know that they are interested in mixed or different races of people." Lee reasons this phenomenon by projecting that these men strategically avoid being seen for having the Asian fetish as they socialize in and across gay sexual cultures. Perhaps, some all-American-looking men save their (White) masculine ideal faces by having exclusively around all-American-looking men in the public. There is a material reality of the gay clique working with the politics of difference.

However, the stigmatization of sticky rice as both inadequately gay and un-American also provides us an opportunity to realize the complex contradictions of the racialized Asian queer male subjects *being simultaneously desired and undesired* in and across gay sexual cultures. Chun also echoes Lee's perspective by saying that "especially living in New York City, it's all about sex….People only fuck instead to have relationships." Hence, the vernacular discourses around sticky rice point to the temporal and spatial contradictions of sexual desires and pleasures that complicate productions and constitutions of queer relationalities. Put simply, cultural contexts through which queer relationalities emerge and reemerge matter.

In this section, I have explicated how the co-researchers utter the social limits of the racialized Asian queer male subjects through their negotiations with the stigmatization of sticky rice as a vernacular. Specifically, the co-researchers are collectively dissatisfied with social boundaries of who/what we are attracted to and who/what we are not attracted to. The historically constructed relations of power that produce the vernacular discourses around sticky rice as both *inadequately gay* and *un-American* hinder possibilities of our (queer) freedom. We cannot easily break free of power that discipline, control, and surveil our queerness. Hence, sticky rice is a pedagogy of unfreedom that allows us to acknowledge what we are missing from our desires implicating the political, economic, and historical conditions of where we socialize.

Building Queer Relationalities

At the same time, because of the pedagogical aspect of sticky rice described above, the co-researchers are aware of how sticky rice provides a moment of coalitional possibility among the racialized Asian queer male subjects. The vernacular discourses around sticky rice point to relational spaces where the racialized Asian queer male subjects can collectively do something. Thus, I turn the attention to sticky rice as a site of a coalitional possibility that troubles the constraints and restraints of (queer) freedom next.

In speaking with the co-researchers for this study, it is clear to me that a gay vernacular sticky rice – Asian men loving Asian men – does not strictly reference to the cisheteronormative construct of "relationship" rooted in privacy, monogamy, marriage, and nuclear family. Instead, sticky rice implicates a much larger intellectual and geopolitical connection (and disconnection) among racialized Asian queer subjects than the cisheteronormative defining of relationship. A New York-based Japanese male Taro tells me the following:

> To be queer and Asian, and I think you just have to remind yourselves that it's beautiful to be a queer and Asian....Especially if you're dating other queer Asians, and I think that's really the fundamental thing. You should be proud. I'm proud, although I'm not dating [now] ...I'm proud to be one because, especially because I can represent. I can go out and I can represent my people [implicating the racialized Asian queer male subjects].... I think I have a good understanding of what it's like to be double

minority in this country and be queer and Asian, and be proud to be who I am, be proud to be 46 and single and still continuing my work and accomplish things, that I'm setting example to younger people.

To resist the internalization of social stigmas associated with being queer and Asian, Taro believes that reminding himself to be proud of being queer and Asian is extremely important. Especially for sticky rice pairings, Taro urges them to be proud of their unapologetic choices to go against the U.S. gay sexual cultural values of desire working with the White masculine ideal. Here, Taro suggests the importance of the way in which each racialized Asian queer male subject actively recognizes the body representing multiply marginalized positionalities. While the racialized Asian queer male subjects may not have necessarily in common, they similarly experience the racialized gender politics within the U.S. imagination (e.g., Han, 2015; Nguyen, 2014; Wu, 2018). Consequently, Taro see the need for recapitalizing "queer" and "Asian" as anchoring points to change the highly stigmatized narratives for newer generations of people who represent "queer" and "Asian." The spaces point toward queer relationalities that antagonize and shuffle the inner-workings of cisheteronormativity with whiteness, patriarchy, capitalism, and more.

This is where I find that vernacular discourses around sticky rice point toward coalitional possibilities. Lee tells me that "in the gay community, everyone's gay.... There's no longer that discomfort level of gay or straight; everyone's the same. But the blatant disregard for or the discrimination would be because I'm Asian." The Lee's sense making of being Asian is what Han and Rutledge (2020) has suggested that "gay men of color experience more racism from gay white men from the larger society is wide spread" (p. 33). As I have mentioned in the previous chapters, the sexual rejections of men of color through phrases such as "No Asians" and "no Blacks" are ordinary narratives that continue to be seen in gay online dating scenes (e.g., McBride, 2005; Nguyen, 2014). This racist phenomenon points to power and privileges associated with the White masculine ideal that organize the gatekeeping activity. In speaking with me, Polo brings up about his Asian American friend he knows through his Los Angeles-based queer social circle. Polo notes:

> He's definitely chased after that glossy West Hollywood ideal [meaning, the White masculine ideal], and he's been burned a lot. A lot of it is chalked up to the fact that well, he's not White enough to get through the gate. At the end of the day, there isn't room for a lot of minorities in the circles that he's trying to be part of. I feel like his encountering gay racism in West Hollywood is much stronger than mine, but he actually lives in West Hollywood.

Polo's friend's experience reinforces the way Polo finds that the sexual minoritarians are super competitive for sex and romance in the West Hollywood designed as one of the major global gay meccas. He continues:

> People came here because they are ambitious… And they would like to win at all things, not just dating but their jobs, their houses, their lifestyle, their clothes, their cars, all that stuff. There's a definite reach for a glamorous life.

Here, it is important to note that the U.S. political economy of capitalism shapes and reshapes what is globally constructed as a fabulous gay lifestyle. By this means, male sexual minoritarians engage in gay sexual cultural consumptions of the high-end luxurious lifestyle, including but not limited to shopping, partying, drinking, dining out, and traveling (e.g., Buckland, 2002; Eguchi, Files-Thompson, & Calafell, 2018; McCune, 2014). This money-driven culture that reinforces social inequalities drives the gay sexual cultural competition that collectively disadvantages the racialized Asian queer male subjects. Hence, I find that, because the trope of sticky rice unequivocally insinuates the stigmatized experiences of being Asian in gay dating scenes, there is the potential through which the racialized Asian queer male subjects collectively recapitalize sticky rice to antagonize and shuffle social and performative forms of gay racism.

To showcase my argument further, I turn the attention to the political significance of sticky rice that regenerates the *stickiness (or sameness)* of the racialized Asian queer male subjects. For example, Taro begins his interview with me by saying:

> I prefer Asian men. I don't necessarily find it [sticky rice] offensive.….I would imagine non-Asians would find it offensive. Especially if they like Asians, they may feel that they are…not the target of affection. Or… they're not included in that sense that … Obviously, I'm not, I won't be interested. They may feel offended that they're excluded.

Here, I am intrigued by Taro telling me that non-Asians who are interested in meeting, dating, and having sex with Asian men can be offended by a vernacular sticky rice. While I can see it happening, I am also uncomfortable to support the idea of sticky rice that uncritically offends non-Asians, especially White men, in the historical continuum of racial formation. As I have laid out in this book, it is important to recognize that everyone is not given equal opportunities to participate in the U.S. gay dating and hookup scene that privileges the White masculine ideal.

However, another New York-based Japanese male Yoshi also asks me if sticky rice is "a bad word." He says, "is it kind of like a racist kind of word?" So, I explain to him that sticky rice is about Asian men loving Asian men. He responses, "Okay, it is like 'Rice Queen,' that kind of stuff." The way Yoshi instantly equates sticky rice to rice queen – a White man who is interested in meeting, dating, and having sex with Asian men –reinserts the color-blinded rhetoric of racial diversity that does not fully elaborate ongoing histories of gay racism. As Han (2015) reminds, because of the small pool of rice queens available, the racialized Asian men tend to compete against each other to meet, date, and have sex with White men. Hence, Yoshi's language ignores how the logic of whiteness that organizes gay sexual cultures construct an easier path for White men meeting, dating, and having sex with Asian men than Asian men meeting, dating, and having sex with White men.

Yet, Chun provides me a different reason to be uncomfortable with a vernacular sticky rice. He says,

> For me, it [sticky rice] is like a little bit racial derogatory thing to say. It's kind of like, "Oh, so you are using the food that we are eating to define who we are?" Okay? Then, that's even asking around, not every Asian eat rice. So that's for me, it's really racial derogatory.

I can relate to Chun's frustration with the racialized semantic of sticky rice that equates people with food. The discriminatory targets of Asian foods as filthy historically manifest the blatant forms of anti-Asian racism. The COVID-19 pandemic though which the U.S. 45th president Trump names it as "a China virus" re-stigmatizes and decreases the global consumption of Chinese and East Asian foods (Fernando & Mumphery, 2020).

At the same time, hearing Taro, Yoshi, and Chun's perspectives all together, what I value is the politically incorrected offensiveness of sticky rice as a vernacular. Returning to the methodological foundation of queer theory that reclaims an offensive word queer (Yep, Lovaas, & Elia, 2003), I value the possible way in which reclaiming the offensiveness of sticky rice that represents the racial exclusiveness of Asian men loving Asian men works as a rhetorical strategy to sideline or ostracize the White masculine ideal. Because the politics of respectability that recenters whiteness promotes the politically correct condition of social interactions, the offensiveness of sticky rice not only breaks the silence of White privileges materialized in the gay dating and hookup market. But it also allows the racialized Asian queer male subjects to recognize, reevaluate, and work with their internalizations of anti-Asian racism (e.g., Han, 2015; Nguyen, 2014; Wu, 2018).

More specifically, the co-researchers and I are required to question and critique the paradox of how we reproduce anti-Asian racism through our embodied performances of queer desires. So, we can take further steps toward recapitalizing the *stickiness (or sameness)* of the racialized Asian queer male subjects to perform queer relationalities that develop *the collective*. For example, Lee reminds me of the pervasiveness of the femininized Asian stereotype by saying that "I think just as Asian people in general, we're still kind of objectified as this soft, delicate, de-masculined, [and] not very strong." Polo also tells me that Asians are not expected to be "an alpha male" in and across gay sexual cultures. Because of this racialized gender imagination, the Asian queer male subjects are often left out. Lee tells me that "the majority would be interested in a very well-groomed, physically fit or in shape, masculine or somewhere in the middle." However, as I have showcased earlier, the racialized Asian queer male subjects also participate in the gay sexual and romantic aspiration toward the (White) masculine ideal. Yoshi says to me, "I like men like a normal guy. If you see the guy [Yoshi likes], you don't know [if he is] gay or straight. Some people always look always gay. I don't like that." Because effeminacy is historically constructed as a sign of homosexuality (Johnson, 2003), the logic of anti-Asian racism working with the feminization highly disadvantages the racialized Asian queer male subjects seen as feminine in gay dating scenes. Hence, Taro tells me the following:

> There has been documented stories and experiences of Asians being labeled as lesbians. Asian men like other Asians... That's sort of interesting because it's really a stereotype put upon by ourselves. I think that's within Asian community that you're expected to not date other Asians [because] maybe we're seen as feminine. I don't know where that came from. Again, maybe that came from our own community.

Taro's elaboration on sticky rice as a "lesbian" pairing reinforces what Nguyen (2014) has previously said is the logic of whiteness that organizes the patriarchal architectures of gay sexual cultures constructs sticky rice as inappropriately gay. Two effeminate subjects are not expected to meet, date, and have sex with one another (Wu, 2018). At the same time, I appreciate Taro points out that the racialized Asian queer male subjects also remake the stigmatization of sticky rice because we are not supposed to meet, date, and have sex with one another. *Once again, we are a part of the problem.* So, as Taro articulates this, he also questions that "may be there has never been a stigma. May be, that was internalized homophobia and internalized racism combined that sticky rice at one point was frowned upon within the likes of community." This is where Taro alludes to the way the *stickiness (or sameness)* of sticky rice pushes the racialized Asian queer male subjects to be critically reflexive of our desires. We must refuse and reject internalizing the settler colonial logic of whiteness that produces the gay sexual cultural narratives about being Asian. It is the time for us to collectively fight back and change the oppressive narratives implicated by vernacular discourses around sticky rice.

To do so, turning the attention to a transnational context of queer Asia can be a productive step. Taro tells me "Thanks to internet. Thanks to more empowered queer Asians in Asia that they [queer Asians] are finding better role models." Because of various narratives about being queer and Asian available, Taro believes that queer Asians can feel proud to desire someone who look like them. I find this Taro's shifting attention to queer Asia quite interesting. On the one hand, I can relate to Taro's perspective on queer Asia that provides an alternative framework of desire. As I have briefly mentioned in the introductory chapter of this book, I did not have the racial hang-ups to negatively judge the trope of sticky rice while in Japan. Loving someone who looks me was quite ordinary. Most people around me were phenotypically Japanese to begin with. On the one hand, as a number of scholars (e.g., Fung, 2005; Lim, 2014; Puar, 2007; Suganuma, 2012) have suggested before, the U.S. politics of homonationalism as a symbol of imperialism promotes power and privilege of the White masculine ideal in and across queer Asia. Queer Asians in Asia are not really free from the White masculine ideal that functions as a global gay beauty standard in the historical continuum of the U.S. imperialism. However, turning the attention to queer Asia that centralizes minoritarian sexualities and genders in and across Asia can offer an alternative space of possibility through which the racialized Asian queer male subjects reevaluate and reconfigure their "colonized" paradigms of sexual and romantic desire. At least, performative manifestations and implications of sticky rice in and across queer Asia are quite different from the White, Western, and U.S. paradigms of sticky rice, recentering anti-Asian racism. The trope of sticky rice does not automatically signal the lesser status of desire in and across queer Asia. Perhaps, this is why the foreign-born-and-raised co-researchers Chun, Taro, and Yoshi are much more open to the trope of sticky rice than the rest of the co-researchers. To support this, the U.S.-born-and-raised Polo reminds himself of the following:

> To put all gay men into a category is silly. We share our preference, but then there's so much diversity within the group that to address that as a monolith, as a category, feels silly because it's just so diverse within.... For the Asian-American community specifically, a lot of [difference] is just an educational opportunity not only for others but for yourself to know a little bit more about the history of gays in India or China or Japan or the Philippines [for example]. Then we do that a lot in our culture of history and design. We are stronger and more authoritative in this space because we know our history. It's a thing that America in particular begs you to forget. It begs you to forget everything. It's become a whole new thing. I think we can find unity in the fact that we can appreciate each other's stories without having to shoehorn ourselves into some blobby combination of things, that we can celebrate and unify ourselves within the really particular moments and stories and maybe qualities that we all have from being disparate parts of Asia.

Here, Polo reiterates the way turning the attention to queer Asia offers an alternative paradigm of possibility. The connections (and disconnections) among the racialized Asian queer male subjects can be used to resist against the supremacy of whiteness that normalizes the assimilation. The vernacular discourses around sticky rice pedagogically put the racialized Asian queer male subjects in their places for being non-White in and across gay sexual cultures. As Asians, we should not forget how the U.S. settler colonial institution historically racializes our bodies for its systematic sustainability. Hence, the trope of sticky rice points to a moment of a coalitional possibility that elaborates the connections (and disconnections) among the racialized Asian queer male subjects.

This is where, along with co-researchers, I call to contemplate the *stickiness (or sameness)* of the racialized Asian queer male subjects as a potential site of the collective resistance. Taro says the following:

> White people, simply being a majority, really don't help them being aware of that racism dynamics or sensitivity ... They may be offended [by sticky rice] because they expect to be found attractive by everybody, especially from the [racial] minority because that [whiteness] is the normative. That's sort of like a majority experience, I would imagine. I'm not speaking on behalf of white people because I wouldn't know. But I'm sort of imagining that may be the reason they would feel that way.

Here, Taro reminds of the way in which the racialized Asian queer male subjects should not be attracted to White men just because they are White. The racialized Asian queer male sexual and romantic attention toward White men reinserts the unquestioned and unearned sets of White privileges. Hence, the trope of sticky rice that shifts the sexual and romantic attention away from the logic of whiteness marginalizes the power and privilege of White men in the gay dating scene.

This mechanism of sticky rice also creates a path for the racialized queer Asian male subjects to relate to various people of color who are differently disadvantaged by the supremacy of whiteness. Taro continues to express:

> Generally, I would be open to all races. But I prefer people of color... While I was dating a White guy who couldn't really understand the meaning of safe space, being amongst our people to be able to share issues within ourselves. Since then, I found it easier in intimate relationship with people of color or Asians, that way I don't have to explain my personal experiences. There's no trying to explain what it means to be a person of color or Asian, or both.

At this juncture, Taro reiterates the historical implication of Asians as non-Black people of color disadvantaged by White supremacy. Regardless of the current model minority stereotype that misrepresents Asians and Asian Americans as successful and "almost White" (e.g. Eguchi, 2013; Eguchi & Ding, 2017; Kawai, 2005; Sun, 2007), Asians and Asian Americans are subjected to microaggressions that recenters anti-Asian racism. In the word of another co-researcher Lee, Asians and Asian Americans are often cattle-called as "Ching Chong" and "Jackie Chen." Consequently, Taro seeks a safe space through which he does not need to explain about being a person of color or Asian in his relationships. So, he can temporally and spatially have a break from the logic of whiteness that disadvantages him.

At the same time, because of anti-Asian racism manifested in everyday social interactions, Taro feels a sense of queer kinship with the racialized Asian queer male subjects who do not necessarily have in common. Taro goes:

> It [being around the racialized Asian queer male subjects] is like a little family...It's a surrogate family...Especially in the big city like New York or elsewhere, you really need to have that close knit community to call upon if you need help or vice-versa. That's for survival. I think you can say that for non-queers, but I mean I think our issue is being very specific to this whole group of people. I think it's more important to have that kind of support system. We can share any issues without being afraid of being stereotyped or all that.

For Taro, the racialized Asian queer male subjects who simultaneously experience multiple sets of marginalization from the mainstream, ethnic diasporic, and gay sexual cultural contexts are someone whom he can depend on. Particularly, Taro feels that the racialized Asian queer male subjects will easily understand his culturally specific issues and concerns.

Another co-researcher Yoshi also expresses that this kind of sense of kinship Taro has described above is the reason why Yoshi finds being in sticky rice relationships is easier and more comfortable than interracial relationships. Yoshi says to me that he is interested in being around someone "who can always count on no matter what happen." He continues, "I can ask something to do something. Also, I want to do the same thing, too. Support each other." Because of this, Yoshi feels that he easily can depend on the racialized Asian queer male subjects who would understand his culturally specific issues and needs. Hence, there is something about the *stickiness (or sameness)* of the racialized Asian queer male subjects that generates a collective sense of queer kinship. By this means, the racialized Asian queer male subjects develop an alternative web of social relationships that transgresses the cisheteronormative structures of marriage, family, and kinship.

Consequently, the trope of sticky rice offers possible pathways to build queer relationalities as forms of disjunctive modernities through which various racialized

Asian queer male subjects perform intellectual and geopolitical coalitions. To counter the stigmatization of sticky rice, Polo notes:

> Specifically for Asian-Americans, gay Asian-Americans, I think the fight for visibility is still on in a major way. There is a lot of value still to finding any sort of representation on a broader level. So… it means a lot when you see someone out there whose modeled a life that is successful, that is fruitful, that's positive. You have this thing in common, and it didn't hold you back, and even within the gay community, it didn't hold you back. I think the only way to change minds and perceptions about what defines Asian-American men and what specifically defines gay Asian-American men, it will only come through increased presence and visibility.

Once again, Polo reminds me of the way historically specific operations of anti-Asian racism make Asians and Asian Americans invisible in the U.S. settler colonial nation-state normalizing the Black-White binary paradigm. As Delgado and Stefancic (2012) suggested, "'Race' means, quintessentially African Americans. Other groups such as Asians, American Indians, and Latinos/as, are minorities only insofar as their experience and treatment can be analogized to those of blacks" (p. 75). More specifically, the logic of whiteness that represents Black/African Americans as problems strategically constructs Asians and Asian Americans as non-threating, quiet, passive model minorities (Eng, 2001). In so doing, Asians and Asian Americans become invisible. This is exactly what the Stop Asian Hate movement re-highlighted under the COVID-19 pandemic fights against. The White supremacy strategically ignore, erase, and marginalize everyday occurrences of anti-Asian racism in order to maintain historical continuities of anti-Blackness. Hence, Polo emphasizes that various racialized Asian queer male subjects must come together to resist and fight against the invisibility of Asians and Asian Americans in the U.S. racial paradigm that normalizes the logic of whiteness organizing gay sexual cultures.

For these reasons, I end this section by suggesting that sticky rice can be a moment of a coalitional possibility that connects (and disconnects) the racialized Asian queer male subjects with one another in and across time, space, and context. As Polo reminds me, representation matters. Thus, the racialized Asian queer male subjects must be politically cognizant of the material realities where each of us represents the very notion of being "queer" and "Asian." While we may never meet one another in person in life, each of us must resist and fight against the invisibility of Asians and Asian Americans in and through our lived experiences. *In doing so, we are always already in sticky rice relationships with one another.* Hence, the trope of sticky rice suggests possible pathways toward building queer relationalities that collectively resist and fight against the constraints and restraints of (queer) freedom.

Concluding Remarks

In this chapter, I have returned to examine the vernacular discourses around sticky rice emerged from my auto/ethnographic approaches to in-depth interviews with the seven racialized Asian queer male co-researchers. Specifically, I have showcased how the co-researchers articulate the gay sexual cultural stigmatization of sticky rice as inadequately gay and un-American. At the same time, because the stigmatization of sticky rice requires disruption, the co-researchers are aware of coalitional possibilities of sticky rice that remake the stickiness of the racialized Asian queer male subjects to trouble the *business-as-usual* aspects of gay sexual cultures. The stickiness indeed points to the "shared critical dissatisfactions" (Muñoz, 2009, p. 189) with the constraints and restraints of (queer) freedom. The queerness of sticky rice can generate and regenerate pathways to develop *the collective* among the racialized Asian queer male subjects.

Before ending this chapter, I turn the attention to the implications of sticky rice to queer Asia. As I have mentioned earlier, queer Asia privileges intraregional flows of power to promote the self-fashioning of queerness in and across Asia in order to trouble the White, Western paradigms of minoritized sexualities and genders (e.g., Chiang & Wong, 2017; Yue, 2017; Yue & Leung, 2017). Given queer Asia is a temporal and spatial concept of intellectualism and geopolitics, I expand the genealogy of queer Asia by having examined the vernacular discourses of sticky rice that largely occur in queer Asian America. This is because ongoing histories of globalization promote the intraregional flows of power circulated in and across Asia and Asian diasporas. And the sticky rice trope of Asian men meeting, dating, and having sex with Asian men offers a continually shifting space of borderland that alters, shapes, and reinforces connections between homeland, diaspora, and hostland.

At the same time, in speaking with a Washington D.C.-based Indian American male Tayo about sticky rice, I once again question, "*What is Asia?, What is Asian?*" For example, Tayo tells me that "it [sticky rice] tends to be, you know, more with Asian, meaning like kind of Chinese or you know, Southeast Asian, or like East Asian." As I have showcased in the previous chapter, Tayo believes that sticky rice can be used to signify all Asians loving Asians. Yet, he also thinks that the stigmatization of sticky rice specifically points to the historical feminization of the male subjects who look like East or Southeast Asian. Being a hairly thick Brown male, Tayo continues, "they [gay sexual cultural participants] do not see me as effeminate. They just seem me as another masculine." Tayo's experience hints to the paradox of Asia as a White, Western, cisheteronomative, and colonized cartography. While India is classified to be in the region of Asia, the logic of whiteness that organizes gay sexual cultures differently racializes Brown subjects like Tayo from someone like me who phenotypically looks East Asian. Asia is a largely vague concept. *All Asians are not the same.*

Simultaneously, queer Asia is about challenging the normative cartography of Asia through the self-fashioning of queerness. Thus, a vernacular sticky rice that provides a temporal moment of transgression can go beyond the geopolitical boundaries of the East and Southeast Asian subjects. Because the logic of whiteness separate people of color from people of color in order to thrive, the trope of Asian men meeting, dating, and having sex with Asian men should be kept as a multiple, dynamic, and unfinalized concept. Remaking sticky rice from queer Asia has the potential to build *the queer relational collective* among different kinds of Asians in and across time, space, and context. As Tayo tells me, a Brown Asian man like Tayo meets, dates, and have sex with a Yellow Asian man and vice versa. Therefore, the trope of sticky rice that generates the *stickiness (or sameness)* of the racialized Asian queer male subjects suggests the intraregional flows of power that help self-fashion queer Asia. Sticky rice is one of many anchoring points toward (re)building queer Asia.

Note

1   See, Appendix I for Co-Researchers' Demographic Information.

References

Alexander, B. K. (2021). Dense particularities: Race, spirituality, and queer/quare intersectionalities. In M. Niles Goins, J. F. McAllister, & B. K. Alexander (Eds.), *The Routledge handbook of gender and communication* (pp. 18–44). Routledge.

Bailey, M. M. (2016). Black gay (raw) sex. In E. P. Johnson (Ed.), *No tea no shade: New writings in black queer studies* (pp. 239–261). Duke University Press.

Baudinette, T. (2016). Ethnosexual frontiers in queer Tokyo: The production of racialised desire in Japan. *Japan Forum, 28*(4), 465–483. https://doi.org/10.1080/09555803.2016.1165723

Buckland, F. (2002). *Impossible dance: Club culture and queer worldmaking.* Wesleyan University Press.

Calafell, B. M. (2015). *Monstrosity, performance, and race in contemporary culture.* Peter Lang.

Calafell, B. M., & Moreman, S. (2010). Iterative hesitancies and Latinidad: The reverberances of raciality. In R. Halualani & T. K. Nakayama (Eds.), *Handbook of Critical Intercultural Communication* (pp. 400–416). Wiley-Blackwell.

Chávez, K. R. (2013). *Queer migration politics: Activist rhetoric and coalitional possibilities.* University of Illinois Press.

Chambers-Letson, J. (2018). *After the party: A manifesto for queer of color life.* New York University Press.

Chiang, H., & Wong, A. K. (2016). Queering the transnational turn: Regionalism and Queer Asias. *Gender, Place and Culture: A Journal of Feminist Geography, 23*(11), 1643–1656. https://doi.org/10.1080/0966369X.2015.1136811

Chiang, H., & Wong, A. K. (2017). Asia is burning: Queer Asia as critique. *Culture, Theory and Critique, 58*(2), 121–126. https://doi.org/10.1080/14735784.2017.1294839

Delgado, R., & Stefancic, J. (2012). *Critical race theory: An introduction* (2nd ed.). New York University Press.

Eguchi, S. (2013). Revisiting Asiacentricity: Toward thinking dialectically about Asian American identities and negotiation. *Howard Journal of Communications, 24*(1), 95–115. https://doi.org/10.1080/10646175.2013.748556

Eguchi, S. (2015). Queer intercultural relationality: An autoethnography of Asian-Black (dis) connections in White gay America. *Journal of International and Intercultural Communication, 8*(1), 27–43. https://doi.org/10.1080/17513057.2015.991077

Eguchi, S., & Ding, Z. (2017). "Uncultural" Asian Americans in ABC's *Dr. Ken. Popular Communication, 15*(4), 296–310. https://doi.org/10.1080/15405702.2017.1326604

Eguchi, S., & Kimura, K.* (2021). Racialized im/possibilities: Intersectional queer-of-color critique on Japaneseness in Netflix's *Queer Eye: We're in Japan! Journal of International and Intercultural* Communication, *14*(3), 221–239. https://doi.org/10.1080/17513057.2020.1829675

Eguchi, S., & Long, H. (2019). Queer relationality as family: Yas fats! yas femmes! yas Asians! *Journal of Homosexuality, 66*(11), 1589–1606. https://doi.org/10.1080/00918369.2018.1505756

Eguchi, S., Files-Thompson, N., & Calafell, B. M. (2018). Queer (of color) aesthetics: Fleeting moments of transgression in VH1's *Love & Hip-Hop: Hollywood Season 2. Critical Studies in Media Communication, 35*(2), 180–193. https://doi.org/10.1080/15295036.2017.1385822

Eng, D. L. (2001). *Racial castration: Managing masculinity in Asian America.* Duke University Press.

Eng, D. L. (2010). *The feeling of kinship: Queer liberalism and the racialization of intimacy.* Duke University Press.

Fernando, C., & Mumphery, C. (2020, December 20). Racism Targets Asian Food, Business During COVID-19 Pandemic. USnews. https://www.usnews.com/news/us/articles/2020-12-20/racism-targets-asian-food-business-during-covid-19-pandemic

Fung, R. (2005). Looking for my penis: The eroticized Asian in gay video porn. In R. Guins & O. Z. Cruz (Eds.), *Popular culture: A reader* (pp. 338–348). Sage Publications.

Gopinath, G. (2018). *Unruly visions: The aesthetic practices of queer diaspora.* Duke University Press.

Han, C. W. (2015). *Geisha of a different kind: race and sexuality in gaysian America.* New York University Press.

Han, C. W., & Rutledge, S. E. (2020). They don't date any dark people: The queer case of gay racism. In J. G. Smith & C. W. Han (Eds.), *Home and community for queer men of color* (pp. 31–48). Lexington Press.

Johnson, E. P. (2003). The specter of the black fag. *Journal of Homosexuality, 45*(2/3/4), 217–234. http://doi.org/10.1300/J082v45n02_10

Kang, D. B. (2017). Eastern orientations: Thai middle- class gay desire for 'white Asians'. *Culture, Theory and Critique, 58*(2), 182–208. https://doi.org/10.1080/14735784.2017.1288580

Kawai, Y. (2005). Stereotyping Asian Americans: The dialectic of the model minority and the yellow peril. *Howard Journal of Communication, 16*(2), 109–130. https://doi.org/10.1080/10646170590948974

Keeling, K. (2019). *Queer times, black futures.* New York University Press.

Lim, E.-B. (2014). *Brown boys and rice queens: Spellbinding performances in the Asias.* New York University Press.

Mackintosh, J. D. (2010). *Homosexuality and manliness in postwar Japan.* Routledge.

Martin, F., Jackson, P. A., McLelland, M., & Yue, A. (2008). Introduction. In F. Martin, P. A. Jackson, M. McLelland, & A. Yue (Eds.), *AsiaPacifiQueer: Rethinking genders and sexualities* (pp. 1–27). University of Illinois Press.

McBride, D. A. (2005). *Why I hate Abercrombie & Fitch: Essays on race and sexuality.* New York University Press.

McCune Jr., J. Q. (2014). *Sexual discretion: Black masculinity and the politics of passing.* University of Chicago Press.

Morris, C. E., & Sloop, J. M. (2006). "What lips these lips have kissed": Refiguring the politics of queer public kissing. *Communication and Critical/Cultural Studies, 3*(1), 1–26. https://doi.org/10.1080/14791420500505585

Muñoz, J. E. (2009). *Cruising utopia: The then and there of queer futurity.* New York University Press.

Nakayama, T. K. (1994). Show/down time: "Race," gender, sexuality, and popular culture. *Critical Studies in Media Communication, 11*(2), 162–179. https://doi.org/10.1080/15295039409366893

Nguyen, H. T. (2014). *A view from the bottom: Asian American masculinity and sexual representation.* Duke University Press.

Ono, K. A. (2005). From nationalism to migrancy: The politics of Asian American transnationalism. *Communication Law Review, 5*(1), 1–17. https://commlawreview.org/Archives/v5i1/From%20Nationalism%20to%20Migrancy.pdf

Puar, J. K. (2007). *Terrorist assemblages: Homonationalism in queer times.* Duke University Press.

Rodriguez, J. M. (2014). *Sexual futures, queer gestures, other Latina longings.* New York University Press.

Sekimoto, S. (2014). Transnational Asia: Dis/orienting identity in the globalized world. *Communication Quarterly, 62*(4), 381–398. https://doi.org/10.1080/01463373.2014.922485

Snorton, C. R. (2014). *Nobody is supposed to know: Black sexuality on the down low.* University of Minnesota Press.

Suganuma, K. (2012). *Contact moments: The politics of intercultural desire in Japanese male-queer cultures.* Hong Kong University Press.

Sun, W. (2007). *Minority invisibility: An Asian American experience.* University Press of America.

Toyosaki, S. (2011). Critical complete-member ethnography: Theorizing dialectics of consensus and conflict in intercultural communication. *Journal of International and Intercultural Communication, 4*(1), 62–80. https://doi.org/10.1080/17513057.2010.533786

Toyosaki, S., & Eguchi, S. (2017). Powerful uncertainty for the future of Japan's cultural diversity: Theorizing Japanese homogenizing discourses. In S. Toyosaki & S. Eguchi (Eds.), *Intercultural communication in Japan: Theorizing homogenized discourse* (pp. 1–23). Routledge.

Velasco, G. K. (2019). *Queering the global Filipina body: Contested nationalisms in the Filipina/o diaspora.* University of Illinois Press.

Welker, J. (2017). Toward a history of 'lesbian history' in Japan. *Culture, Theory and Critique, 58*(2), 147–165. https://doi.org/10.1080/14735784.2017.1282830

Wu, C. (2018). *Sticky rice: A politics of intraracial desire.* Temple University Press.

Wu, F. H. (2002). *Yellow: Race in America beyond black and white.* Basic Books.

Yep, G. A., Lovaas, K. E., & Elia, J. P. (2003). Introduction: Queering communication: Starting the conversation. In G. A. Yep, K. E. Lovaas, & J. P. Elia (Eds.), *Queer theory and communication: From disciplining queers to queering the discipline(s)* (pp. 1–10). Harrington Park Press.

Yep, G. A., Alaoui, F. Z. C., & Lescure, R. (2020). Relationalties in/trhough difference; Explorations in queer intercultural communication. In S. Eguchi & B. M. Calafell (Eds.), *Queer intercultural communication: The intersectional politics of belonging in and across differences* (pp. 19–45). Rowman & Littlefield.

Yu, T.-F. (2020). Reconfiguring Queer Asia as disjunctive modernities: Notes on the subjective production of working-class gay men in Hong Kong. *Journal of Homosexuality, 67*(6), 863–884. https://doi.org/10.1080/00918369.2018.1560126

Yue, A. (2017). Trans-Singapore: Some notes towards Queer Asia as method. *Inter-Asian Cultural Studies, 18*(1), 10–24. https://doi.org/10.1080/14649373.2017.1273911

Yue, A., & Leung, H. H.-S. (2017). Notes towards the queer Asian city: Singapore and Hong Kong. *Urban Studies, 54*(3), 747–764. https://doi.org/10.1177/0042098015602996

PART III

RETURNING TO THE SELF

CHAPTER FIVE

Monstrous Onē Performance: Sticking with *Hikawa Kiyoshi* [氷川きよし]

Performance is capable of providing a ground-level assault on a hegemonic world vision that substantiates the dominant public sphere --- (Muñoz, 1999, p. 196).

Performance [is] a space of radical creativity, accountability, and social justice…..Performance provides the possibility to learn and unlearn. --- (Calafell, 2015, p. 29).

Performance doesn't just rehearse a different world, it makes it anew, again and again --- (Chambers-Letson, 2018, p. 24).

On December 31st, 2000, I was watching the 51st kouhaku uta gassen (第５１回 紅白歌合戦, [literally, red and white singing contest]) between 7pm and 11:45pm. The government owned Nippon Housou Kyoukai known as NHK (日本放送協会 [literally, Japan Broadcasting Corporation]) started its signing contest as a New Year's celebration programming in 1951. The introduction of this music programming highlights the post-WWII context of Japan where the U.S. and its allied occupation (1945–1952) took place. The promotion of popular culture and music was used to reenergize the social and performative aspects of Japanese people defeated by the war (Dower, 1999). Since then, the consumption of NHK's kouhaku uta gassen on New Year's Eve has become a major cultural ritual during the holiday season. This programming assembles female singers and bands into an aka gumi (紅組 [literally, a red group]) and male singers and bands groups into a shiro gumi (白組 [literally, a white group]). Unisex bands are grouped into an aka gumi or a shiro gumi based on their lead singers' genders. This grouping reinforces an essentialist, biologically assigned male-female cisgender binary. Then, each signer or band performs his/her/their own song by each. At the conclusion of all performances, judges who are composed of actors/actresses, entertainers, artists, athletes, intellectuals, and/or celebrities vote for either an aka gumi or a shiro gumi that represents the best performance of the year.

During the middle of this 51st NHK kouhaku uta gassen described above, I heard a melody of the classical style Japanese music genre Enka (演歌). However, unlike *the usual*, I saw a tall cisgender man in mid 20's who represents a Shiro-Gumi was about to sing. So, I thought, "*Who is singing Enka today? Isn't it a dying music genre?*" My late maternal grandparents based in Hiroshima City who had gone through the World War II (1941–1945), the atomic bombing (August 6, 1945), and the U.S. and its allied occupation of Japan (1945–1952) loved listening to Enka. However, my parents born and raised in Hiroshima were no longer interested in Enka. They are in the post-WWII generation of Japanese people who consume the modern popular music influenced by the Western/U.S. cultures and instruments. Hence, as I turned my attention to the TV screen, I "accidentally" encountered *Hikawa Kiyoshi* (氷川きよし)[1] for the first time. Born in Fukuoka on September, 6, 1977, Hikawa debut as an Enka singer in February, 2000 (Nippon Colombia Co. LTD, n.d.). I could not understand why someone like him wanted to be an Enka singer to begin with. So, I said to my family "*Who is this ji dai okure (時代遅れ [literally, outdated]) singer?*"

My reaction to Hikawa mirrors what Darling-Wolf (2000), Sekimoto (2014), and Toyosaki (2011) have suggested is the normative cultural logic of time progress that normalizes the Americanization of Japan as its future in the post-WWII context. The linear progression of Japan's modernization and social change that catches up with the U.S. outdates Enka. By 2000, I was a major fan of Mariah Carry, Destiney Child, Ricky Martin, and Backstreet Boys. Hence, a brief moment through which my "accidental" interest in Hikawa emerged during the 51st Kouhaku Uta Gassen was immediately shut down. Associating Enka as a signifier of Japan's past, I turned away from the *depressive memory* of the Empire of Japan's wartime. Born in early 80's, I was taught not to let Japan go "back" to the wartime while in the schooling. Similar to Sekimoto (2014) born in my generation, I was subjected to gaze toward the Americanization of Japan. Thus, I "forgot" about Hikawa as I moved to the U.S. in May, 2001. Still, after his debut, Hikawa has become a "Prince of the Enka world" (Kouno, 2020). So, Hikawa has been appearing in various media programs such as NHK Kouhaku-Uta-Gassen.

However, two decades later, my attraction to Hikawa suddenly grows fast. As ORICON News (2020) has suggested, Hikawa presents his "natural" atheistic to show who he *really* is. Starting from summer 2019, Hikawa has begun to up-load social media images that are much more *genderqueer* than before. By gen-derqueer, I mean an embodied performance of gender that radically re/mixes both masculinities and femininities. In particular, Hikawa's white-color wed-ding dress shoot, uploaded into his Instagram, surprises his fans and followers in November, 2019 (ORICON News, 2019b). Additionally, Hikawa's first non-Enka, Rock 31st single song genkaitopa X survivor (限界突破×サバイバー) released on October 25, 2017 regains its popularity. A record company *Nippon Columbia* [literally, Japan Columbia] uploaded Hikawa's performance of the song to YouTube in May 2019 (Murakami, 2020). Hence, Japan's celebrity tab-loid magazines and websites has been paying attention to the recent Hikawa's transformation.

As an effeminate queer subject born and raised in Japan, I am drawn to the mediated displays of Hikawa's genderqueerness. Both queer and transgender discourses are becoming visible in the ever-changing landscape of Japanese pop-ular culture. Hikawa's genderqueerness points out the impacts of human rights movement that promotes the concept of coming out. This implicates what Chávez (2013) suggested is that "Western queer formations travel, by choice and by coercion, imposing Western values and ideals on non-Western cultures within and outside of Western countries" (p. 87). Japan's social institutions are not any exceptions from the global phenomenon. Japanese popular media broadcasts the Western LGBT modernity rooted in the logics of individualism and sexual freedom through its programming (see, for example, Maree, 2017; Suganuma, 2012; Welker, 2017). The Western paradigm of coming out of the closet shape minoritized sexual and gender subjects to be publicly proud of their human rights in global localities where cultural organizations of sexuality, gender, and the body have been historically different (Puar, 2007). Here, the paradigm of closet signifies a *depressive* space where minoritized sexual and gender subjects "hide" who they are. Discourses around Hikawa's genderqueerness mirror the way the current globalization pressures Japan to adapt the Western modernity of being *out* and *proud*.

Hikawa's genderqueerness emerges out of his music career. Japanese music en-tertainment industry has been a capitalist system of paradox that not only maintains Japanese cisheteropatriarchal values but also creates some spaces to facilitate a brief moment of transgression. For example, cross-dressing singers such as Miwa Akihiro (美輪明宏), Carrousel Maki (カルーセル麻紀)and Mikawa Kenichi (美川憲一) have been vital to establish the contemporary genre of *onē-kei* (オネエ系 [queeny or sisterly]) talent in the post-WWII context of Japanese entertainment industry (see, for example, Eguchi, 2017). The *onē-kei* talent is an essentialized, umbrella term of minoritized sexual and gender performers, including but not limited to male-to-female (MTF) transgender, non-binary, cross-dressing, and cismale same-sex loving subjects (Yukimi, 2013). This genre implicates a Japan's derogatory vernacular okama (オカマ [literally meaning, a slang of anus]) during the pre-industrial, samurai period (McLelland, 2000). Okama means *a man who gets fucked.* Yet, after the industrialization of Japan had taken place after the fall of Edo samurai period, sexualities strictly became private matters (McLelland, 2000). The publicizations of sexualities were considered as shameful (Suganuma, 2012). Hence, okama is "humorous but ultimately sad and pathetic women manqué who try to act like or perform as women, but ultimately fail" (McLelland, 2000, p. 59). This hints to the way the culturally saturated logic of masculinist patriarchy conflates gender and sexuality privileging cisheterosexuality (Eguchi & Kimura, 2021). Still, the *onē-kei* talent is a genre that counters the majoritarian codes of (cis)gender conduct. Hikawa's genderqueerness breaks through the industrial complex of *onē-kei* talent.

In this chapter, I interrogate impossible possibilities of Hikawa's genderqueerness that indexes the *onē-kei* talent genre. To accomplish this task, I methodologically deploy an evocative, creative, and artistic method of performative writing. Guided by women of color feminists (e.g., Madison, 1993, 1999; Pollack, 1998), I juxtapose my narrative of being an effeminate Japanese American queer with Hikawa's genderqueerness. To solidify the quality of my intersubjective relationship with Hikawa, I operate the concept of sticky rice that is an intraracial homoeroticism of an "Asian" man falling in love with another "Asian" man. However, my *Japanese-to-Japanese* attraction to Hikawa is not sexual and romantic. Instead, it is an idolized worship of the celebrity who represents some social and performative aspects of who I am, what I do, and how I make sense of what I do. From this methodological process, I question and critique discourses around impossible possibilities of Hikawa's genderqueerness. At the same time, I unpack the way Hikawa's genderqueerness offers a brief moment of transgression against the majoritarian codes of (cis)gender conduct. In so doing, my overall goal of writing this chapter is to refashion Hikawa's genderqueerness as a form of revolt.

In what follows, I contextualize the historically saturated and culturally specific constructions of *onē-kei* talents as *monstrous queers.* In addition, I offer how I orient the concept of sticky rice as a bridge methodology in my performative writing. Then my presentations of performative writing follow. I end this chapter by discussing my building of a bridge with Hikawa to organize the *queer Japanese collective.*

Onē-Kei Talents as Monstrous Queers

Japan's minoritized sexual and gender cultures are rich and diverse. The ongoing histories of both cisgender and transgender subjects who do not subscribe the logics of cisheteronormativity exist (see, for example, Suganuma, 2012; Summerhawak, McMahill, & McDonald, 1998; Welker, 2010). For example, many categorical divisions among minoritized sexual and gender subjects who participate in what is known as Japan's queer cultures can be seen in Tokyo (e.g., Mitsuhashi, 2006). However, the mainstream popular media ignores, erases, and marginalizes these sexual and gender differences that are shored under Japan's queer cultures. The *onē-kei* genre is essentially used to represent MTF transgender, non-binary, cross-dressing, and cismale same-sex loving subjects (see, Eguchi, 2017; Maree, 2008). At the same time, it is important to emphasize that, while the representations of female-to-male (FTM) transgender, non-binary, cross-dressing, and cisfemale same-sex loving subjects are increasing (see, for example, Eguchi & Kimura, 2021; Mackie, 2008; Maree, 2017; Welker, 2017), there is no major genre given to the demography. Unlike the *onē-kei* genre, the mainstream popular media do not operationalize any particularized categories that represent these minoritized sexual and gender subjects who participate in Japan's queer cultures.

The aforementioned landscape of Japanese media and popular culture implicates the strategic function of cisheteropatriarchy that requires the subordination of MTF transgender, non-binary, cross-dressing, and cismale same-sex loving subjects as *onē-kei* (Eguchi, 2020). These subjects are threats to Japan's patriarchal society that maintains the power of cisgender heterosexual men. According to My Navi News (2020), an extremely well-known fat cross-dressing talent Matsuko Deluxe (マツコデラックス) recently calls out the popular cultural production of *onē* in their primetime TV show Matsuko & Ariyoshi Karisome Heaven (マツコ&有吉かりそめ天国) aired on TV Asahi (テレビ朝日). Because *onē* is a politically corrected term of *okama*, Matsuko expresses their discomfort with the term *onē* that subtly sustains the historical (mis)subordination of both queer male and MTF transgender subjects. For Matsuko, *onē* should be used to indicate the genderqueer aesthetic of queeny or sisterly camp speech style, known as *onē-kotoba* (オネエ言葉). This perspective coincides with what Maree (2008) suggested is *onē-kotoba* as "a parody of stereotypical women's language that is generally used by gay (gei) men in a performance of (hyper)femininity" (p. 67). Matsuko who resists the term *onē* makes clear the historical continuities of Japanese heterosexual cismale power that essentially marginalize the minoritized sexual and gender subjects all together. Because the (hetero)normative communication style is indirect and implicit (Eguchi & Kimura, 2021; Toyosaki, 2011), Matsuko is unorthodox and rebellious as they say what others do not normally say. Hence, Matsuko is very queer. Here, by queer, I mean hentai (変態[literally meaning, freak]). The logic of cisheteropatriarchy constructs Matsuko's fat cross-dressing genderqueerness as "outspoken," "bitter," and ultimately "scary" (Eguchi, 2017). These personality characteristics of Matsuko point to the abnormalization of the *onē-kei* talent as the *monstrous* queer. By monstrous, I mean inhuman, outrageous, and/or frightening.

Consequently, I draw Calafell's (2015) scholarship on monstrosity to unpack the performances of Hikawa's genderqueerness. While searching the displays of Hikawa's transformation online, I have repeatedly encountered how some bloggers (mis)translated Hikawa's genderqueerness as *onē*. However, Hikawa has yet said nothing about becoming and being an *onē*. Hence, I elaborate the concept of monstrosity to read how the logic of Japan's cisheteropatriarchy essentializes excessive performances of genderqueerness as an *onē*. By excessive performance, I mean an over-the-top, extra, and exaggerated performance that troubles the *ordinary* and *usual*.

Calafell (2015) draws the women of color feminism (e.g., Boylorn, 2008; Griffin, 2012; Molina-Guzmán, 2010) to suggest how minoritized subjects of color, who disrupt the majoritarian codes of conduct, are almost always constructed as *monstrous*. To showcase this line of argument, Calafell demonstrated her everyday interpersonal intercultural interactions in the U.S. academy through which people almost always mark her as monstrous. She is a short, fat, feminine, queer, cisgender, light-skin Chicana who directly calls out the normative ideas, values, and beliefs. Her embodied politics of disruption is to call for equity and inclusiveness to centralize the issues and concerns of the faculty and students of color (Calvente, Calafell, & Chávez, 2020). By breaking the code of (White) civility that sustains the *business-as-usual* aspects of the academy, she troubles unearned racial privileges structurally given to White people. For that reason, she is framed as unruly. She interrupts the silence that maintains the majoritarian codes of conduct. Hence, White people whom Calafell (2015) calls out marginalize her as a *monstrous* queer ciswoman of color. So, by blaming her for wrongdoings, they do not have to check their racist actions and behaviors. This kind of treatment is a typical narrative for the minoritized subjects who call out social injustice (Calvente, Calafell, & Chávez, 2020).

The ideological mechanism of monstering Calafell (2015) is similar to the logic of Japan's cisheteropatriarchy that otherizes the *onē-kei* talent as the monstrous queer like Matsuko. Femininities, performed by the *onē-kei* talents, signal the embodied signs of difference that redefine the masculinist architectures of cismale heterosexuality (Eguchi, 2017, 2020). As I have mentioned earlier, the

Japanese cultural and communicative norm that values indirectness and implicitness monster Matsuko's MTF cross-dressing performance expressed through
their queeny or sisterly camp speech style of outspokenness and frankness. As
Johnson (2003) suggested, "Because femininity is always already devalued in patriarchal societies those associated with the feminine are also viewed as inferior"
(p. 227). Apparently, the logic of cisheteropatriarchy *both essentially and collectively* feminizes, subordinates, and otherizes MTF transgender, non-binary, cross-
dressing, and cismale same-sex loving subjects as *onē/okama* (e.g., Maree, 2008;
Mitsuhashi, 2006; Suganuma, 2012). *Onē/Okama* implicates Japan's patriarchal society that values the masculinist centrality of heterosexual cismen and undervalue
the subjects associated with femininities. Kimmel (1996) reinforced, "masculinity
has been (historically) defined as the flight from women and the repudiation of
femininity" (p. 123). Hence, I orient monstrous *onē* femininity as a referencing
point to contextualize the historically specific and culturally saturated conditions
of Japanese popular culture from which Hikawa's genderqueerness emerges. Next,
I showcase a detailed description of my methodology.

Methodology: Performative Writing and Sticky Rice

In this chapter, I engage in my performative writing to interrogate discourses
around Hikawa's genderqueerness. Similar to scholars such as Calafell (2015),
Chávez (2009), and Corey (2002), I approach performative writing as a critical
cultural method that questions and critique the effects of existing power relations
on everyday life experiences. Performative writing orients my body as a central
platform of knowledge and analysis to produce my narrative for engaging in the
social and cultural analysis. I unapologetically capitalize my body as a standpoint
of performing the research design, analysis, and writing. Evidently, I am the effeminate queer Japanese American subject who performs a close reading of Hikawa's
genderqueerness. Hence, hiding my body under the rhetoric of research is inauthentic, ingenuine, and quite frankly dishonest (see, for example, Calafell, 2020;
Eguchi, 2019; McIntosh & Eguchi, 2020).

My performative writing attends to what I have discussed in other chapters
is *theories in flesh* proposed by the U.S.-based feminists of color Moraga and
Anzaldúa (1983). It pays careful attention to the material impacts of power on
minoritized subjects who navigate their institutional lives. A Performance studies
scholar Madison (1993) reinforces that theories in flesh "means the cultural, geopolitical, and economic circumstances of our lives engender particular experiences
and epistemologies that provide philosophies about reality different from those

available to other groups" (pp. 213–214). Emphasizing on the everyday operations of differences (i.e., race, gender, sexuality, class, and nation) that organize lived realities, theories in flesh redirects the attention to knowledge emerged from the body that narrates social experiences. The embodied knowledge may suggest the alternative visions of the present-ness constrained by macrostructural relations of power such as cisheterosexism, classism, and racism (e.g., Calafell, 2015; Madison, 1993, 1999; Polluck, 1998). Hence, I share my narratives that demonstrate my embodied knowledge to analyze Hikawa's genderqueerness. This methodological move follows Boylorn (2008) who juxtaposes her narratives of being a Black woman with media representations associated with Black women.

During the sharing of my narratives, I stage the concept of sticky rice as a *bridge methodology* to advance the intersubjective connections (and disconnections) between Hikawa and me. As Carrillo Rowe (2008) suggests, "A bridge methodology attends to the (in)fluencies that inflect our own and our subject's speech as a point of entry into theorizing the relationship between belonging, communication, and self-staging" (p. 80). As I have thus far demonstrated in this book *Asians loving Asians: Sticky Rice Homoeroticism and Queer Politics*, sticky rice is a gay vernacular that describes an "Asian" man falling in love with another "Asian" man. Sticky rice not only points to the settler colonial logic of whiteness that produces the *sameness* among racialized "Asian" men who participate in gay sexual cultures. But it also elaborates *differences* that are essentially shored under the term "Asian." Hence, I figuratively use the contradiction of sticky rice to build a bridge between Hikawa and me in and across times, spaces, and contexts.

I stage my sticky rice relationship with Hikawa as *sisterly*. I capitalize impossible possibilities of sticky rice that "does not quite count as properly homosexual" (Nguyen, 2014, p. 155). I worship Hikawa as a genderqueer celebrity whom I would like to become and be as I age. Since Hikawa is five years older than me, I view Hikawa as my role model for fashion, beauty, and lifestyle. This kind of my queer sociality is similar to the *Yellow Fever*'s (1998) representation of Ernest who is much more interested in hanging out with his "girlfriends" whom he can gossip with than looking for sex and romance, which I have showcased in the chapter one. Hence, I perform sticky rice as a bridge methodology of queerness that produces "a collective political becoming" (Muñoz, 2009, p. 189). Through my performative writing, I remap the configurations of the present organized by Japan's cisheteropatriarchy. By building a bridge with Hikawa who has no idea of who I am, I take a step toward organizing the queer fights against the majoritarian codes of (cis)gender conduct. In order to articulate Hikawa's genderqueerness, next I perform my entry into a digital world of Japanese popular culture.

*****

November 26, 2019 Tuesday

I have just woken up. I am in Albuquerque, NM. It is in the morning that is two days before the U.S. settler colonialist Turkey day. Even though I think I have slept well, I am still exhausted....really exhausted. The 2019's National Communication Association (NCA)'s convention that took place in Baltimore, MD between November 13 and November 17 completely wore me out. As Chakravartty et al. (2018) observed that the Communication discipline is so White, I feel like I always end up fighting against the whiteness of Communication. However, this year's NCA was extremely horrible. So, I eager to mentally escape from where I am right now. At once, through my participation in the digital world, I turn my attention toward where I come from, Japan.

Now, I enter into *Yahoo! Japan*. So, I can read news in Japanese. While I sip my coffee, I am drawn to a news article. ORICON News (2019b) suggests "Hikawa Kiyoshi fascinates with a pure white dress 'like a wedding dress.' 'Beauty awakens.'" As scrolling down the online news article, I see the Instagram post that showcases the performative display of Hikawa in a super flashy, fluffy white wedding dress. I also notice that Hikawa, siting on stairs, looks feminine. The wind, generated by the air circulator, blows his brown-colored long hair. His facial expression suggests a bit sexual too. At least, what I imagine of Hikawa is different from this post. Some fans comment like "Beautiful! It's sexy" and "I thought it was an angel" onto his Instagram (ORICON News, 2019b).

After comprehending what I am seeing on my screen, I go "Wait, What!!!! Is Hikawa coming out?" At this point, I "forgot" that I am exhausted by the NCA. Then, I recall having seen a tabloid news of Hikawa dating another cisgender masculine-presenting actor Matsumura Yuuki (松村雄基) around 2010. However, I have never really cared about Hikawa until this moment. So, I say to myself, "I need to follow Hikawa on Instagram. And I need to find out what is going on."

*****

Monstering Hikawa as an *Onē*

Shortly after having followed Hikawa through my Instagram account, I seek more of the information about Hikawa's aesthetic transformation by inserting three key terms such as 氷川きよし (Hikawa Kiyoshi), インスタ (Insta [literarily, meaning Instagram]), and ドレス (Dress) in the search engine. Even though Hikawa's official Instagram page was first opened on November 17, 2019, I already see a number of media and social media reactions to Hikawa's transformation in the digital platform by this time. Scrolling down the screen, I find an interesting title "An onē-zation of Hikawa Kiyoshi comes out! I was amazed at his bare feet in ceremonial first pitch, Instagram posts, and visual costumes!" (Tori Chan's Outlook Report, 2019). So, I click this page and read through what a blogger Tori Chan summarizes Hikawa's transformation. Apparently, Tori Chan details differences of Hikawa's aesthetic presentation between 2017 and 2019 in two public stages; ceremonial first pitch and music concert in the page. While I do not fully agree with Tori Chan's tone that reinforces the logic of cisheterosexism, I can see some aspects of Tori Chan's (2019) reading of Hikawa's transformation.

For example, Hikawa looks boyish for the ceremonial first pitch for Tokyo Yakult Swallows' game with Yokohama DeNA Baystars on August 25th 2017 (ORICON News, 2017). Hikawa wears a light yellow-green color Yakult jersey top and a regular-length white color short pant with a pair of gray colored sport sneakers. He has a typical cismale short haircut. However, two years later Hikawa looks *onē-kei* in Tori Chan's (2019)'s word. For his ceremonial first pitch for Tokyo Yakult Swallows' game with Hanshin Tigers on August 8th 2019 (See, ORICON News, 2019a), Hikawa wears a white color Yakuruto's jersey top tackled into a black-color mini short pants with a pair of red-color sneakers. Because of the mini short pants, Tori-Chan (2019) notices how Hikawa's hairless legs may appeal to "otoko no me sen" (男の目線 [literally meaning, the male gaze]). Hikawa's legs that may be completely shaved draws the cisheteronormative constructs of female beauty standard. He also has a brown-colored long wavy hair. From the back, I can see how the audience may mistake Hikawa as a "woman."

Additionally, Tori-Chan (2019) refers to Hikawa's performances of his first non-Enka, Rock 31st single song *genkaitopa X Survivor* [限界突破×サバイバー] originally released on October 25, 2017. At the time of release, Hikawa's outfit for the performance is a red-color leather jacket and pants with a pair of black-color long boots. His makeup is natural. In Tori-Chan's word, Hikawa's performance is *manly* in 2017. However, in 2019 Hikawa's outfits are much flashy and shiny. Some are see-through clothing outfits. At the same time, Hikawa's make up is extra. His eyeshadow is clearly visible. And, his lip is obviously shining. As I have mentioned in the previous example, Hikawa has a brown-colored long wavy hair by this time. Thus, Tori-Chan reads the femininizing of Hikawa's nonverbal aesthetics associated with *Genkaitopa X Survivor* as one of the performative elements that evidence Hikawa as *onē*. Therefore, Tori-Chan concludes that Hikawa may come out of the closet near future.

After having read this Tori-Chan's (2019) page concerning Hikawa, I feel I must take a pose. I struggle with the logic of Japan's cisheterosexism that guides

Tori Chan's nonverbal reporting of Hikawa's transformation as *onē-ka* (オネエ 化[literally meaning, onē-zation/feminization]). For example, Hikawa has been unofficially known to be queer before and after his aesthetic transformation. In addition to the tabloid gossip of him having dated another actor in 2010 I have mentioned earlier, Hikawa has never known to get married to or involved in a romantic relationship with a cisgender woman. Hence, I argue that Hikawa is not really coming out through the aesthetic transformation. He is *always already* queer, at least, from my perspective. At the same time, Tori-Chan (2019) insinuates Hikawa has been "hiding" his *onē* femininity because he has "accidentally" used a femininized word watashi (私 [meaning, I]) to describe himself in the previous media appearance in August 2019. Yet, there is no consideration of Hikawa who could have used watashi to draw the audience's attention to his genderqueer aesthetic at this point of his career. *Is it possible if Hikawa strategically capitalizes his genderqueerness to survive in a highly competitive landscape of Japan's entertainment industry through which the singing career is never stable?* As I have mentioned earlier, Hikawa has established his position as the "Prince of the Enka world" whom mature women worship over the last two decades (Kouno, 2020). Still, Enka is becoming an outdated genre for younger generation. Thus, Hikawa must cultivate new markets to maintain his entertainment career. *Isn't this why Hikawa's 31st song* genkaitopa X survivor *(限界突破×サバイバー) is non-Enka, Rock to begin with?* Therefore, I call to locate the structural system of Japan's entertainment industry to read Hikawa's embodied performance of genderqueerness.

I reject the individualization of Hikawa's embodied performance as his own personal desire to come out as an *onē*. Tori-Chan (2019) emphasizes a gossip of Hikawa wearing female panties, which is reported by a major tabloid publisher Shukannbunshu (週刊文春) (2019). This gossip not only points to the way the logic of Japan's cisheterosexism otherizes queers as hentai [freak]. But it also automatically suggests the essentialization of MTF transgender, non-binary, crossdressing, and cismale same-sex loving subjects as *okama/onē* who ultimately want to be women (e.g., McLelland, 2000). Yet, Hikawa has not shared the way he makes sense of his genderqueerness. However, Hikawa is rumored to be wanting to reveal his "true" self. Here, it is important to note that, given the visibility of the *onē-kei* talent genre, revealing Hikawa's true self is never about his self-fashioning of genderqueerness. Instead, it is about revealing *onē monstrosity* that disrupts the Japan's cisheterosexualized comfort. People who are affected by cisheterosexism are entitled to feel in need of being clear with Hikawa's hen-tai monstrosity. While popular media representations of cisgender male same-sex loving subjects are increasing in and across TV dramas and movies, the entertainers who fill in the characters are known to be "straight" (e.g., Eguchi & Kimura, 2021). In addition, the logic of Japan's cisheterosexism shapes the entertainment industry to cover up the existence of cisgender male same-sex loving entertainers for the purpose of profit-making (e.g., Eguchi, 2020). Hence, the industrial complex forces Hikawa to choose either a heterosexualized cismale or an *onē* entertainment career. Hikawa cannot just perform unnamable and unintelligent aspects of his genderqueerness. Hikawa cannot do what he wants to do. Hence, the logic of Japan's cisheterosexism that essentializes MTF transgender, non-binary, cross-dressing, and cismale same-sex loving subjects as *onē* requires ongoing critical discussions.

Then again, I appreciate and embrace the discourses around Hikawa's *onē-ka* that direct the attention to overlooked issues and concerns of minoritized sexualities and genders in Japan. A couple of weeks after having learned about Hikawa's transformation, I return to Japan for the winter break. So, as the *usual*, I am watching the 70th NHK's kouhaku uta gassen on December 31, 2019 with my parents. Toward the end of the show, it is another turn for a shiro gumi male singer to perform his song. So, Hikawa appears on the TV screen. Hikawa, who has a brown-colored long wavy hair, begins with his Enka song called daijyoubu (大丈夫). He only sings this song for a few seconds. Then, he disappears from the stage. As soon as the illumination goes dark, I once again find Hikawa who changes to his shiny, flashy, black-color outfit in the stage. Then, the lighting vividly spots at Hikawa. Now, Hikawa stands on a huge human-made monstrous dragon machine set up on the stage. As the dragon gradually moves, Hikawa starts to sings his Rock song genkaitopa X survivor (限界突破×サバイバー). At the juncture, the camera focuses on other shiro-gumi male signers who stand at the right corner of the stage. They look very surprised by Hikawa's theatrical stage production of a huge human-made monstrous dragon moveable machine. *Right now, Hikawa is so extra and dramatic. Hikawa is a monster.* Hikawa's fearless performance troubles the cisheteropatriarchal architecture of NHK's kouhaku-uta-gassen. I am falling in love with Hikawa who unapologetically performs fearless.

*****

January 6, 2020 Monday

I am at a Chinese restaurant in Tokyo's Ginza district. I am having dinner with my bougie married cisgender female friend "Teruko" who is a thirteen-year older than me. She has not only established her career in the cisheteropatriarchal architecture of finance, but also has been modeling on the side. She is a very strong Japanese woman. I look up to her as a life mentor. During the dinner, she asks me, "How is your personal life going on lately?" By personal life, she specifically means a dating life. So, I respond to her that "nothing has changed yet." Then, I share the way I feel I sacrifice my personal life for my professorate. Since I started my current job in August 2012, I have not been able to focus on my personal life. There have been many political challenges associated with my current job that took my spiritual energies. Quite frankly, I have been exhausted from the academic drama. Yet, I tell her, "I am actually looking forward to my 40's. I do not know why. I feel positive about my 40's because I feel I can finally focus on me. Or at least I feel something can change in my 40's." So, I bring Hikawa into my conversation with Teruko to explain what I mean by looking forward to my 40's. I mention that the way Hikawa's unapologetic and fearless performance of genderqueerness in the 70th NHK's kouhaku uta gassen inspires me. Then, I say, "I fell in love with Hikawa! And, I really want to be unapologetic and fearless like Hikawa when I enter into 40's." Apparently, Teruko has watched NHK's kouhaku uta gassen as well. So, she agrees with me that Hikawa's performance was extra, theatrical, and fabulous. But then, she reminds me of Japan's queerphobia. She goes, "however unfortunately someone like my husband thinks that Hikawa is kimochiwarui (気持ち悪い [meaning, yucky])." For the Japanese "straight" cisgender male gaze, Hikawa's genderqueerness that signifies okama (オカマ [a slang of anus] and/or hentai [freak]) is revolting. At large, Japan's masculinist politics that sustains the power of cisheterosexuality abnormalizes Japan's ongoing histories of sexual and gender minoritarians. So, I rethink of kimochiwarui as an idea associated with MTF transgender, non-binary, cross-dressing, and cismale same-sex loving subjects.

*****

Hikawa's "Genderless" Transgresses

Since the dinner with Teruko, I have been struggling to recognize the way Japan's masculinist politics that maintains the power of cisheterosexism makes Hikawa's performance of genderqueerness yucky. From my standpoint, Hikawa's genderqueerness that creates an alternative genre of gender being in Japan's entertainment industry is far from kimochiwarui. As a music journalist Shiba (2020) states, "Without being bound by the stylistic beauty of an Enka singer, he [Hikawa] has pursued 'expressing himself as he is,' including make-up and fashion." Shiba characterizes Hikawa's transformatiom as "genderless." Here, it is important to mention the way waseieigo (和製英語 [meaning, Japanglish/English Made in Japan]) works. This use of genderless means lacking masculine qualities in Japan's social institutions that rigidly maintain the cisheteropatriarchal systems. Genderless means how Hikawa revises the historically homogenized imagining of Japanese cisheteromaleness through his unorthodox and rebellious presentation of genderqueerness. Accordingly, gender exists under the name of Hikawa's genderless. Simultaneously, this naming of Hikawa's gender subtly separates him from the *onē-kei* (or *okama*) talents who perform pejorative humors. Hikawa performs his own vision of who he is as he likes (Shiba, 2020). Hence, Hikawa's performance of genderless can be beyond the historically homogenized constructs of cisheterogenders. Hikawa's genderless does neither identify nor counter-identify with Japan's entertainment industry that produces the *onē-kei* talent genre. This is what Muñoz (1999) said is that "[d]isidentification resists the interpellating call of ideology that fixes a subject within the state power apparatus" (p.97). The rhetoric of Hikawa's genderless that can be neither masculine nor feminine implicates the way Hikawa positions himself as *a different kind of monster*.

This is further evident as Hikawa performs his genderless in and across the media platforms. Generally, I observe that the *onē-kei* talents mostly appear in variety and information programs (バラエティー情報番組) such as talk shows, game shows, and cooking shows because they are fashion/beauty experts, singers, dancers, artists and more. The *onē-kei* talents rarely appear in TV dramas and movies unless they are featured to play *onē* characters. Regardless, the *onē-kei* talents are framed to take roles that are extra or "quite out there." Specifically, the ways they perform who they are do not conform to Japan's cisheteropatriarchal norms of communication, maintaining civility and respectability through nuanced uses of indirectness and implicitness. They pejoratively disrupt unspoken and unwritten rules of what they are culturally expected to say, act, and/or behave. As the *onē-kei* talents violate the cisheteropatriarchal norms of communication in and across programs, they collectively become a *monstrous genderqueer* genre. However, even though Hikawa expresses his genderless through his make-up and fashion (Shiba, 2020), I have not seen the way Hikawa participates in the pejorative mechanism of monstrous genderqueerness associated with the *onē-kei* talents in and across media programs he appears. By using the language of genderless that characterizes his aesthetic transformation, Hikawa seeks out an *alternative path* to make genderless unintelligibility intelligible beyond the *onē* pejorative. Perhaps, this is why Hikawa has not officially responded to tabloid gossips around Hikawa being an *onē*. Hence, by reformatting his gender(less) within the cisheteropatriarchal present moment, Hikawa can offer an additional space of transgression through which monstrous genderqueerness, which is often unnamable and unintelligent, can be performed in Japan's entertainment industry.

Then again, I contemplate the majoritarian subjects like Teruko's husband reductively read Hikawa's genderless through the cisheterosexist discourse. Kimochiwarui [yucky] literally means *feeling bad*. So, I normally use the phrase to describe when I feel nauseous or am about to throw up. Hence, I urge the readers to imagine when people use the phrase to describe the sexual and gender minoritarian subjects. Kimochiwarui can be discursively weaponized to control, punish, and discipline the monstrosity of sexual and gender minoritarian subjects for their failures to conform to Japan's cisheterosexist society's expectations. As Toyosaki (2011) highlights, social conformity is a major social and performative aspect of Japan's nationalism valuing the myth that *everyone should be the same*. If the subject fails to comply the cultural expectation of social conformity, he/she/they will be immediately constructed as *lacking self-discipline* (Gannon, 2001). This interpersonal communication system points to the historical continuum of Japan's social structure as zokushakai (俗社会[literally meaning, common/popular society]) that values collectivism over individualism. Embodying and performing harmonies of social interactions that embrace the group identity over each individual identity is a key element of Japaneseness. Hence, the sexual and gender minoritarians who disrupt the harmonies become revolts as they break the majoritarian codes of conduct that value Japan's family and kinship system rooted in cisheteropatriarchy. This ideological mechanism that monsters the sexual and gender minoritarians also oppresses unmarried/divorced cisgender women who are over thirty-year old. As Maeda and Hecht (2012) argued, Japan's social institutions position single ciswomen as makeinu (負け犬[meaning, loser dog]). These women who are "left over" in the cisheterogendered marriage market implicate their personal characters who fail to comply Japan's social conformity. Hence, cisheterosexist discourses of kimochiwarui around Hikawa's genderless explicate the way social conformity is used to maintain the historically homogenized and culturally saturated imaginings of Japaneseness.

Simultaneously, Hikawa's genderless that points to the way the logic of cisheterosexism maintains social conformity demonstrates an alternative path toward reconsidering genderqueerness. As I have explained the term okama earlier, Japan's social institutions historically conflate gender and sexuality. More precisely, sexuality is always already gendered; Gender is always already sexualized. Valentine (1997) reiterated, "[Japan's] sexuality (unlike gender) is not a major source of identity, an those whose sexual orientation is toward the same sex are identified as differently gendered" (p. 97). Japan's popular cultural production of the *onē-kei* talent implicates the way gender operates a much more salient identity marker than sexuality (e.g., McLellan, 2000).

For example, well-known *onē-kei* talents such as Haruna Ai (はるな愛) and Kaba Chan (Kaba. ちゃん) have publicly disclosed their transitioning experiences of going through the gender conformation surgery. Hence, they perform being *onē* through the paradigm of transgender embodiment. Yet, other well-known talents such as Ikko (イッコー) and Mitz Mangrove (ミッツマングローブ) engage in crossdressing to play *onē* in and across media and social media. Still, cisgender male presenting talents such as Tano Shingo (楽しんご) and Chris Matsumura (クリ ス松村) who perform extra, campy effeminacies are categorized as *onē* as they are publicly known to be same-sex loving subjects. Here it is important to note, "due to the historical association between cross-dressing and the entertainment world, not all cross-dressed or cross-gendered individuals in that world are understood to be homosexual" (McLelland, 2000, p. 44). However, what the *onē-kei* talents have in common is their genderqueer nonconformity that can be temporally expressed, performed and/or embodied in and across public platforms. Because sexuality is a private matter, genderqueerness, materialized onto the body, is a major sign of social nonconformity that troubles the historically homogenized and culturally saturated imagining of Japanese cisheteromaleness. Hence, the brief and/or lasting displays of genderqueerness that can be publicly visualized become the social domains to articulate and rearticulate issues and concerns of homosexuality, cross-dressing, and transgenderism in Japan.

Consequently, Hikawa's genderless that disidentifies with the *onē-kei* talent genre creates an additional space of queer possibilities. More specifically, I view Hikawa is trying to be the queer author to write his own narrative about gender(less) under the constraints of Japan's social conformity. Hikawa was born and raised as a cisgender male. Hikawa has established his entertainment career as a cisgender male. At the same time, now Hikawa's genderless may provide an alternative paradigm of becoming and being genderqueer redefining the historical continuum of *okama* emerged from Japan's pre-industrial period, that is, before 1868. The construction of *okama* who performs a gender and sexual nonconformity onto the body constrained at the birth is extremely cisheterosexist. Hence, Hikawa's *less* of genderless allows us to return to add a new category of genderqueer nonconformity that transgresses the logic of Japan's cisheteropatriarchy.

While articulating my thought on Hikawa's genderless that suggests queer im/possibilities, *I find myself falling in love with Hikawa once again.* I want to be like Hikawa as I enter into 40's. No matter what the macro-structural relations of difference constrain my aging body, I want to be able to express myself as I am through my gender queer aesthetics.

*****

October, 25, 2020 Sunday

It has been almost over ten months since my first articulation of "love" for Hikawa. During the time, I have been in Seattle for my sabbatical between January and July in 2020. My stay in Seattle was not as easy as I originally thought. Shortly after I started to stay in Seattle, the COVID-19 pandemic became globally visible, killed large numbers of people across the world, and required people to stay home. So, while I appreciate my economic capital that allows me to be safely sheltered, I have ended up spending my time in a tiny studio in Capitol Hill where I originally planned more to go out to gay cultural sites than to stay home. Then, the Death of George Floyd that demonstrates the historically recurring episodes of killings of Black/African American people by the police prompted the Capitol Hill Autonomous Zone (CHAZ)/the Capitol Hill Occupied Protest (CHOP). It took place in Cal Anderson Park where was a block from my studio apartment. My physical proximity to CHAZ/CHOP pushed me to reflect my voluntary participation in the U.S. settler colonialism that occupies the Native Lands and sustains the logic of anti-blackness. As a non-Black, non-indigenous queer immigrant-becoming-citizen of color, I must be conscious of the way the settler colonialism necessitates my unthreatening, model minority existence for the maintenance of the system. Hence, my stay in Seattle has literally forced me to think of the following questions: *Why am I in the U.S? Why don't I want to return to Japan?* My answers to these questions are constantly changing. However, I must admit that the reason why I decided to go on to pursue MA/PHD degrees upon the completion of my undergraduate degree was that *I wanted to enjoy my gay life* in the U.S. I thought going back to Japan that reiterates the value of social conformity would restrict my (queer) freedom. Little did I know that gay life would almost always require the White, masculine, middle-class social capital that sustains the U.S. settler colonialism.

However, I have gradually become aware of my glass ceiling as an effeminate queer Japanese American subject over the years. I can never achieve the perfect vision of gay life designed by the logic of whiteness. Hence, my falling in love with Hikawa is my critical returning moment to gaze toward where I come from. Until recently I have often described myself as a queer Asian/American subject. This is because I have to frequently check a box of a racialized Asian category as I participate in the U.S. social institutions, in general, and gay sexual cultures, in particular. Yet, having been able to stay Seattle for my sabbatical has pushed me to question my use of Asian/American. What I have enjoyed staying in Seattle is its convenient accessibility to Japanese American cultures and materials. Despite of having been in the U.S. settler nation-state for almost two decades, some parts of me almost always miss my home. I can completely neither forget nor undo the way I was born and raised in Japan. Thus, my falling in love with Hikawa points to how I project uncertain (impossible) possibilities of my Japanese American queerness onto his embodied performance of genderless. As I idolize Hikawa's genderless, I imagine and reimagine if I would permanently return to Japan one day. In so doing, I begin to wonder if I have been running away from the way Japan's social norm monsters me as *okama*. *To me, it is a very derogatory term.* Growing up, I have never seen people using *okama* positively. *Okama* has been and is always already monstrous. Hence, by falling in love with Hikawa, I am seeking an alternative path to reclaim the monstrosity of being *okama* as I am.

*****

Becoming the Queer Japanese Collective

Before ending this chapter, I take a moment to reflect how sticky rice can be a bridge building methodology to advance the intersubjective connections in and across times, spaces, and contexts. As illustrated, my sticky rice desire for Hikawa is not about sexual and romantic. It is about my social aspiration to become and be like Hikawa as I enter into my 40's. My emphasis on ageing should not be read as my desire to maintain my youthfulness. I do not want to go back to my 20's at all. I am much more comfortable with who I am and what I do now than before. At the same time, my emphasis on entering into 40's is about my desire to seek out how to be unapologetically and fearlessly queer as I age. I want to find a way to reclaim and embody the unapologetic, fearless monstrosity of being *okama* because I know life is short and an onetime gift in this material reality. Hence, as Wu (2018) showcased, I have figuratively used sticky rice to suggest an alternative path toward considering the multiple possibilities of "Asians" loving "Asians." My rejection of the hetero/homo-normative relational logic of linear progression, re-centering the cispatriarchal tradition of marriage as an end goal, has organized my figurative use of sticky rice as a bridge methodology. The embodied politics of sticky rice that pays attention to the ways "Asians" love "Asians" are dynamic, multiple, and unstable in and across times, spaces, and contexts. Put simply, there should be no single, correct way for "Asians" to love "Asians." For that reason, my love for Hikawa should be read as one of many forms of sticky rice desires, performances, and politics.

In addition, my goal to centralize sticky rice in performative writing is to take a step toward imagining the *Japanese queer collective*. I am concerned with the way Japan's sexual and gender minoritarians reproduce normative power relations such as cisheterosexism and ethnocentrism. For example, I engaged in an auto/ ethnographic fieldwork of socializing with Japanese cismale sexual minoritarians in New York City in July 2013 (see, Eguchi, 2015). One night at the bar, I was introduced to cisgender masculine-presenting Japanese bisexual man who was with a cisgender feminine-presenting Japanese female friend. As soon as I finished introducing myself and turned away, I heard of them saying "he is super *onē.*" While I embrace their reading of my effeminate queerness or genderqueerness, it also reminds me of the hierarchies of gender presentation that organize Japan's queer cultures. As McLelland (2000) said, "use of this term [*okama*] is extremely loose and it can be used to describe a man who displays any transgender attribute" (p. 8). This coincides with the *onē-kei* talent genre. However, who is invisible through the use of *okama/onē* is the cisgender masculine-presenting male sexual minoritarian subject who can pass as "straight." Said simply, "straight-acting" men who conform to the majoritarian codes of (cis)gender conduct may be able to disidentify with the monstrous stigmatization of *okama/onē* in their everyday social interactions and processes. This kind of disidentification does not entirely trouble the historical subordinations of *okama/onē* subjects who are historically imagined to get fucked by men. Hence, as an effeminately queer subject, I have attempted to reclaim sticky rice as a "sisterly" concept. So, I can intimately build a bridge with Hikawa who also violates the majoritarian codes of (cis)gender conduct for demonstrating my step toward the *Japanese queer collective*, embracing differences shored under.

Here, I end this essay by critiquing on my sticky rice attraction to Hikawa that occurs as I gaze toward my homeland, Japan. As an immigrant-becoming-citizen in the U.S. settler colonial nation, I must be carefully aware of the way my returning attention to Japan joins in an already established imperialist path from the West to the non-West and from the U.S. to Japan. There is no doubt that I carry out my embodiment of (somewhat) Americanized Japanese queer-ness as I digitally and physically enter into Japan's queer cultures. However, my shifting attention that is from Global North to Global North is quite privileged under the current political economy of liberal capitalism that enables discourses around LGBT rights around the world. Simultaneously, my sticky rice attraction to Hikawa can be ethnocentric by nature. Because I was born and raised in Japan, I may idolize Hikawa's Japanese genderless much more than other forms of Asian and Asian American genderqueerness that are currently available in and across media and social media. I am spatially limited to a transnational border in-between the U.S. and Japan through which my embodied site of knowledge production currently occurs. As a scholar who values performative writing, I am personally, intellectually, and politically committed (and limited) to working from the cultural context of my body as a part of my ethical responsibility. Still, it is my hope that the readers of this chapter from various localities can relate to the way my performative writing refashions Hikawa's genderless as a queer form of revolt against the majoritarian codes of (cis)gender in Japan.

Note

1 Following the typical practice in the Japanese language system, I list last name first and given name second.

References

Boylorn, R. M. (2008). As seen on TV: An autoethnographic reflection on race and reality television. *Critical Studies in Media Communication*, *25*(4), 413–433. https://doi.org/10.1080/15295030802327758

Calafell, B. M. (2015). *Monstrosity, performance, and race in contemporary culture*. Peter Lang.

Calafell, B. M. (2020). The critical performative turn in intercultural communication. *Journal of Intercultural Communication Research*, *49*(5), 410–415. https://doi.org/10.1080/17475759.2020.1740292

Calvente, L. B. Y., Calafell, B. M., & Chávez, K. R. (2020). Here is something you can't understand: the suffocating whiteness of communication studies. *Communication and Critical/Cultural Studies*, *17*(2), 202–209. https://www.tandfonline.com/doi/full/10.1080/14791420.2020.1770823

Carrillo Rowe, A. (2008). *Power lines: On the subject of feminist alliances*. Duke University Press.

Chakravartty, P., Kuo, R., Grubbs, V., & McIlwain, C. (2018). #CommunicationSoWhite. *Journal of Communication*, *68*(2), 254–266. https://doi.org/10.1093/joc/jqy003

Chambers-Letson, J. (2018). *After the party: A manifesto for queer of color life*. New York University Press.

Chávez, K. R. (2009). Remapping Latinidad: A performance cartography of Latina/o identity in rural Nebraska. *Text and Performance Quarterly*, *29*(2), 165–182. https://doi.org/10.1080/10462930902774866

Chávez, K. R. (2013). Pushing boundaries: Queer intercultural communication. *Journal of International and Intercultural Communication*, *6*(2), 83–95. https://doi.org/10.1080/17513057.2013.777506

Corey, F. C. (2002). "Alexander." *Communication Quarterly*, *50*(3/4), 344–358. https://doi.org/10.1080/01463370209385668

Darling-Wolf, F. (2000). Texts in context: Intertextuality, hybridity, and the negotiation of cultural identity in Japan. *Journal of Communication Inquiry*, *24*(2), 134–155. https://doi.org/10.1177/0196859900024002003

Dower, J. W. (1999). *Embracing defeat: Japan in the wake of World War II*. W. W. New York: Norton.

Eguchi, S. (2015). Queer intercultural relationality: An autoethnography of Asian-Black (dis) connections in White gay America. *Journal of International and Intercultural Communication*, *8*(1), 27–43. https://doi.org/10.1080/17513057.2015.991077

Eguchi, S. (2017). Japanese male-queer femininity: An autoethnographic reflection on Matsuko Deluxe as an *onē-kei talent*. In S. Toyosaki & S. Eguchi (Eds.), *Intercultural communication in Japan: Theorizing homogenized discourse* (pp. 73–85). Routledge.

Eguchi, S. (2019). Queerness as strategic whiteness: A queer Asian American critique of Peter Le. In D. M. D. McIntosh, D. G. Moon, & T. K. Nakayama (Eds.), *Interrogating communicative power of whiteness* (pp. 29–44). Routledge.

Eguchi, S. (2020). Japan's masculinist politics: An intersectional queer critique of actor Narimiya Hiroki's retirement from the entertainment industry. *Women & Language*, *43*(2), 317–324. https://doi.org/10.34036/WL.2020.027

Eguchi, S., & Kimura, K. (2021). Racialized im/possibilities: Intersectional queer-of-color critique on Japaneseness in Netflix's Queer Eye: We're in Japan! *Journal of International and Intercultural Communication*, *14*(3), 221–239. https://doi.org/10.1080/17513057.2020.1829675

Gannon, M. J. (2001). *Understanding global cultures: Metaphorical journeys through 23 nations* (2nd ed.). Sage.

Griffin, R. A. (2012). I am an angry Black woman: Black feminist autoethnography, voice, and resistance. *Women's Studies in Communication*, *35*(2), 138–157. https://doi.org/10.1080/07491409.2012.724524

Johnson, E. P. (2003). The specter of the black fag: Parady, blackness, and hetero/homosexual b(r) others. *Journal of Homosexuality*, *45*(2/3/4), 217–234. https://doi.org/10.1300/J082v45n02_10

Kimmel, M. S. (1996). *Manhood in America: A cultural history*. Free Press.

Kouno, Y. (2020, June 10). Hikawa Kiyoshi conflict between "Enka Fan's dream ..." and "Enka in the Enka world." *AnAn News*. https://ananweb.jp/news/292574/

Mackie, V. (2008). How to be a girl: Mainstream media portrayals of transgendered lives. *Asian Studies Review*, *32*(3), 411–423. https://doi.org/10.1080/10357820802298538

Madison, S. D. (1993). "That was my occupation": Oral narrative, performance, and black feminist thought. *Text and Performance Quarterly*, *13*(3), 213–232. https://doi.org/10.1080/10462939309366051

Madison, D. S. (1999). Performing theory/embodied writing. *Text and Performance Quarterly*, *19*(2), 107–124. https://doi.org/10.1080/10462939909366254

Maeda, E., & Hecht, M. L. (2012). Identity search: Interpersonal relationships and relational identities of always-single Japanese women over time. *Western Journal of Communication*, *76*(1), 44–64. https://doi.org/10.1080/10570314.2012.637539gy

Maree, C. (2008). Grrrl-queens: One-kotoba and the negotiation of heterosexist gender language norms and lesbo(homo)phobic stereotypes in Japan. In F. Martin, P. A. Jackson,

M. McLelland, & A. Yue (Eds.), *Asiapacific queer: Rethinking genders and sexualities* (pp. 67–84). University of Illinois Press.

Maree, C. (2017). Weddings and white dresses: Media and sexual citizenship in Japan. *Sexualities, 20*(1/2), 212–233. https://doi.org/10.1177/1363460716645790

McIntosh, D. M. D., & Eguchi, S. (2020). The troubled past, present disjunctures, and possible futures: Intercultural performance communication. *Journal of Intercultural Communication Research, 49*(5), 395–409. https://doi.org/10.1080/17475759.2020.1811996

McLelland, M. J. (2000). *Male homosexuality in modern Japan: Cultural myths and social realities.* Routledge.

Mitsuhashi, J. (2006). The transgender world in contemporary Japan: the male to female cross-dressers' community in Shinjuku. *Inter-Asia Cultural Studies, 7*(2), 202–227. https://doi.org/10.1080/14649370600673847

Molina-Guzmán, I. (2010). *Dangerous curves: Latina bodies in the Media.* New York University Press.

Moraga, C., & Anzaldúa, G. (Eds.). (1983). *This bridge called my back: Writing by radical women of color.* Kitchen Table.

Muñoz, J. E. (1999). *Disidentifications: Queers of color and the performance of politics.* Minneapolis: University of Minnesota Press.

Muñoz, J. E. (2009). *Cruising utopia: The then and there of queer futurity.* New York University Press.

Murakami, M. (2020, February 19). *Hikawa Kiyoshi "I'm no longer aiming for a singer loved by everyone":Free from the complex. From now on, be yourself.* https://fujinkoron.jp/articles/-/1616

My Navi News. (2020, February 29). *Matsuko confesses the reason "I really don't want to say" to onē.* https://news.mynavi.jp/article/20200229-984942/

Nguyen, H. T. (2014). *A view from the bottom: Asian American masculinity and sexual representation.* Duke University Press.

Nippon Colombia. (n.d). *Hikawa Kiyoshi.* Profile. https://columbia.jp/hikawa/prof.html

ORICON News. (2017, August 25). *Hikawa Kiyoshi challenges the opening ceremony of the last 30's. "25 points modestly."* https://www.oricon.co.jp/news/2096189/?ref_cd=newsphotorelation

ORICON News. (2019a, August 8). *Hikawa Kiyoshi, Noban pitching "99 points" for 4 consecutive years at Jingu Stadium.* https://www.oricon.co.jp/news/2141901/full/

ORICON News. (2019b, November 25). *Hikawa Kiyoshi fascinates with a pure white dress "Like a wedding dress." "Beauty awakens."* https://www.oricon.co.jp/news/2149506/full/

ORICON News. (2020, June 2). *Hikawa Kiyoshi frankly talks about changes and challenges, I want to be key natural.* https://www.oricon.co.jp/news/2163524/full/

Pollack, D. (1998). Performing writing. In P. Phelan & J. Lane (Eds.), *The ends of performance* (pp. 73–103). New York University Press.

Puar, J. K. (2007). *Terrorist assemblages: Homonationalism in queer times.* Duke University Press.

Sekimoto, S. (2014). Transnational Asia: Dis/orienting identity in the globalized world. *Communication Quarterly, 62*(4), 381–398. https://doi.org/10.1080/01463373.2014.922485

Shiba, T. (2020, August 7). Kiyoshi Hikawa, Tsuyoshi Domoto, new areas of expression for popular artists. *Fujinkouron*. https://fujinkoron.jp/articles/-/2360

Shukanbunshu. (2019, September 12). *The first person is "Watashi [I]", showing off his bare feet in shorts ... Hikawa Kiyoshi has finally come out "serious."* https://bunshun.jp/articles/-/20345

Suganuma, K. (2012). *Contact moments: The politics of intercultural desire in Japanese male-queer cultures*. Hong Kong University Press.

Summerhawak, B., McMahill, C., & McDonald, D. (1998). *Queer Japan: Personal stories of Japanese lesbians, gays, bisexuals, and transsexuals*. New Victoria Publishers.

Toyosaki, S. (2011). Critical complete-member ethnography: Theorizing dialectics of consensus and conflict in intercultural communication. *Journal of International and Intercultural Communication, 4*(1), 62–80. https://doi.org/10.1080/17513057.2010.533786

Tori-chan's Outlook Report. (2019, November, 25). *An onē-zation of Hikawa Kiyoshi comes out! I was amazed at his bare feet in ceremonial first pitch, Instagram posts, and visual costumes.* https://green-3-triangle.com/hikawakiyoshi-gay-the-first-pitch-ceremony/

Valentine, J. (1997). Pots and pans: Identification of queer Japanese in terms of discrimination. In A. Livia & K. Hall (Eds.), *Queerly phrased: Language, gender, and sexuality*. Oxford University Press.

Welker, J. (2010). Telling her story. Narrating a Japanese lesbian community. *Journal of Lesbian Studies, 14*(4), 359–380. https://doi.org/10.1080/10894161003677265

Welker, J. (2017). Toward a history of 'lesbian history' in Japan. *Culture, Theory and Critique, 58*(2), 147–165. https://doi.org/10.1080/14735784.2017.1282830

Wu, C. (2018). *Sticky rice: A politics of intraracial desire*. Temple University Press.

Yukimi, K. (2013, March 1). Explain the difference between onē talents who are active in the entertainment world! Excite News. https://www.excite.co.jp/news/article/Ren_ai_10249/

Coda: Turning Points: Queer Desire in Progress

Queerness should and could be about a desire for another way of being in both the world and time, a desire that resists mandates to accept that which is not enough --- (Muñoz, 2009, p. 96).

To expand the circumferences of Critical Intercultural Communication Studies promoted by scholars such as Calafell (2021), Halualani (2014), and Nakayama (2008), *Asians loving Asians: Sticky Rice Homoeroticism and Queer Politics* has deployed queerness as a conceptual lens to engage in the multi-level analyses of sticky rice as a gay vernacular. To be precise, I have carefully examined the vernacular discourses around sticky rice produced, constituted, and negotiated in and across personal (micro), relational/communal (meso), and mediated (macro) contexts. In the examination processes, queerness has methodologically allowed me to unpack how the trope of sticky rice displays moments of transgressions against the social orders in and across time, space, and context.

More specifically, "Part I Reading Media Representation" has paid careful attention to the gay sexual cultural representations of sticky rice in *Yellow Fever* (1998) and *Front Cover* (2016) and Here TV's *Falling for Angeles'* episode *Koreatown* (2017, S1E2). Then, by centering my body as a major platform of knowledge and analysis in "Part II Speaking with Racialized Asian Queer Male Subjects", I have analyzed the vernacular discourses around sticky rice emerged from in-depth interviews with the seven co-researchers. Lastly, I have deployed sticky rice as a bridge building methodology of performative writing to examine impossible possibilities of genderqueerness being represented by a well-known Japanese Enka singer Hikawa Kiyoshi to begin "Part III Returning to the Self."

With all of the five chapters described above, I have argued how the trope of sticky rice as a gay vernacular is both powerful and problematic at the same time. This reinforces Muñoz' (1999) theorizing of disidentification as "a mode of *recycling* or re-forming an object that has already been invested with powerful energy" (p. 39, emphasis in original). More specifically, I have demonstrated how the racialized Asian queer male subjects both reify and resist the stigmatization of sticky rice as they participate in and across gay sexual cultures. While sticky rice can disrupt the logic of whiteness that organizes the gay masculine ideal, it can also reinsert the mundane operations of cisgenderism working with masculinism, patriarchy, and phallic hegemony. Still, there are "somethings" about the *stickiness* (or *sameness*) of sticky rice that work as *intersectional queer politics of race*. Politicizing the *stickiness* (or *sameness*) of sticky rice that point to connections and (disconnections) among racialized Asian queer subjects is quite necessary in the historical continuum of colonization that normalizes the White masculine ideal. Hence, complexities and contradictions of sticky rice as a multiple, dynamic, and unfinalized vernacular require the attention further.

Before closing this book, I continue "Part III Returning to the Self" as I critically turn my attention to the *behind-the-door* story of writing about and analyzing the trope of sticky rice as a gay vernacular. Since I am a transnational queer of color scholar who unapologetically orients my body as a central platform of knowledge and analysis, I believe that showcasing my critical reflexivity of doing this research is a major ethnical commitment (see, Eguchi, 2020). As suggested by scholars such as Adam (2017) and Boylorn (2016), my sharing of the self that points to the social, the cultural, the political, and the historical is to offer an honest space of intersubjectivity through which you (as the reader) relate to where I come from as the writer of this book. Hence, in this closing chapter I share my embodied performance of racialized queerness that prompts me to write this book. Simultaneously I reflect the way the COVID-19 pandemic shapes my desire to complete writing this book. In so doing, my overall goal of this closing chapter is to end *Asians loving Asians: Sticky Rice Homoeroticism and Queer Politics* by leaving some possibilities for both the readers and me to continue to question and critique the trope of sticky rice in the future.

*****

Writing about sticky rice is…
SO HARD!
Why did I want to write about sticky rice to begin with?
WHAT….
    WAS…
       I…
          THINKING?

*****

A Turning Point

Sometimes in late summer during the year of 2014 when I completed revising my publication on an autoethnography of Asian-Black (dis)connections in White gay America (Eguchi, 2015), I began to question myself as to why I had been openly and frankly writing about my autoethnography of queer relationships with cisgender men of color in the academic writings (see, for example, Eguchi, 2011a, b; 2014). By cisgender men of color, I mean mostly Black/African American cisgender men born and raised in the U.S. Apparently, coming to the U.S. as an international student from Japan, everyday negotiations of my racialized queerness in relation to significant others drove my passion to pursue both undergraduate and graduate educations in Communication. I wanted to know about myself in relation to this settler colonial nation because I had experienced *culture shocks* in many ways. In particular, the racialization of my body as an Asian subject in and across gay sexual cultures have been a major site of struggle for me to make sense of who I am, what I do, and what I make sense of what I do in relations to people around me. So, I dove into autoethnography without any doubt. Little did I know that people could use my autoethnographic writings against me *out of the context* in the higher education. In the word of Griffin (2012), I have learned how the higher education is a full of toxic, unnecessary competition.

At the same time, what I came to be critically aware of writing my autoethnography was that the logic of whiteness that produces racialized gender imaginations in and across gay sexual cultures frames the contextual settings of interpersonal intercultural encounters between queer people of color. In other words, the gay sexual cultural categories of "Asian" and "Black" that normalize the White masculine ideal shaped my everyday experiences. To be precise, I could not escape from the historical fetishization of "Asian" shaping how Black/African

American men whom I came across interacted with me. Simultaneously, I was also subjected to the fetishization of Black hypermasculinity shaping how I interacted with them. Here, I must be critically reflexive of the way my desire has undeniably reproduced the U.S. racialized gender imagination of the Black male body. Hence, although my resistance against the White masculine ideal originally caused my shifting attention to men of color, I was also required to check how my embodied performances of queerness could not escape from the gay sexual politics of racial fetish. Thus, when I completed the manuscript (Eguchi, 2015), I was drawn (back) to the trope of sticky rice – Asian men loving Asian men.

More specifically, my reading of Nguyen's (2014) examination of sticky rice pushed me to critically question myself. *When did I stop being attracted to men who look like me?* As I have said in the introductory chapter, intra-ethnic/racial/cultural homoeroticism is normal and ordinary in Japan. Hence, taking a step to answer my own question required me to be reflexive of how I was socialized into the logics of whiteness that organizes the U.S. gay sexual cultures. Similar to what my co-researchers Lala and Yoshi says in the Chapter 4, I have been gazing toward *non-Asian men* for the most parts. My relational proximity to non-Asian men signified my being away from Japan as it is geographically located in Asia. Not being around Asians has been the coping mechanism for me to resist the stigmatization of being Asian in the gay sexual cultures. As I remember, by the time I was living in New York City (2006–2008), I had already internalized the negative discourses around sticky rice thinking that I wouldn't date and hook up with racialized Asian queer male subjects. Hence, I felt in need of studying about the trope of sticky rice to challenge my own internalization of gay racism that marginalizes racialized Asian queer male subjects including myself. Put simply, I felt in need of combatting the self-hatred.

However, the overall course of writing *Asians loving Asians: Sticky Rice Homoeroticism and Queer Politics* originally began in 2014 has been challenging for me. Because the body as a central platform of my knowledge and analysis drives my passion for doing the scholarship, I felt I was missing my "embodied" knowledge to critically examine the trope of sticky rice. Quite frankly, I could not even picture how I am supposed to feel doing sticky rice. Since I have not been a sticky rice subject like my co-researchers Chun, Taro, Yoshi, I felt I could not fully question and carefully critique the trope of sticky rice to begin with. So, I felt connected to the U.S. born and raised co-researchers like Tayo, Lee, and Polo who distanced themselves from the trope of sticky rice. Hence, I very much felt I was lost in thinking and writing about sticky rice. And, my being unable to critically think of sticky rice was indeed the embodied product of gay racism I had been subjected to.

*****

Wow....I am lost....
Why...Why did I choose this topic?
...Should I quit?.... Should I continue?
At this point, I am stuck with this topic...
AGAIN
WHAT....
WAS...
I...
THINKING?

*****

Another Turning Point

At the same time, starting from early 2020, the COVID-19 pandemic that once again highlights ongoing histories of America's race problems forces me to reevaluate why I have been drawn to the trope of sticky rice. As I have mentioned in some of the previous chapters, the COVID-19 misnamed as "a China Virus" globally increased happenings of anti-Asian hate crimes and harassments. Under the conditions, I am once again reminded that Asian Americans are indeed the minoritized subjects as *Others* in the historical continuum of the U.S. racial formation. Asian Americans are not White. Even when Asian Americans are framed to be almost White, they are still people of color. And this is why I was interested in studying the trope of sticky rice as a minoritarian sexual politics to begin with.

My sabbatical stays in Seattle, Washington between January and July in 2020 have particularly given me a chance to rearticulate and remember the historical marginalization and stereotyping of Asian Americans that shape the contextual backgrounds of sticky rice. Take, for example, I enter into a Pharmacy store Rite Aid on the corner of Broadway and John Street on a night of February 4, 2020 in Seattle's Capitol Hill. Once I grab what I need to buy, I stand in line to wait for a casher. Then, a White cisgender masculine man is waiting for a casher behind me. As I turn my face to the entrance, I see that three cisgender women who look East Asian descents in 20's enter into the store. Then, a White cisgender male cashier suddenly uses his hands to gesture the masks. And he shouts "we do not have masks" to the women. However, the women do not even ask him about masks. They just pass by the cashier. At this moment, I immediately feel I am about to lose myself. I feel my anger boiling up from the body as a site of knowledge about and analysis about anti-Asian racism. Then, it is my turn to check out. So, I walk

toward the cashier. I ask him, 'Why did you say about the masks to the women?"
So, he replies to me "oh, we do not have masks." So, I instantly tell him that "I
am Asian. I am not looking for masks. I think what you say is a racist. In fact,
you discriminated against them when they didn't ask you for anything." Then, a
White cisgender masculine-presenting man waiting for a casher after me makes
this situation worse. He scolds me that "he [the casher] was trying to be helpful
for those girls." I immediately said, "how is it helpful when they did not ask him
for anything?" At this point, because I am extremely mad, I angrily exist myself of
the store. As I walk back to my apartment, I vent about the incident on Facebook
by tagging the store.

The surreal moment of anti-Asian aggression immediately reminds of
how I have come to develop my queer critical race awareness while especially
participating in the U.S. gay sexual cultures last two decades. When I lived in
San Francisco (2003–2005), the bartenders ignoring me were quite ordinary in
gay clubs. When I was skipped for ordering drinks, my non-Asian friends who
are mostly White ordered them for me. This kind of gay bar experience through
which people of color patrons are ignored for ordering drinks is quite common
(Han, 2007). And Asians and Asian Americans are often framed to be invisible
in and across gay sexual cultures. Because of this racial climate, I recognized how
the racialized Asian queer male subjects tended to socialize in the corners of gay
clubs such as San Francisco's Badlands. Moreover, it was quite normal for me to
encounter a common phrase "No Asians" in and across gay online dating sites just
like Han (2015) and Nguyen (2014) showcased the sexual and romantic rejections
of racialized Asian queer male subjects. Hence, my experiences reinforce what Han
and Rutledge (2020) write is that gay sexual cultural manifestations of racism toward queer people of color are super visible everyday.

Still, because of my racial consciousness, I feel connected to the three "Asian"
women who walk into a Rite Aids store. I have no clue of who these women are.
I have no idea of what cultural, ethnic, linguistic, and sexual identifications they
claim. However, when I see the casher says "we do not have masks," I intuitively
feel in need of *sticking with* them. I felt how the language, uttered by the cashier,
reinforces the performative rhetoric of anti-Asian racism in Seattle where is historically known as one of the U.S. cities with the most Asian American populations.
Perhaps, the racist architecture of the U.S. settler colonial nation-state rooted in
White supremacy instantly produces my desire for *sticking with* the women.

This incident once again reminds me of *somethings about* the body that play
into everyday social interactions and processes. Because race is a social construct
of meanings attached to the body, I cannot ignore the way in which people read
me though my racialized gender body that represents historically specific and

culturally particular meanings of being "Asian." As Eng (2001) has detailed be-fore, the particular portraits of the Asian eyes and cheekbones were used to es-sentially discern Japanese Americans from the rest of Asian Americans such as Chinese Americans during the time of Japanese American isolation and inter-ment. This example points to ongoing continuities of the U.S. settler colonial in-stitution through which the figure of the Asian immigrant body is strategically manipulated to produce xenophobic anxieties to maintain *the nation* in and across time, space, and context (Lowe, 1996). At the same time, the recent happenings of anti-Asian hate crimes and harassments showcase that hate crime perpetuators randomly target different kinds of Asians and Asian Americans. It does not matter what cultural and ethnic backgrounds they identify with. *What matter is how they look.* Hence, even though race is never a singular, fixed, and essentialist concept, the racialized framings of the body in a way it is read by others matter. The discourses around the body cannot be ignored.

Thus, the trope of sticky rice that turns the attention to the body as a pos-sible site of resistance against the supremacy of whiteness that organizes (global) gay sexual cultures require more investigations than now. The *stickiness* of sticky rice implicates vernacular possibilities of queerness that challenge socially ac-ceptable and taken-for-granted ideas, beliefs, and values. Hence, sticky rice is not only about a gay vernacular suggesting racialized Asian men dating, meeting, and having sex with racialized Asian men. But it is also beyond just an impossible pos-sibility of the present moment that constrains and restraints (queer) freedom. Thus, I join Wu's (2018) advocacy for sticky rice as a critical cultural methodology that examines much larger political, economic, and historical conditions of connections and disconnections between the racialized Asian subjects than (global) gay sexual cultures. Sticky rice politics is quite dissident in the contemporary globalization that circulates the logic of whiteness, patriarchy, cisheteronormaivity, and neolib-eral capitalism across the world.

Temporal Closing

With the realization of sticky rice described above, I have written on *Asians loving Asians: Sticky Rice Homoeroticism and Queer Politics* mostly under the COVID-19 pandemic that made me stay home. No matter what critiques I may be going to receive from you as the reader, I feel responsible of putting my racialized gender body on the line. So, I can help create an additional space to reimagine vernac-ular possibilities of sticky rice. Still, Wu (2018) reiterates the complexity of sticky rice. She notes, "Despite a contemporary politics of sticky among certain Asian

Americans, a racially congruent combination is still almost unthinkable" (p. 166). While writing this book forces me to be critical of my queer desire that points to my internalization of upward mobility and racial hang-ups, I yet engage in sticky rice. Disembodying the embodiment of whiteness that organizes gay sexual cultures is an extremely challenging task. However, queer desire is a multiple, dynamic, and fluid product that cuts across time, context, space. *Queer desire is always already in progress.* Hence, as I continue to gaze toward the trope of sticky rice in the future, I am personally, intellectually, and politically committed to challenge my embodied performance of queerness. As Muñoz (2009) reminds, the future is an unknown and unknowable destination. So, I never know what I will be doing and how I will be making sense of what I will be doing in relation to people around me. I may be going to become and be a sticky rice subject like some of my co-researchers introduced in this book. Anything is possible.

Still, as I close *Asians loving Asians: Sticky Rice Homoeroticism and Queer Politics*, I once again invite you (as the reader) to join me to study lived experiences of racialized queer desire, in general, sticky rice desire, in particular. This is of great consequence in Communication. As large numbers of scholars such as Calvente, Calafell, and Chávez (2020), Chakravartty and Jackson (2020), Flores and Gomez (2020), and McCann, Mack, and Self (2020) have argued, Communication is a discipline that almost always normalizes the logic of whiteness. Simultaneously, the pervasiveness of whiteness recenters patriarchy, cisheteronormativity, capitalism, and U.S. Americanism in Communication (Calafell, Eguchi, & Abdi, 2020). Therefore, as a transnational queer of color scholar, it is my hope that *Asians loving Asians: Sticky Rice Homoeroticism and Queer Politics* will help sustain critical spaces for queer of color scholarships in the discipline. *Let's stick together!*

*****

....ACUTUALLY......
I WAS THINKING RIGHT!!!!
BECAUSE....finally....
I FEEL....I FEEL...I FEEL ...

Having written about sticky rice sets me FREE from the PAST.....

By the past...
I mean.....
how I have come to be who I am.....
NOW
I...

AM....
"READY"
....TO RE/ENTER INTO...
QUEER ASIA
QUEER JAPAN
See you "THERE"!!!!

References

Adams, T. E. (2017). Autoethnographic responsibilities. *International Review of Qualitative Research, 10*(1), 62–66. https://doi.org/10.1525/irqr.2017.10.1.62.

Boylorn, R. M. (2016). On being at home with myself: Blackgirl autoethnography as research praxis. *International Review of Qualitative Research, 9*(1), 44–58. https://doi.org/10.1525/irqr.2016.9.1.44

Calafell, B. M. (2021). On invitations and possibilities. *Journal of International and Intercultural Communication, 14*(1), 1–2. https://doi.org/10.1080/17513057.2020.1748881

Calafell, B. M., Eguchi, S., & Abdi, S. (2020). Introduction: De-whitening intersectionality in intercultural communication. In S. Eguchi, B. M. Calafell, & S. Abdi (Eds.), *De-Whitening Intersectionality: Race, Intercultural Communication, and Politics* (pp. xvii–xxvii). Lexington Press.

Calvente, L. B. Y., Calafell, B. M., & Chávez, K. R. (2020). Here is something you can't understand: The suffocating whiteness of communication studies. *Communication and Critical/Cultural Studies, 17*(2), 202–209. https://doi.org/10.1080/14791420.2020.1770823

Chakravartty, P., & Jackson, S. J. (2020). The disavowal of race in communication theory. *Communication and Critical/Cultural Studies, 17*(2), 210–219. https://doi.org/10.1080/14791420.2020.1771743

Eguchi, S. (2011a). Cross-national identity transformation: Becoming a gay 'Asian American' man. *Sexuality & Culture, 15*(1), 19–40. https://doi.org/10.1007/s12119-010-9080-z

Eguchi, S. (2011b). Negotiating sissyphobia: A critical/interpretive analysis of one 'femme' gay Asian body in the heteronormative world. *Journal of Men's Studies, 19*(1), 37–56. https://doi.org/10.3149/jms.1901.37

Eguchi, S. (2014). Coming in/out of the closet: Living in-between singlehood and relationship(s) through a gay Asian body. In S. Howard (Ed.), *Critical articulations of race, gender, and sexual orientation* (pp. 5–21). Lexington Press.

Eguchi, S. (2015). Queer intercultural relationality: An autoethnography of Asian-Black (dis)connections in White gay America. *Journal of International and Intercultural Communication, 8*(1), 27–43. https://doi.org/10.1080/17513057.2015.991077

Eguchi, S. (2020). A transnational queer of color vision: Toward the "future" of autoethnography. *Journal of Autoethnography, 1*(3), 309–314. https://doi.org/10.1525/joae.2020.1.3.309

Eng, D. L. (2001). *Racial castration: Managing masculinity in Asian America.* Duke University Press.

Flores, L. A., & Gomez, L. A. (2020). Disciplinary containment: Whiteness and the academic scarcity narrative. *Communication and Critical/Cultural Studies, 17*(2), 236–242. https://doi.org/10.1080/14791420.2020.1770818

Griffin, R. A. (2012). Navigating the politics of identity/identities and exploring the promise of critical love. In N. Bardhan & M. P. Orbe (Eds.), *Identity research and communication: Intercultural reflections and future directions* (pp. 207–221). Lexington Books.

Halualani, R. T. (2014). Editor's introduction: Critical interventions in urgent times. *Journal of International and Intercultural Communication, 7*(4), 259. https://doi.org/10.1080/17513057.2014.964143

Halualani, R. T., & Nakayama, T. K. (2010). Critical intercultural communication studies: At a crossroads. In T. K. Nakayama & R. T. Halualani (Eds.), *The handbook of critical intercultural communication* (pp. 1–16). Wiley-Blackwell.

Han, C. (2007). They don't want to cruise your type: Gay men of color and the racial politics of exclusion. *Social Identities, 13*(1), 51–67. https://doi.org/10.1080/13504630601163379

Han, C. W., & Rutledge, S. E. (2020). They don't date any dark people: The queer case of gay racism. In J. G. Smith & C. W. Han (Eds.), *Home and community for queer men of color* (pp. 31–48). Lexington Press.

Lowe, L. (1996). *Immigrant acts: On Asian American cultural politics.* Duke University Press.

McCann, B. Mack, A. N., & Self, R. (2020). Communication's quest for whiteness: The racial politics of disciplinary legitimacy. *Communication and Critical/Cultural Studies, 17*(2), 243–252. https://doi.org/10.1080/14791420.2020.1770822

Muñoz, J. E. (1999). *Disidentifications: Queers of color and the performance of politics.* University of Minnesota Press.

Muñoz, J. E. (2009). *Cruising utopia: The then and there of queer futurity.* New York University Press.

Nakayama, T. (2008). Editor's statement: On (not) feeling rebellious. *Journal of International and Intercultural Communication, 1*(1), 1–2. https://doi.org/10.1080/17513050701837865

Nguyen, H. T. (2014). *A view from the bottom: Asian American masculinity and sexual representation.* Duke University Press.

Wu, C. (2018). *Sticky rice: A politics of intraracial desire.* Temple University Press.

Co-Researchers' Demographic Information

Name	Age	Location	Race	Ethnicity	Birthplace	Document Status
Tayo	36	Washington, DC	Asian	Indian	U.S.	Citizenship
Lala	26	Atlanta	Asian/White	Vietnamese	Vietnam	Permanent Residency
Taro	46	New York	Asian	Japanese	Japan	Permanent Residency
Lee	37	New York	Asian	Chinese/Vietnamese	U.S.	Citizenship
Chun	36	New York	Asian	Taiwanese	Taiwan	Permanent Residency
Yoshi	45	New York	Asian	Japanese	Japan	Permanent Residency
Polo	34	Los Angeles	Asian	Filipino	U.S.	Citizenship

About the Author

Shinsuke Eguchi (They/He) is Associate Professor in the Department of Communication and Journalism at the University of New Mexico. They studied Culture, Power, and Communication throughout their undergraduate and graduate trainings at San Francisco State University (B.A.), New York University (M.A.), and Howard University (Ph.D.). Prior to the current position, they were the post-doctoral fellow of Transnationalism, Diasporas, and Migration in the Department of Communication studies at the University of Denver. Their research and teaching interests center on Global and Transcultural studies, Queer of Color Critique, Intersectionality and Racialized Gender Politics, Asian/American studies, and Performance studies. They are a recipient of the 2019 Randy Majors Award – annually recognizing an individual who has made outstanding contributions to Lesbian, Gay, Bisexual, and/or Transgender scholarship in Communication Studies – bestowed by NCA's (National Communication Association's) Caucus on Gay, Lesbian, Bisexual, and Transgender Concerns.

Index

A

accent 24, 93, 113
aesthetic 50, 69, 70, 87, 92, 139, 143–145, 148, 150
affect 9, 64, 83, 121
Albuquerque 143
alternative 4, 7, 9, 15, 17, 30, 51, 61, 66–67, 69–70, 77, 79, 81, 83–85, 87, 89, 91, 93, 95, 97, 99–101, 103, 106, 108, 110–111, 113, 124, 126, 142, 147–149, 152
anti-Asian 2–4, 29, 34–35, 62, 64–65, 90, 116–117, 122–124, 126–127, 163–165
anti-Blackness 127, 151
auto/ethnographic 13–14, 16, 84–85, 99, 106, 128
autoethnography 161

B

beauty 3, 51, 54, 57, 79, 124, 142–144, 147–148
belonging 8, 33, 91–93, 99–100, 114, 142

body 2, 5, 10, 13–14, 16–17, 30, 33, 42, 51, 53, 55–57, 59, 64, 78, 82–85, 91, 93, 106, 116–117, 120, 137, 141–142, 150, 154, 159–165
borderland 29, 31, 34, 45, 49, 79, 81–83, 88, 91, 106, 128
bottom 3, 27, 35, 39–41, 52–53, 57–59, 93
bridge methodology 138, 142, 152, 160
brown 86, 88, 113, 128–129, 143–144, 146
buffed 50, 56, 65

C

California 90, 94, 99
capitalism 5–6, 8, 49, 55, 77, 81, 96, 107, 120–121, 153, 165
cartography 68–69, 79, 94, 105, 129
China 29, 31, 34–36, 38–39, 43–44, 62, 95, 116, 122, 124, 163
Chineseness 36, 44
cisgenderism 6, 50, 53–54, 160
cisheteropatriarchal 4, 15, 49–51, 56–60, 68, 83, 137, 146, 148

citizenship 6, 36, 80, 83, 169

coalitional possibility 16, 107, 110–111, 119, 125, 127

colonialist 3–4, 9, 42, 45, 49, 52, 54–55, 79, 143

condom 58–59, 63, 65

coupling 3, 11, 89–90, 92, 95, 97, 109–11

crip 10–11

critical cultural 13, 84, 141, 165

Critical Intercultural Communication 4, 11–14, 159

culture 2–4, 6, 9, 12–13, 15, 27–30, 32, 37, 39–45, 50–55, 57–58, 64–65, 68–69, 77–80, 83–85, 87, 91–92, 94–97, 99, 105–106, 109, 110, 112–114, 117–118, 121–125, 127–129, 135–137, 139, 141–142, 151, 153, 160–162, 164–166

D

dating 1–2, 11, 28, 30, 36, 50, 53, 59, 62, 64, 66, 86–90, 94–95, 97, 109–110, 113, 115, 117–123, 125, 128–129, 143, 147, 164–165

depress 30, 82, 91, 136–137

desire 1–4, 8, 15–16, 35, 40–41, 43, 45, 51–53, 55, 69–70, 72–73, 77, 80, 82, 86–89, 91, 94–98, 107, 109, 111–114, 117–120, 122–124, 145, 152, 159–167

diaspora 4, 15, 38, 69–70, 77–83, 88, 91–93, 95–96, 98–100, 110, 112, 128

difference 3, 5–8, 10–12, 27, 31–34, 38, 44, 51, 54–55, 62, 64, 78–79, 84–86, 91–92, 97–100, 106, 110, 112, 118, 124, 139–140, 142, 144, 150, 153

disadvantage

disidentification 4, 6, 8–10, 153, 160

diversity 10, 32, 115, 122, 124

E

East Asian 87–88, 96, 98, 122, 128–129, 163

effeminate 16, 27, 35, 116, 123, 128, 137–138, 141, 151, 153

embodiment 2, 11, 43, 69, 90–91, 150, 153, 166

equity 86, 140

ethnicity 7, 30, 51, 64, 81, 84

F

family 6, 30, 36, 39, 42–44, 56–57, 60, 65, 68–69, 79–80, 82–83, 86, 88, 97–98, 107, 115, 199, 126, 130, 136, 149

feeling 17, 28, 42, 50, 88–89, 93–94, 97–98, 117, 149

feminine 9, 27, 37, 39–42, 52–53, 55, 58, 65, 87, 123, 140, 141, 143, 153

femininity 36, 139, 141, 145

foreign 2, 29, 33, 36–37, 40, 44, 52, 60, 68, 93–95, 98–99, 108, 114–115, 124

freedom 7, 15–16, 35, 44–45, 86–87, 97, 105, 107–108, 110–111, 119, 127–128, 137, 151, 165

Fresh off the Boat (FOB) 93

front cover 14–15, 17, 27–45, 50, 54, 64, 66, 70, 159

futurity 30, 78, 107

G

gay and Asian 15, 51–54, 56, 63, 65–67, 70, 92

genderless 147–150, 152–154

genderqueerness 14, 16, 137–138, 140–142, 145–150, 153, 160

globalization 5, 10, 52, 80, 108–109, 112, 128, 165

H

Hikawa Kiyoshi 14, 16, 135–154, 160

homeland 29, 31, 39, 44, 68–69, 79–83, 91, 110, 128, 153
homosexuality 42, 65, 123, 150
hostland 69, 79, 81–83, 91, 110, 128

I

ideality 85–86, 89, 92, 110
imperialism 37, 49, 82, 106, 112, 124
impossibilities 17
indigenous 87, 151
inequality 86, 109
interpersonal communication 149
interracial 2, 11, 28, 42, 53, 66, 88, 126
intersectionality 4, 6, 9–11, 15, 30–32, 51–54, 56, 63, 66, 70, 72
intersubjective 16, 142, 152
intersubjectivity 160
interview 14–16, 28, 78–79, 84–85, 96, 99–100, 106, 110, 121, 128, 160
intraracial 1, 45, 89–90, 115, 138
intraregional 62, 94–96, 98, 108–110, 128–129

J

Japan 1–2, 62, 93, 95–96, 98, 105, 109, 112, 114, 124, 135–154, 161–162, 167
Japaneseness 93, 95–97, 105, 149

K

knowing 7, 17, 56, 68–69
knowledge 2, 4, 6–8, 11, 13–14, 16, 30, 32, 51, 78, 84, 106–107, 141–142, 153, 159, 162–163
Korean 15, 50–51, 58, 60–65, 69, 72, 82, 95, 103, 108–109
Koreatown 15, 49–70, 82, 159

L

land 29, 31, 79
language 2, 5, 10, 27, 30, 33, 39, 51, 60–61, 64, 67, 84, 86, 91, 96, 98, 122, 139, 148, 164
Latino 87, 113
liberalism 35, 53, 86–87, 91, 101
liberation 5–6, 43, 49, 55
Los Angeles 50, 53, 57, 60–61, 63–64, 66, 68, 90, 94, 115, 120
love 1, 28–29, 31, 35–37, 44, 50, 64, 66, 77, 136, 138, 142, 146–147, 150–152

M

marriage 6, 30–31, 42–44, 52–53, 68, 107, 119, 126, 149, 152
masculine 2–3, 9, 27, 37, 41–42, 50–55, 65, 67, 87–88, 91, 111–114, 116–118, 120, 122–124, 128, 143, 147–148, 151, 153, 160–164
masculinity 9, 15, 35, 41, 49–51, 53, 55, 63, 65–67, 70, 77, 87, 116
migration 80–81, 83, 113
military 114
model minority 112, 151
modernity 69, 108, 137
monstrous 16, 135–154
multidimensional 5

N

negotiation 4, 14–15, 61, 79, 84–85, 91–92, 94, 96, 119, 161
New York 28, 31, 34, 36, 43, 50, 53, 55, 89, 92–93, 96–97, 99, 113–116, 118–119, 121, 126, 130–131, 153, 162

O

occupation 38, 112, 135–136
online 1–2, 56–58, 60, 65, 85–86, 94, 120, 140, 143, 164

P

pandemic 2, 14, 16, 85, 116, 127, 151, 160, 163, 165
paradox 4, 15, 77–100, 109, 122, 128, 137
past 2, 12, 30–31, 35, 42–43, 45, 67, 69, 77, 81, 94, 99, 108, 136, 166
pedagogy 15, 56, 67, 105–129
performance 6–7, 14, 16, 34–35, 40, 43, 50–52, 56, 58–59, 78, 87, 90, 135–154, 160, 166
performative writing 13, 16, 138, 141–142, 152–153, 160
phallus 3, 41, 52, 57, 59, 64, 66
possibilities 7, 14–16, 29–31, 33, 44–45, 51, 55, 62, 66, 69, 77–79, 81, 83, 91–95, 97, 99–101, 110, 113, 119–120, 128, 138, 142, 150, 152, 160, 165
present 1, 4, 30–31, 33, 36, 40–45, 51, 54, 56, 62, 65, 67, 69, 78, 81, 92, 94, 99, 107–108, 110, 142, 148, 165
privilege 3, 5–6, 32–33, 36, 38–39, 51–52, 55–56, 62–64, 68–69, 93, 98, 108, 124–125

Q

quare 4, 6–8, 10–11
queer Asia 16, 106–108, 110, 123–125, 128–129, 167
queer of color 4–8, 10, 17, 28, 30, 32, 51, 77–78, 105, 160, 166
queerness 5, 7–8, 10–13, 15–16, 27, 30–33, 40–45, 49, 51, 55, 68–69, 77–79, 81–83, 85–88, 90–92, 94–95, 97–100, 106–108, 110, 119, 128–129, 142, 152–153, 159–162, 165–166

R

racialized gender 3, 15, 29, 31–33, 37, 39–42, 44–45, 49, 53–54, 57–58, 60, 64, 87, 114, 117, 120, 123, 161–162, 164, 165
reflexivity 160
representation 14, 39, 42, 51, 54, 70, 82, 114, 127, 142, 159
resistance 7–8, 14, 51, 78, 83, 125, 155, 162, 165
rhetoric 29–30, 35, 66, 87–89, 117, 122, 141, 148, 164
rice queen 122
romance 63, 89, 91, 121, 142

S

San Francisco 28, 50, 90, 164
Seattle 28, 90, 151, 163–164
semen 58–59
settler colonialism 11, 53, 81, 151
sexuality 5–7, 10–12, 30, 42–43, 55, 69, 83–84, 106, 118, 137–138, 142, 149–150
social institutions 11, 51, 66, 70, 86, 93, 137, 148–149, 151
social interactions 62, 65, 77–78, 85, 88, 100, 122, 126, 149, 153, 164
South Asian 87–88
Southeast Asian 98, 128–129
Stonewall 55

T

Taiwan 10, 28, 35, 38, 60–61, 95–96, 98, 109
Thai 98, 109–111
theories in flesh 7, 78, 141–142
Tokyo 1, 28, 108–109, 139, 144, 146
top 35, 40–41, 57–59, 140, 144

trans 10–11, 15, 28, 45, 50–51, 54–55,
   63, 110
transgender 13, 16, 43, 50, 55, 86, 108, 137,
   139, 141, 145–147, 150, 153
transgression 3, 15–16, 30, 51, 54, 68, 129,
   137, 148
transnational 2, 13, 16–17, 28–29, 31, 45,
   61, 77, 80–82, 94–95, 98, 108–109, 112–
   114, 123, 130–131, 153, 160, 166
transnationalism 80–81

V

vernacular 1–4, 10–11, 14–15, 27–29, 31, 37,
   40, 42, 44–45, 49–52, 55, 77–79, 84–87,
   93–95, 98–100, 106, 110–111, 114, 116,
   119–121, 123, 125, 128–129, 138, 142,
   159–160, 165
versatile 3, 57–58

W

white supremacy 2, 29, 31, 33, 44, 66, 117,
   125, 127, 164
whiteness 3–9, 15, 27–29, 32–37, 39–42,
   44–45, 50–57, 59–63, 65–67, 69–70, 77,
   79, 81, 83, 87, 91, 93–94, 96, 106–108,
   113, 115–116, 120, 122–123, 125–128,
   142–143, 151, 160–162, 165–166
women of color 7, 10, 138, 140

X

xenophobia 3, 30, 109, 117

Y

yellow fever 1–2, 14–15, 17, 27–45, 50, 54,
   64, 66, 70, 142, 159

Critical Intercultural Communication Studies

Thomas K. Nakayama and Bernadette Marie Calafell, General Editors

Critical approaches to the study of intercultural communication have arisen at the end of the twentieth century and are poised to flourish in the new millennium. As cultures come into contact—driven by migration, refugees, the internet, wars, media, transnational capitalism, cultural imperialism, and more—critical interrogations of the ways that cultures interact communicatively are needed to understand culture and communication. This series will interrogate—from a critical perspective—the role of communication in intercultural contact, in both domestic and international contexts. This series is open to studies in key areas such as postcolonialism, transnationalism, critical race theory, queer diaspora studies, and critical feminist approaches as they relate to intercultural communication, tuning into the complexities of power relations in intercultural communication. Proposals might focus on various contexts of intercultural communication such as international advertising, popular culture, language policies, hate crimes, ethnic cleansing and ethnic group conflicts, as well as engaging theoretical issues such as hybridity, displacement, multiplicity, identity, orientalism, and materialism. By creating a space for these critical approaches, this series will be at the forefront of this new wave in intercultural communication scholarship. Manuscripts and proposals are welcome that advance this new approach.

For additional information about this series or for the submission of manuscripts, please contact:

Thomas K. Nakayama, General Editor | *T.Nakayama@neu.edu*
Bernadette Marie Calafell, General Editor | *calafell@gonzaga.edu*

To order other books in this series, please contact our Customer Service Department at:

peterlang@presswarehouse.com (within the U.S.)
orders@peterlang.com (outside the U.S.)

or browse online by series: www.peterlang.com